Populism in Europe and the Americas

Although 'populism' has become something of a buzz word in discussions about politics, it tends to be studied by country or region. This is the first book to offer a genuine cross-regional perspective on populism and its impact on democracy. By analysing current experiences of populism in Europe and the Americas, this edited volume convincingly demonstrates that populism can be both a threat and a corrective to democracy. The contributors also demonstrate the interesting similarities between right-wing and left-wing populism: both types of populism are prone to defend a political model that is not against democracy per se, but rather at odds with liberal democracy. *Populism in Europe and the Americas* offers new insights into the current state of democracy from both a theoretical and an empirical point of view.

Cas Mudde holds a Ph.D. from Leiden University and teaches in the Department of International Affairs of the University of Georgia. His most recent book, *Populist Radical Right Parties in Europe* (Cambridge University Press, 2007), won the Stein Rokkan Prize and was named a *Choice* Outstanding Academic Title in 2008.

Cristóbal Rovira Kaltwasser holds a Ph.D. from the Humboldt University of Berlin, has worked for the United Nations Development Programme (UNDP), and was a post-doctoral fellow at the Social Science Research Center Berlin (WZB). He is the recipient of the Marie Curie Intra-European Fellowship for a two-year research project on populism in Europe and Latin America, which he is currently undertaking at the University of Sussex. His research interests include populism, democracy, and Latin American politics, and his work has been published in *Democratization* and the *Latin American Research Review*, among others.

Populism in Europe and the Americas

Threat or Corrective for Democracy?

Edited by

Cas Mudde & Cristóbal Rovira Kaltwasser

University of Georgia and University of Sussex

CAMBRIDGE UNIVERSITY PRESS
Cambridge, New York, Melbourne, Madrid, Cape Town,
Singapore, São Paulo, Delhi, Mexico City

Cambridge University Press
The Edinburgh Building, Cambridge CB2 8RU, UK

Published in the United States of America by Cambridge University Press, New York

www.cambridge.org
Information on this title: www.cambridge.org/9781107699861

First published 2012
Reprinted 2013
First paperback edition 2013

A catalogue record for this publication is available from the British Library

Library of Congress Cataloguing in Publication Data
Populism in Europe and the Americas : threat or corrective for democracy? /
edited by Cas Mudde & Cristóbal Rovira Kaltwasser.
    p. cm
Includes bibliographical references and index.
ISBN 978-1-107-02385-7
1. Populism–Europe–Case studies.   2. Democracy–Europe.
3. Populism–America–Case studies.   4. Democracy–America.
I. Mudde, Cas, editor of compilation.   II. Rovira Kaltwasser,
Cristóbal, editor of compilation.
JN40.P673 2012
320.56´62094–dc23   2012003069

ISBN 978-1-107-02385-7 Hardback
ISBN 978-1-107-69986-1 Paperback

To Peter Mair (1951–2011)

Contents

Figures

Tables

Notes on contributors

TJITSKE AKKERMAN is Assistant Professor of Political Science at the University of Amsterdam. Her research focuses on democratic theory and on populist radical right parties. Recent publications include (with A. Hagelund) "Women and Children First! Anti-immigration Parties and Gender in Norway and the Netherlands," *Patterns of Prejudice* (2007); "Friend or Foe? Right-wing Populism and the Popular Press in Britain and the Netherlands," *Journalism* (forthcoming in 2011), and "The Impact of Radical Right Parties in Government. A Comparative Analysis of Immigration and Integration Policies in Nine Countries (1996–2010)," *West-European Politics* 2012.

KATHLEEN BRUHN is Professor of Political Science at the University of California, Santa Barbara. She focuses her research on the politics of leftist parties and movements in Latin America, particularly Mexico. She has published extensively on the foundation and development of Mexico's Party of the Democratic Revolution, beginning with her first book, *Taking on Goliath* (1997). Her most recent book, *Urban Protest in Mexico and Brazil* (2008), looks at the causes and implications of leftist party victories for protest strategies.

KEVIN DEEGAN-KRAUSE is Associate Professor of Political Science at Wayne State University. His publications include *Elected Affinities: Democracy and Party Competition in Slovakia and the Czech Republic* (2006) and, co-edited with Zsolt Enyedi, *The Structure of Political Competition in Western Europe* (2010). He is co-editor of the 2012 *Handbook on Political Change in Eastern Europe* and co-editor of the forthcoming online version of the *European Journal for Political Research: Political Data Yearbook*. His ongoing research, including ongoing projects on populism and party change, concerns the origins and consequences of political divides in new democracies.

SARAH L. DE LANGE is Assistant Professor of Comparative Politics at the University of Amsterdam. She has previously been a Jean Monnet

Fellow in the Robert Schuman Centre for Advanced Research at the European University Institute. Her main research interests concern political parties, party families, and party systems and her publications have appeared in *Acta Politica*, *Communist and Post-Communist Studies*, *Comparative European Politics*, *Ethical Perspectives*, *European Political Studies*, *Party Politics*, and *West European Politics*.

FRANZ FALLEND is Senior Scientist at the Department of Political Science and Sociology at the University of Salzburg, Austria. His research focuses on Austrian politics, comparative federalism, and regional policy. His recent publications include "Austria" in Political Data Yearbook 2009, special issue of the *European Journal of Political Research*, Vol. 49, Nos. 7–8, 2010, pp. 880–98, and "Austria: From Consensus to Competition and Participation?" in John Loughlin, Frank Hendriks, and Anders Lidström (eds.), *The Oxford Handbook of Local and Regional Democracy in Europe*.

SEÁN HANLEY is Senior Lecturer in East European politics at University College London. His interests include the development of new anti-establishment parties and right-wing politics in Central and Eastern Europe. He has a special interest in Czech politics and is author of *The New Right in the New Europe: Czech Transformation and Right-wing Politics, 1989–2006* (2007). He also writes an occasional blog on Central and East European politics: http://drseansdiary.wordpress.com.

DAVID LAYCOCK is Professor of Political Science at Simon Fraser University, Canada. His research focuses on political ideologies, democratic theory, populism, and Canadian party politics. He has published *Populism and Democratic Thought in the Canadian Prairies* (1990), *The New Right and Democracy in Canada* (2001), *Representation and Democratic Theory* (2004), and articles on populism in *Party Politics* and *Commonwealth and Comparative Politics*.

STEVEN LEVITSKY is Professor of Government at Harvard University. His research interests include political parties, political regimes and regime change, and weak and informal institutions, with a focus on Latin America. He is author of *Transforming Labor-Based Parties in Latin America: Argentine Peronism in Comparative Perspective* (2003), and co-author (with Lucan Way) of *Competitive Authoritarianism: Hybrid Regimes after the Cold War* (2010).

JAMES LOXTON is a Ph.D. candidate in the Department of Government at Harvard University. His fields of interest are comparative politics and Latin American politics, particularly the intersection between regime transitions and party formation. He is writing his dissertation on post-authoritarian political parties in Latin America following the Third Wave of democratization.

CAS MUDDE is Assistant Professor in the Department of International Affairs at the University of Georgia. His previous publications include *Populist Radical Right Parties in Europe* (2007), which won the 2008 Stein Rokkan Prize and was a *Choice* Outstanding Academic Title. He is currently working on various projects related to the overarching question: How can liberal democracies defend themselves against political challenges without undermining their core values?

KENNETH M. ROBERTS is Professor of Government at Cornell University with a specialization in Latin American politics. He is the author of *Deepening Democracy? The Modern Left and Social Movements in Chile and Peru* (1998) and co-editor of *The Diffusion of Social Movements* (2010) and *The Resurgence of the Latin American Left* (2011). His research on political parties and popular movements in Latin America has been published in a number of scholarly journals.

CRISTÓBAL ROVIRA KALTWASSER is Marie Curie Research Fellow at the Department of Politics of the University of Sussex. He holds a Ph.D. from the Humboldt University of Berlin and has worked at the Social Science Research Center Berlin (WZB) and the Chilean Bureau of the United Nations Development Programme (UNDP). With research interests that include democracy, elite theory, populism, and Latin American politics, he has published in, among others, *Democratization* and the *Latin American Research Review*.

Preface

As holds true of so many things today, the origins of our scholarly collaboration and of this edited volume can be traced to a random match on the Internet. In 2009 Cristóbal had just started a post-doc – financed by the Alexander von Humboldt Foundation – on populism in Europe and Latin America at the *Wissenschaftszentrum Berlin für Sozialforschung* (WZB) and was surfing the Web for scholars of and texts on this topic. He came across the page of Cas, who had just started a similar project as a visiting fellow at the Helen Kellogg Institute for International Studies at the University of Notre Dame. We started an extensive exchange of e-mails, in which we discussed the challenges of undertaking cross-regional research on populism. Beyond these virtual discussions, we met in the fall of 2009 in Berlin and decided to collaborate on various related topics, one being this book.

After developing a rough theoretical framework, of which a significantly revised version is published as Chapter 1, we started to apply for funding and to invite potential collaborators. We were very lucky not only to find such a great team of esteemed experts, but to convince everyone we invited that this was worth their time. Thanks to the financial support of the *Volkswagen Stiftung*, we organized a workshop titled "Populism in Europe and the Americas: Threat or Corrective for Democracy?" at the WZB in Berlin in August 2010, where all collaborators presented the first versions of their chapters, which were discussed by the collaborators and a broad group of colleagues from Germany and beyond. Our workshop discussants all took their role very seriously and provided invaluable feedback to all authors. We want to thank Carlos de la Torre, Wolfgang Merkel, Emilia Palonen, Karin Priester, Hans-Jürgen Puhle, Paul Taggart, Peter Učeň, and Kurt Weyland once again for their great and thoughtful contributions to this project. We also want to thank the Alexander von Humboldt Foundation, the *Volkswagen Stiftung*, and the *Wissenschaftszentrum Berlin für Sozialforschung* for their generous financial and practical support for the workshop.

After the workshop we gave all contributors a couple of months to re-write their chapters for the edited volume. While not everyone made the original deadline, all contributors not just stayed close to the deadline, they also provided excellent second drafts of their respective chapters. This was confirmed by the two anonymous reviewers of Cambridge University Press, who addressed problems in the framework chapter rather than in the individual country chapters. We want to thank all authors for being so engaged with and so open to our project, despite legitimate concerns about, and differences of opinions on, the key definitions used in this volume. It truly was a pleasure to work with all of you. Similarly, we want to thank the people at Cambridge University Press, in particular editor John Haslam, for their cooperation and support for our book. Moreover, we discussed the subject of this book with different friends and colleagues, who gave us invaluable comments and ideas. In this regard, we are particularly grateful to Martin Beckstein, Nancy Bermeo, Giovanni Capoccia, Matias Dewey, Klaus Eder, Raimundo Frei, John Keane, Alan Knight, Kirk Hawkins, Herfried Münkler, Pierre Ostiguy, and Laurence Whitehead.

As we were in the final stages of editing this book, we were, like many in the discipline, shocked by the devastating news of the sudden death of Peter Mair. Peter was a professor of comparative politics at the European University Institute and one of the leading scholars on parties and party systems and European democracy. Most of the collaborators of this book knew Peter and/or were heavily influenced by his work. Peter was also the Ph.D. supervisor of one of the editors at Leiden University, who remembers him not just as an exceptional scholar, but also as a kind and warm *Doktorvater* who will always be an inspiration to him. We dedicate this book to him.

Cas Mudde & Cristóbal Rovira Kaltwasser
Greencastle, U.S. & Brighton, U.K.

1 Populism and (liberal) democracy: a framework for analysis

Cas Mudde and Cristóbal Rovira Kaltwasser

> Populist movements are widely regarded, especially in Europe and Latin America, as threats to democracy. Yet New Populists explicitly claim to be true democrats, setting out to reclaim power for the people.
>
> – Canovan 2004: 244

Introduction

One of the most used and abused terms inside and outside of academia is undoubtedly *populism*. At times it seems that almost every politician, at least those we do not like, is a populist. The term has been applied to both Venezuelan left-wing president Hugo Chávez and American right-wing vice presidential candidate Sarah Palin, and to both the radical left Scottish Socialist Party (SSP) and the radical right Austrian Freedom Party (FPÖ). It has also been hailed as a way to include the underclass and scorned as a programme to exclude minorities. No wonder some authors have called for the abandonment of the use of the allegedly meaningless term (e.g. Roxborough 1984).

We acknowledge the broad usage of the term populism, and the problems associated with that, but attempt to construct a framework within which the term populism has a clear meaning and its relationship to democracy can be studied *empirically*. In fact, most studies that have analysed the tension between populism and democracy tend to make normative and theoretical arguments, but little has been said from an empirical point of view. Moreover, although it is true that this growing body of literature has generated new insights, it relies on very different, and sometimes even contradictory, concepts of both populism and democracy (e.g. Abts and Rummens 2007; Albertazzi and McDonnell 2007; Conniff 1999; de la Torre and Peruzzotti 2008; Decker 2006; Laclau 2005a; Mény and Surel 2000, 2002a; Panizza 2005; Taggart 2000). Having this in mind, this framework ensures the broad applicability (in time and place) of the key concepts of this research topic by adhering to Giovanni Sartori's approach (1970) of so-called minimal definitions (cf. Collier and Gerring 2009). Accordingly, the main aim of this chapter is to provide a clear conceptual and theoretical framework to guide the individual case studies of the book, ensuring a common core yet leaving space for individual accents.

In the first two sections we define the key terms in the framework: populism and (liberal) democracy. We briefly discuss the main trends in the literature and present clear minimal definitions. In the third section we discuss the different ways in which the relationship between populism and (liberal) democracy has been described in the academic debate. Through a critical analysis of the scholarly literature, and the application of our own definitions, we set out our own position on the relationship between the two. In the next two sections we discuss the two key research questions underlying this edited volume: (1) What are the effects of populist actors on liberal democracies? and (2) under which circumstances do populists constitute a corrective or a threat to the liberal democratic system?

It is critical to understand that our primary concern is populism, not the host ideology it has attached itself to or the person who expresses it. One of the crucial tasks is therefore to separate populism from features that might regularly occur together *with* it, but are not part *of* it. For example, populist radical right parties in Europe share a core ideology of nativism, authoritarianism, and populism (Mudde 2007); all three features have a strained relationship with liberal democracy, but we are only interested in the effect of *populism* (even though, admittedly, the effects are not always easy to disentangle in reality).

In a similar vein, scholars have convincingly demonstrated that populism in Latin America is compatible with both neoliberalism and state-centred development (Roberts 1995; Weyland 1996, 2001). In fact, even contemporary Europe hosts both left-wing and right-wing populist parties (e.g. Albertazzi and McDonnell 2007; March and Mudde 2005). Accordingly, there is no reason to assume that a certain economic doctrine is a defining attribute of populism. This implies that it makes little sense to define the latter on the basis of a specific set of economic and/or social policies.

Finally, it is important to underline that populism and clientelism are not synonymous. As Herbert Kitschelt and Steven Wilkinson (2007) have recently pointed out, clientelism involves a whole organizational structure (mostly of informal character) in charge of both monitoring voter behaviour and delivering the expected goods to the clientele. Without a doubt, populist leaders in Latin America have shown a propensity to use clientelist linkages, but this does not mean that populism is necessarily related to this kind of linkage (Filc 2010; Mouzelis 1985; Weyland 2001).

1.1   Defining populism

One of the reasons that so many different politicians have been called populist is that there are so many different understandings and usages of the term populism. Some are extremely broad and vague, including most of the popular usages that equate populism with campaigning, demagoguery, or 'the mob' (e.g. Canovan 2004; Laclau 2005a; Mudde 2004). But even in the academic literature *populism* is used to refer to a range of very different phenomena and is attached to a broad variety of 'host ideologies' and political actors. While it is impossible, and unnecessary, to debate all existing definitions, we will provide a short overview of the main historical manifestations of populism and a concise discussion of three conceptual approaches – populism as a movement, as a political style, and as a discourse – that are commonly used. Finally, we will provide the *minimal* definition of populism to which we adhere and which is employed by all authors in this volume.

1.1.1   A brief conceptual history of the term populism

The origins of the concept of populism are normally traced back to the end of the nineteenth century, when the Populist Party in the United States and the so-called Narodniki in Russia emerged (Canovan 1981: 5–6). Although the word *populism* appears as a self-description in both cases, the two experiences were very different: While the U.S. Populist Party was, first and foremost, a mass movement commanded by farmers who demanded a radical change of the political system (Hofstadter 1969), the Russian Narodniki was a group of middle-class intellectuals who endorsed a romanticized view of rural life (Walicki 1969). To these two original experiences it is quite common to add a third one, namely the peasant movements that appeared in several parts of Eastern Europe and the Balkans in the inter-war years (Ionescu 1969). The commonality of these movements was in their defence of an agrarian programme in which the peasantry was seen as the main pillar of both society and economy (Mudde 2002: 219).

With the rise of the Great Depression of the 1930s, populism started to emerge also in Latin America. Indeed, it is in this region that populism gained most visibility during the twentieth century, with the cases of Juan Domingo Perón in Argentina and Getulio Vargas in Brazil as the most famous examples (Germani 1978; Weffort 1978). These leaders were actually part of a new generation of politicians, who by appealing to 'the people' rather than to the 'working class' were able to build multi-class coalitions and mobilize lower-class groups (Drake 2009: chapter 6).

In effect, populist parties and movements represented a major challenge to the Marxist left in Latin America, since they were never constrained by ideological orthodoxy, and were thus capable of developing a profile appealing to a broad electorate rather than an intellectual vanguard (Angell 1998).

In Western Europe populism jumped onto the scene only at the end of the last century. Among the few exceptions is the case of Poujadism in France, a populist movement with an eclectic ideology that made a brief breakthrough in the 1950s and did not have a major impact on the political landscape (Priester 2007: 142–58). Between the 1930s and 1970s populism also took root in both Canada and the United States. While in the former populism appeared most notably in the form of the Social Credit movement (Laycock 2005a), in the latter populism gained momentum with the rise of very different figures such as Huey Long, Father Coughlin, and George Wallace (Kazin 1995).

Though this brief and schematic overview of populism's main historical manifestations before the 1980s is far from complete, it is helpful for illustrating that the concept of populism has been applied to a wide range of experiences. Hence, developing a plausible and useful definition of populism is anything but simple. To confront this problem, more than forty years ago a group of well-known scholars participated in a conference held in London under the title 'To Define Populism.' As the report of this conference (Berlin, Hofstadter, MacRae et al. 1968) and the famous edited volume resulting from it (Ionescu and Gellner 1969) reveal, the participants used the term *populism* for such a perplexing variety of phenomena that the organizers seem to have made little effort to establish a minimum definitional agreement. More than forty years later the number of scholars of populism has increased manifold and we are probably even further from a definitional consensus within the scholarly community. This notwithstanding, can we identify a central core present in all the manifestations of populism?

Although certain authors have answered this question negatively (e.g. Canovan 1982; Hermet 2003), many others have tried to develop a conceptual approach with the aim of identifying the elements present in all manifestations of populism. Given that a thorough overview of the existing approaches is beyond the scope of this framework, we will critically examine three notions of populism that are very influential not only inside and outside of academia, but also in the analysis of Europe and the Americas.[1]

---

[1] Strictly speaking, in the case of Latin America it is possible to identify a fourth approach, which relies on an economic perspective. This approach defines populism as a particular

The first approach conceives of populism as a particular type of political movement. In this respect, the foundational work is probably Seymour Martin Lipset's *Political Man* (1960), which proposed a definition of populism that became highly popular in the study of Latin American politics. According to Lipset, the rise of Perón in Argentina and Vargas in Brazil should be analysed as a phenomenon similar to the rise of fascism in Europe, since both cases stand for the emergence of extremist mass movements. Nevertheless, he argues that there is one key difference between Latin American populism and European fascism: While the former relied on the lower classes, the latter hinged on the middle classes. Following this perspective, Gino Germani (1978) defined populism as a *multi-class* movement organized around a charismatic leader. Seen in this light, the main feature of populism is not only the presence of a strong leader but also, and mainly, the formation of a movement appealing to very heterogonous social groups (Collier and Collier 1991; Conniff 1999; Drake 1978; Oxhorn 1998).

Certainly, the idea that populism tends to foster multi-class alliances is not unjustified. By making use of the notion of 'the people,' populist leaders and parties claim to represent a variety of different groups sharing a common idea: Popular sovereignty has been corrupted by the elites. However, the formation of multi-class alliances is not a defining attribute of populism, but rather a central element of mass politics. As Alan Knight (1998: 238–40) has pointed out, successful political parties such as the Christian democratic and social democratic parties in Europe are characterized precisely by their capacity to mobilize and represent a plethora of social groups, yet we do not refer to these cases as examples of populism. Not by coincidence, Otto Kirchheimer (1965; cf. Krouwel 2003) developed the notion of *Volksparteien* (catch-all parties) to describe those parties able to build a programme that is appealing to voters with very different socio-economic and socio-cultural backgrounds.

The second approach defines populism as a political style characterized by the promotion of a particular kind of link between political leaders and the electorate, a link structured around a loose and opportunistic

---

type of macroeconomic policy that is extremely harmful, since in the short run it generates growth and redistribution via increasing state expansion, but in the long run it leads to rising inflation and public debt and thus a major economic crisis (Dornbusch and Edwards 1991; Edwards 2010; Sachs 1989). Although this interpretation has some plausibility for analysing specific cases (e.g. the first government of Alan García in Peru), it is difficult to see why this type of macroeconomic policy is the essential attribute of populism. As Roberts (1995) and Weyland (1996) have pointed out, in the 1990s some Latin American populist actors have employed neoliberal recipes, which were neither 'irresponsible' nor very popular among the electorate (Panizza 2009: chapter 3). Put briefly, it is flawed to assume that a particular type of (economic) policy is a definitional attribute of populism (Mudde and Rovira Kaltwasser 2011).

appeal to 'the people' in order to win and/or exercise political power. For instance, Peter Mair (2002: 84) defines populism as "a means of linking an increasingly undifferentiated and depoliticized electorate with a largely neutral and non-partisan system of governance." According to this approach, populism designates a dimension of political action or discourse, and in consequence, it is compatible with all forms of leaders, movements, and parties (Taguieff 1995). Social democratic governments such as those of Tony Blair in the United Kingdom (e.g. Mair 2006) and Gerhard Schröder in Germany (e.g. Jun 2006) are seen as prime examples of this populist style of politics, since in both cases political leaders ruled not only based on surveys and spin doctors, but also against (rather than with) their political parties in order to enact reforms that were allegedly relevant for 'the people.'

The main problem of this approach lies in its propensity to conflate phenomena like demagogy or opportunism with populism, so that the latter is defined in a way that almost all political actors, particularly in campaign periods, can be labelled as populist (Mudde 2004: 543). Hence, by proposing such a broad concept of populism, this approach develops more a catchword than an analytical concept that has discriminating power for undertaking comparative research. In other words, neither the use of spin doctors and surveys, nor the development of pragmatic positions and the avoidance of partisan conflicts is specific to populism.

The third and last approach is a discursive one, whose main exponent is Ernesto Laclau (1977, 2005a, 2005b). Criticizing the economic determinism present in most interpretations of Marx, he developed a theory of populism whereby the latter is understood as a particular political logic, not as the result of particular class alliances. In a nutshell, Laclau maintains that this political logic is characterized by the confrontation of the existing hegemony by means of a discursive construction capable of dividing the social into two camps, namely 'the power bloc' versus 'the people.' This discourse does not emerge by accident, but is rather the product of a three-step process involved in radical politics: first the linking of very different demands, then the formation of a collective identity through the recognition of an enemy (e.g. the establishment), and finally the affective investment in an element (e.g. the leader) that represents 'the people' (Kleis Nielsen 2006: 89).

Although Laclau's theory of populism is interesting, it has serious problems when it comes to analysing populism in more concrete terms. As Yannis Stavrakakis (2004) has indicated, since Laclau – particularly in his last writings – equates populism with politics, the very concept of populism is defined in a way that is not helpful for undertaking empirical analysis. In effect, if populism should be seen as synonymous with the political, only two very doubtful pathways for research remain possible: Either populism is something omnipresent, or anything that is not populist cannot be considered political. To sum up, Laclau's theory of populism is, on the one hand, extremely abstract, and on the other hand, it proposes a concept of populism that becomes so vague and malleable it loses much of its analytic utility (Mouzelis 1978).

1.1.2 Towards a minimal definition of populism

Obviously, populism is not the only contested concept in the social sciences. In fact, most concepts are contested at some level. Nevertheless, in most cases some basic aspects are above discussion; for example, despite all debate about the true meaning of conservatism, virtually all definitions consider it an ideology or an attitude. But, as we noted before, even this kind of consensus cannot be found in the literature on populism. Since the end of the 1990s, however, an important development in the debate on how to define populism has occurred. This development is related to the rise of new contributions aiming to develop a definition of populism capable of avoiding the problems of conceptual travelling (i.e. the application of concepts to new cases) and conceptual stretching (i.e. the distortion that occurs when a concept does not fit the new cases). To cope with these problems, two main approaches have been employed: radial and classical categorization (Collier and Mahon 1993).

Both radial and classical categorizations seek to confront Sartori's (1970) dilemma of the inversely proportional relation between the intension and extension of concepts: The more defining attributes a concept has (i.e. greater *intension*), the fewer instances it encompasses (i.e. more limited *extension*). The main difference between both types of categorization relies on the way in which they deal with the Sartorian intension–extension dilemma. Given that the radial categorization follows Wittgenstein's idea of family resemblance, it assumes that a phenomenon can be conceptualized on the basis of a pool of defining attributes, which are not shared by all the cases. In other words, none of the cases are exactly the same, but each family member shares several defining attributes with all other members. By contrast, the classical categorization postulates that the defining attributes of a concept must be seen as necessary and sufficient criteria; that is, *all* 'family members' should share *all* defining variables. This means that the classical categorization aims to identify the lowest common denominator between all manifestations of a particular phenomenon.

Although the radial categorization has significant potential in certain areas of the social sciences, we are sceptical about its advantages for the study of populism.[2] First of all, since the populist label has been attached to such a wide variety of phenomena, it is hard to reach a consensus on the defining attributes of populism in order to build a family resemblance (Sikk 2009). In other words, radial definitions of populism may foster a sort of pseudo-consensus: "Agreement on a term may disguise disagreement on its meaning. In encompassing conceptual diversity, they may perpetuate rather than reduce confusion" (Weyland 2001: 3). In fact, by employing a radial definition it might be the case that different authors stick to their own conceptualizations instead of trying to arrive at a common understanding of the core aspects of populism. Hence, classical categorization is the best way to enhance conceptual clarity and foster cumulative knowledge, particularly when it comes to studying populism from a comparative perspective.

This begs the following question: How do we reach a *minimal* definition of populism? In this regard, it is worth mentioning that at least implicitly almost all concepts of populism share the idea that the latter always alludes to a confrontation between 'the people' and 'the establishment.' As Margaret Canovan (1981: 294) has indicated, "[A]ll forms of populism without exception involve some kind of exaltation of and appeal to 'the people', and all are in one sense or another anti-elitist." Seen in this light, it seems that every manifestation of populism criticizes the existence of powerful minorities, which in one way or another are obstructing the will of the common people.

Following this intuition, and in line with the earlier work of one of the authors, populism is defined here as *a thin-centred ideology that considers society to be ultimately separated into two homogeneous and antagonistic groups, 'the pure people' and 'the corrupt elite,' and which argues that politics should be an expression of the* volonté générale *(general will) of the people* (e.g. Mudde 2007: 23, 2004: 543). This means that populism is in essence a form of *moral* politics, as the distinction between 'the elite' and 'the people' is first and foremost moral (i.e. pure vs. corrupt), not situational (e.g. position of power), socio-cultural (e.g. ethnicity, religion),

---

[2] One of the few examples of the use of a radial categorization to define populism can be found in Roberts (1995), who maintains that Latin American populism should be conceptualized on the basis of five defining attributes that are not always present. These defining attributes are: (1) a personalistic and paternalistic, though not necessarily charismatic, pattern of political leadership; (2) a heterogeneous, multi-class political coalition concentrated in subaltern sectors of society; (3) a top-down process of political mobilization that either bypasses institutionalized forms of mediation or subordinates them to more direct linkages between the leader and the masses; (4) an amorphous or eclectic ideology characterized by a discourse that exalts subaltern sectors or is anti-elitist and/or anti-establishment; (5) an economic project that utilizes widespread redistributive or clientelistic methods to create a material foundation for popular sector support.

or socio-economic (e.g. class). Moreover, both categories are to a certain extent 'empty signifiers' (Laclau 1977), as it is the populists who construct the exact meanings of 'the elite' and 'the people' (de la Torre 2000; Stanley 2008). In more specific terms, we conceive populism as a thin-centred ideology that has three core concepts (the people, the elite, and the general will) and two direct opposites (elitism and pluralism) (Mudde and Rovira Kaltwasser forthcoming).

As populism is a 'thin-centred ideology,' exhibiting 'a restricted core attached to a narrower range of political concepts' (Freeden 1998: 750), it can be attached to other ideologies, be they thick (e.g. liberalism, socialism) or thin (e.g. ecologism, nationalism). This ideological flexibility is what Paul Taggart (2000) refers to as the chameleonic nature of populism. However, this should not distract us from the clear and distinctive core of populism itself. And, to re-state, we are interested here, first and foremost, in what the populist part of political actors contributes to the political agenda, not the nationalist or socialist or whatever other parts.

It is important to note that this minimal concept is close to many definitions used to study populism in both the Americas (e.g. de la Torre 2000; Hawkins 2009, 2010; Kazin 1995) and Europe (e.g. Art 2011; Pankowski 2010; Stanley 2008). In addition, this minimal concept can and has been applied in empirical research around the globe (e.g. Filc 2010; Jagers 2006; Mudde 2007). Furthermore, Kirk Hawkins (2009, 2010) has proposed a very similar approach for the analysis of Latin American populism and offers an interesting methodology to measure populism through the speeches of chief executives.

How does this minimum definition of populism relate to alternatives put forward in the literature? First, it comes very close to most definitions of populism as a discourse and political style/strategy, in the sense that it agrees on the content, but disagrees on the importance or sincerity. Still, whether the populist really believes in the message distributed or whether populism is a strategic tool is largely an empirical question, which is often almost impossible to answer conclusively (without getting into the populist's head). Second, the definition says nothing about the type of mobilization of the populist actor, an aspect that is central in several definitions of populism in Latin American studies (e.g. Roberts 2006; Weyland 2001). While we do acknowledge a logical connection to certain types of mobilization (e.g. charismatic leadership, direct communication leader to masses, suspicion of strong party organizations), we are as yet unconvinced of the exact status of the relationship: Is it a constitutive element of populism or an empirical consequence? We have encouraged the authors in this volume to investigate this relationship in their empirical analyses.

As we have stated elsewhere (Mudde and Rovira Kaltwasser 2011), by criticizing Kurt Weyland's (1996, 2001) definition, we are not downplaying the role of leadership in populism. Populist leaders are indeed very relevant. They not only try to mobilize the electorate, but are also one of the main protagonists in the process of defining the morphology of populist ideology. However, an excessive focus on leadership narrows the analysis to the supply-side of the populist phenomenon, generating a kind of modern version of Carlyle's 'great man theory,' which presupposes that the leader is the main and almost only factor that explains political development. In contrast, an ideological definition of populism takes into account both the supply-side and the demand-side of the populist phenomenon, since it assumes that the formation, propagation, and transformation of the populist ideology depends on skilful political entrepreneurs and social groups, who have emotional and rational motives for adhering to the populist ideology.

1.2   Defining democracy

Just like populism, democracy is a highly contested concept in the social sciences (e.g. Keane 2009; Tilly 2007). The debates do not only refer to the correct definition of 'democracy,' but also to the various 'models of democracy' (Held 1996) or the discussion on the so-called 'democracy with adjectives' (Collier and Levitsky 1997). Although this is not the place to delve too deep into this debate, we believe that, to clarify our own position, it is relevant to say something about the way in which democracy has been conceptualized, particularly when it comes to studying its relationship with populism. In other words, we are not interested here in developing a new concept of democracy, or in offering a thorough overview of the existing definitions and theories of democracy. Instead, we will provide a brief outline of our understanding of three key concepts used in the debates on populism: democracy, liberal democracy, and radical democracy.

1.2.1   Democracy

Democracy without adjectives is a term often used and seldom defined. Moreover, in most day-to-day usage it refers to liberal democracy, or at least representative or indirect democracy, rather than democracy per se. In our opinion, democracy (*sans* adjectives) refers to *the combination of popular sovereignty and majority rule*; nothing more, nothing less. Hence, democracy can be direct or indirect, liberal or illiberal. In fact, the very etymology of the term 'democracy' suggests that it alludes to the idea of 'self-government of the people,' a political system in which people rule (Przeworski 2010: 8–9).

The most common definition of democracy without adjectives, often used in the literature on democratization, follows Austrian economist Joseph Schumpeter, who defined democracy as 'an institutional arrangement for arriving at political decisions which realizes the common good by making the people itself decide issues through the election of individuals who are to assemble in order to carry out its will' (1949: 250). In this tradition, democracy means first and foremost a *method* by which rulers are selected in competitive elections. Free and fair elections thus correspond to the defining property of democracy. Instead of changing rulers by violent conflict, the people agree that those who govern them should be elected by majority rule. Although this concept might appear to be too minimalistic for certain scholars, it is worth remembering that billions in the world currently live without this narrow form of democracy (Przeworski 1999).

Moreover, while this certainly is a minimal concept, it is a definition of *representative* democracy, not democracy per se. As Nadia Urbinati and Mark Warren (2008: 392) have rightly pointed out, Schumpeter's and other 'thin' concepts of democracy can be criticized for portraying citizens as a passive entity, but not for denying the problem of representation. Since the contemporary world is marked by the existence of political communities that are much bigger than the old Greek and Italian city–states, the implementation of democracy implies the formation of a political system whereby the people elect representatives who – ideally – defend their interests (Pitkin 1967). To what extent and in which ways (e.g. retrospectively and/or prospectively) this ideal process takes place, is one of the main questions debated in the scholarly literature on democracy (e.g. Alonso, Keane, and Merkel 2011).

1.2.2   Liberal democracy

As already stated, most day-to-day use of the term *democracy* actually refers to liberal democracy (or constitutional democracy), a much more elaborate political system. Since it is almost impossible to find a definition that is above debate, we settle for second best and seek inspiration in the seminal work of Robert Dahl. Although sometimes criticized as conservative (e.g. Skinner 1973) or too minimalistic (e.g. Merkel 2010: 30), Dahl's concept of democracy is not only a very elaborate and demanding system of political freedoms and rights, but also sufficiently parsimonious for undertaking empirical and comparative research. Not by coincidence, his approach is probably the one most widely accepted, particularly in terms of providing a useful definition for the analysis of democracy worldwide (Doorenspleet and Kopecký 2008: 699; Norris 2011: 27).

Before continuing, it is worth mentioning that Dahl reserves the concept of 'democracy' for an ideal political system, which is fully responsive to all its citizens and does not exist in actuality. By contrast, the notion of 'polyarchy' denotes regimes in the real world that ensure certain minimal standards, but fall considerably short of the ideal model. Polyarchies, then, may be thought of as relatively (but incompletely) democratized regimes (Dahl 1971: 8). From this perspective, democracy alludes not only to a particular type of political system, but also to a dynamic and open-ended process that always remains incomplete (Tilly 2007; Whitehead 2002). This is a relevant point, because many citizens might value the democratic order, but at the same time they might be dissatisfied with the way existing democracy works. Therefore, it is impossible to avoid the gap between democratic ideals and existing democracies, so that the latter inevitably lead to 'broken promises,' which in turn may be a positive force for scrutinizing governments and demanding reforms (Bobbio 1987). In the words of Dahl (2001: 3408):

Because the ideal democratic criteria set extraordinarily high and perhaps unattainable standards, it is altogether possible than an increasing number of citizens in democratic countries might conclude that the institutions of polyarchal democracy are inadequately democratic. If so, the acceptable level for meeting democratic criteria might continue on the upward trajectory traced during the twentieth century.

While it is true that Dahl's body of work has been strongly influenced by Schumpeter, there are at least two important differences between the two. On the one hand, unlike Schumpeter, Dahl is aware of the fact that the survival of polyarchy depends partly on the existence of 'checks and balances,' constitutional principles seeking not only to guarantee the separation of powers, but also to avoid situations in which majorities threaten the fundamental rights of minorities (e.g. Dahl 1982: 87–92; 2000: chapter 6). On the other hand, by developing the notion of 'polyarchy,' Dahl (1989: chapter 9) openly criticizes Schumpeter, because the latter devotes much more attention on political competition than on the problem of inclusion, leading him to conclude that 'the people' should have the right to demarcate who are entitled to participate. Interestingly, Dahl draws an important lesson from this critical debate with Schumpeter, namely the so-called all-subjected principle. Except for children, transients, and persons proved to be mentally defective, all those subjected to political rule within the state boundaries should have the right to participate in the collective decision making process (Näsström 2011).

Having laid out some of the key aspects of Dahl's democratic theory, it is time to consider his empirical approach. To analyse existing democracies or polyarchies, Dahl maintains that we should be aware that the latter are structured around two separate and independent dimensions: public contestation and political participation. While the former refers to the possibility of freely formulating preferences and opposing the government, the latter alludes to the right to participate in the political system (Coppedge, Alvarez, and Maldonado 2008). Moreover, to ensure the optimization of both dimensions, he believes a set of institutional guarantees is required. The most important of these 'institutional guarantees' are:

(1) Freedom to form and join organizations
(2) Freedom of expression
(3) Right to vote
(4) Right of political leaders to compete for votes
(5) Eligibility for public office
(6) Alternative sources of information
(7) Free and fair elections
(8) Institutions for making government policies dependent on votes and other expressions of preference.

To sum up, liberal democracy is essentially a system characterized not only by free and fair elections, popular sovereignty, and majority rule, but also by the constitutional protection of minority rights. Accordingly, we are dealing with a complex form of government based on the idea of political equality, and consequently, cannot allow a majority to deprive a minority of any of its primary political rights, since this would imply a violation of the democratic process. At the same time, the core aspect of liberal democracy revolves around its ability to provide both public contestation and political participation.[3]

1.2.3   Radical democracy

Radical democracy refers more to an ideal type than to 'real existing democracies.' It is mostly developed in (normative) political theory, but has gained a particular importance in the debate about the relationship between populism and democracy. The two main authors in this respect

---

[3] It is worth mentioning that in his last book, Dahl (2006) maintains that economic inequality has a negative impact on the functioning of 'real existing' democracies. His main argument is that the very existence of the right to participate in the political system does not guarantee that citizens have the capacity to control, contest, and influence the conduct of the government, because important resources, such as political knowledge and skills, are not equally distributed among the population. As Przeworski (2010: xiii–xiv) has recently argued, "[T]oday citizenship is nominally universal, but many people do not enjoy the conditions necessary to exercise it. Hence, we may be seeing a new monster: democracy without effective citizenship."

are Ernesto Laclau and Chantal Mouffe (1985), who do not actually present a clear definition of radical democracy. They conceive the latter as an approach that relies on a reinterpretation of Marxism and that aims to confront the dominance of the notion of 'liberal democracy' within the scholarly research. Since Laclau and Mouffe develop an intricate jargon – at least for those unfamiliar with the work of both authors – we think it is helpful to simplify and summarize their argumentation in the following four points.

First, the link between the liberal tradition (rule of law, respect of individual liberty, etc.) and the democratic tradition (equality, popular sovereignty, etc.) is a contingent historical articulation. This means that a liberal state is not necessarily democratic and that it is possible to have democracy without a liberal state (Bobbio 1990; Møller and Skaaning 2011). From this angle, the link between the liberal and the democratic tradition is the result of bitter struggles, which do not have a clear end and lead to continuous tensions (Mouffe 2000). One of these tensions is the emergence of populist forces that, based on the notion of popular sovereignty, are prone to question the legitimacy of liberal institutions such as the rule of law (Žižek 2008: chapter 6).

Second, liberal democracy tends to the sacralization of consensus and does not acknowledge that democracy inevitably means fighting for something and against someone. In this sense, the idea of radical democracy is close to the notion of the 'democratization of democracy' developed by Boaventura Sousa de Santos and Leonardo Avritzer (2005): While the institutions of liberal democracy represent an important achievement, they have to be amended and complemented by institutional innovations that aim not only to empower excluded sectors of society, but also to strengthen new forms of political participation and representation, such as social movements and global advocacy networks. However, these institutional innovations do not emerge by themselves. They are the outcome of disputes and conflicts that sometimes might even transgress the established liberal institutions.

Third, radical democracy refers to the construction of a new hegemonic project, which intends to articulate quite different demands. Therefore, radical democracy has to build an adversary in order to counter the '*divide et impera*' principle. In fact, Laclau and Mouffe (1985) note that one of the ironies of the contemporary world lies in the fact that, on the one hand, there is a plethora of groups fighting for a growing number of emancipatory demands (from the right of sexual minorities to the ecological discourse and the defense of animal rights), and on the other hand, these different groups are able neither to develop a common identity nor to share an organizational umbrella in order to challenge the current state of affairs.

Fourth and finally, a radical democratic project is based not on the distinction between friend and foe in the sense of Carl Schmitt (1932), but rather on the notion of 'agonistic pluralism,' a clear distinction of adversaries that fight to achieve a better order, although no victory can be final (Mouffe 2005b). Accordingly, it would be erroneous to think that deliberative procedures can offer a proper solution to the current problems of democracy, since the very process of deliberation relies on the idea of rational consensus and leaves no space for taking into account passions, affects, and power struggles. Hence, radical democracy argues that the conflictual dimension of politics is one of the main drivers of democracy. This implies that social antagonisms can be tamed or sublimated, but can (and should) never be completely eliminated.

In conclusion, the core attribute of radical democracy relies on the denunciation of oppressive power relations and the struggles for transforming this situation. Laclau and Mouffe oppose this model of permanent conflict to liberal democracy's model of enforced consensus. Although we do acknowledge the importance of the contributions of Laclau and Mouffe and their many followers to the debate on populism, we do not consider radical democracy a viable concept for the kind of research that we aim for in this book. First and foremost, it lacks a clear definition. Consequently, this approach might be helpful for opening up the canon of democracy, but is problematic when it comes to studying the ambivalent relationship between populism and democracy in empirical rather than in normative and/or theoretical terms.

Moreover, we are not convinced that liberal democracy *by definition* excludes a conflictual model of politics. In essence, Laclau and Mouffe seem to react most directly to the theoretical models of deliberative democracy of Jürgen Habermas and the 'Third Way' of Anthony Giddens, which have only partial relevance in real life. And even against the consensual model of democracy, so prominent within Western Europe (Lijphart 1999), stands the equally viable conflictual model prevalent in the Anglo-Saxon world, which are also liberal democracies. In addition, Dahl (1970, 1989) is not blind to the existence of struggles that do not always have a clear democratic solution, and this is why he argues that under certain conditions (e.g. multi-ethnic states), it may be worth trying to dissolve the political association into more harmonious units or promote a process of secession.

1.3   Populism and democracy: friend *and* foe

In most circles and countries the term *populism* has a negative connotation, whereas *democracy* has a clear positive connotation. Often populism is seen as a threat to democracy, undermining its key values and striving for an alternative, an authoritarian system. As recently as April 2010, European Union President Herman Van Rompuy declared populism the biggest danger to Europe (*Frankfurter Allgemeine Zeitung*, 9 April 2010). However, this negative position is not shared everywhere and, moreover, is something that has evolved. Particularly in the United States, early scholarship on populism was largely sympathetic towards populism (e.g. John D. Hicks), until the emergence of the highly negative 'revisionist' scholarship of the 1960s (e.g. Richard Hofstadter) followed by a more positive 'school of counter revisionists' led by Norman Pollack (Conway 1978: 101–7).

That said, in all times and across all regions opinions have differed on the relationship between populism and democracy; for example, against Gino Germani's negative interpretation of Latin American populism stood Laclau's positive assessment, and Hofstadter's vehement critique of U.S. populism is countered by highly sympathetic accounts by Lawrence Goodwyn or Michael Kazin. Even in contemporary Europe, where right-wing populism is broadly considered a 'normal pathology' (Scheuch and Klingemann 1967; see Mudde 2010), authors like Torbjörn Tännsjö (1992) argue that populism is the purest form of democracy, while Laclau maintains that populism is the '*sine qua non* requirement of the political' (2005a: 154).

Our aim here is to come to a non-normative position on the relationship between populism and democracy based on our definitions (see Sections 1.1 and 1.2).[4] We develop our position primarily on the basis of a conceptual analysis, without of course being blind to the empirical realities. In short, we argue that populism can be both a corrective and a threat to democracy. More specifically, at the theoretical level, populism is essentially democratic (e.g. Canovan 1999; Laclau 2005a; Tännsjö 1992), but it is ambivalent towards *liberal* democracy (e.g. Canovan 2002; Decker 2006; Mudde 2007; O'Donnell 1994; Plattner 2010).[5]

---

[4] We accept the argument that all science is implicitly normative. Our point here is that our prime concern is not normative but empirical, and that we do not define liberal democracy as 'good' or 'better' than populism, even if most of the contributors in this book, including us, might actually think so.

[5] Interestingly, in '*A Preface to Democratic Theory*,' Dahl (1956) implicitly refers to the tensions between populism and liberal democracy, distinguishing and confronting two theories of democracy: the Madisonian approach and the populistic approach. While the first postulates the avoidance of the 'tyranny of the majority' as the goal to be maximized, the second aims to achieve popular sovereignty and political equality at any cost. In addition, Dahl develops here his notion of polyarchy as a type of political rule, which inevitably combines elements of the Madisonian and the populistic approach.

As said, the relationship between populism and democracy is straight-forward and positive. At least in theory, populism supports popular sovereignty and majority rule. Or, as John Green (2006) has stated: "Populism, at its root, is democratic in nature, even if many populist leaders (once they reach power) may not be democratically inclined." Hence, one would expect populists to play a particularly positive role during the first phases of democratization, by giving voice to the people, attacking the authoritarian establishment, and pushing for the realization of free and fair elections (Mudde and Rovira Kaltwasser 2010).

The relationship to representative democracy is also predominantly positive. Many authors have argued that populism is fundamentally opposed to representation (e.g. Taggart 2002), but that is an overstate-ment. Although many populists indeed rally against the representa-tives in their country, or argue that the system of representation fails and should be extended with plebiscitary instruments, they oppose the wrong *kind* of representation, not representation per se (e.g. Mudde 2004). Populists accept representation by someone of 'the people,' not of 'the elite' (remember that this distinction is moral, not situational).

Populism and liberal democracy maintain a much more compli-cated relationship, finally (e.g. Mudde 2007: ch.6). Quintessentially, the ambivalence of the relationship is directly related to the internal contra-diction of liberal democracy, that is, the tension between the democratic promise of majority rule and the reality of constitutional protection of minority rights (e.g. Canovan 1999; Mény and Surel 2002b). In this struggle, populism is clearly on the side of majority rule. Moreover, as an essentially monist ideology that believes in the existence of a 'general will of the people,' populism is hostile towards pluralism and the protection of minorities. Accordingly, populism is based on the primacy of the pol-itical, which means that any other institutional centre of power, including the judiciary, is believed to be secondary. After all, 'the general will of the people' cannot be limited by anything, not even constitutional protec-tions, that is, *vox populi, vox dei* (Mudde 2010: 1175).

In addition, it might be the case that populism emerges partly as a product of the very existence of democracy. Since the latter is based on the periodic realization of free and fair elections, it provides a mechanism by which the people can channel their dissatisfaction with the political establishment. At the same time, democracy generates aspirations, which if not satisfied might well lead to political discontent and thus a fertile soil for the rise of populism. As Benjamin Arditi (2004) has indicated in his dialogue with Margaret Canovan (1999), there are good reasons to think that populism follows democracy like a shadow.

1.4   Populist effects on the quality of democracy: corrective *and* threat

Having laid out the theoretical relationship between populism and democracy, we turn our attention to the empirical question of how populist actors can affect 'real existing democracies,' 'polyarchies' in Dahl's terms. In this regard, it is worth repeating that we use a minimal definition of liberal democracy, which is most useful for distinguishing liberal democracies from competitive autocracies.[6] As O'Donnell (1996: 35) has pointed out, Dahl's concept establishes a crucial cut-off point:

> one that separates cases where there exist inclusive, fair, and competitive elections and basic accompanying freedoms from all others, including not only unabashed authoritarian regimes but also countries that hold elections but lack some of the characteristics that jointly define polyarchy.

Nevertheless, by using Dahl's definition of liberal democracy, we are confronted with the intension–extension dilemma highlighted by Giovanni Sartori (1970): While the notion of polyarchy can be applied to a wide range of cases and avoids conceptual stretching (i.e. high extension), it has little analytical leverage to notice differences within the category of 'real existing democracies' (i.e. low intension). Consequently, we are aware of the fact that liberal democratic regimes, according to Dahl's minimal definition, might show a great level of variety, since they can be organized in very different ways (e.g. parliamentary vs. presidential systems) and might have more or less state capacity to supervise democratic decision making and put its results into practice (Tilly 2007: 15).

Accordingly, the cross-regional nature of this project implies that we are dealing deliberatively with very different liberal democratic regimes. Indeed, the result of the 'third wave of democratization' has been a notable expansion of polyarchies around the world, which share the core attributes of the previously mentioned minimal definition, but differ in many other aspects. Not surprisingly, the academic debate has moved gradually from explaining regime transitions to assessing the *quality* of democracy (Mazzuca 2010; Morlino 2004; Offe 2003). This concern is directly linked to Dahl's approach, since he underlines that (liberal) democracy is first of all an ideal, which never can be fully achieved. In other words, reforms to improve democratic quality are crucial not only

---

[6] Although potentially interesting, we are not interested in analyzing whether authoritarian regimes employ a populist ideology with the aim of consolidating this kind of political systems (e.g. Mahmoud Ahmadinejad in Iran or Aleksandr Lukashenka in Belarus; on the latter, see Matsuzato 2004).

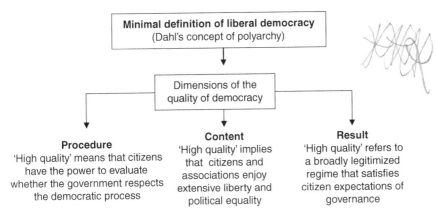

Figure 1.1. Dimensions of the quality of democracy.

for consolidating 'new' democracies, but also for deepening 'old' democracies (Whitehead 2002: 25–7).

In sum, there are very different types of democratic regimes, which can have a higher or lower level of democratic quality. Thus, we are interested in analysing in which ways populism can be a corrective and/or a threat to the quality of democracy. In order to answer this question, it is worth taking into account Larry Diamond and Leonardo Morlino's (2005) distinction of three dimensions of the quality of democracy: procedure, content, and result. Although these three dimensions may well be complementary, it cannot be ruled out that there are certain trade-offs between them. Indeed, populist actors usually claim that the results of the democratic regime are poor, and to remediate this situation they propose to adjust the procedural dimension of the democratic system (e.g. strengthen popular sovereignty at the cost of constitutionalism). Beyond the question of possible tradeoffs, as Figure 1.1. shows, each of these dimensions refers to an ideal state of affairs, that is, areas in which a democracy can improve its performance in order to achieve durable legitimacy and solve its internal problems.

Populism can affect each dimension of the quality of democracy in *both* negative and positive terms. Borrowing Andreas Schedler's (1998) terminology, consider two hypothetical scenarios. In one scenario, populism improves the quality of democracy by facilitating its *deepening* (in the case of consolidated democracies) or its *completion* (in the case of unconsolidated democracies). In the other, populism deteriorates the quality of democracy by facilitating a process of democratic *erosion* (in the case of consolidated democracies) or of democratic *breakdown* (in the case of unconsolidated democracies).

The scholarly literature is full of suggestions of how populism can be a corrective or threat to democracy, but many of these are not necessarily relevant, because they relate to effects of the host ideology (e.g. nationalism or socialism) or to aspects not part of our definition of populism (e.g. type of mobilization or clientelism). Nevertheless, we offer in this chapter some of the positive and negative effects populism is expected to have on the quality of democracy. The term 'positive effect' refers to instances when populism strengthens the quality of democracy, whereas 'negative effects' means that populism weakens the quality of democracy. Given that many of these effects are simply claimed, or follow from studies using different definitions of populism, they are to be treated as hypotheses in the case studies. Moreover, while the authors took these possible effects into account in their country studies, they were encouraged to go further and include whatever other positive or negative effects they came across.

Briefly, we expect populism to strengthen political participation, yet weaken public contestation (Rovira Kaltwasser 2012). In terms of Dahl's two dimensions of polyarchy, populism is believed to increase participation by the *inclusion* of marginalized groups in society but limit (the possibilities for) contestation by *centralizing* power in the executive and *undermining* the power of counter-balancing powers.[7] Seen in this light, populism reminds us that there is always a tension between popular will and constitutionalism: While an excessive emphasis on the former could lead to a 'tyranny of the majority,' too much weight on the latter could bring about opaque processes of decision making and therefore increasing discontent among the population (Plattner 2010). In effect, the very concept of 'checks and balances' suggests the existence, or at least the real possibility, of an imbalance (Armony and Schamis 2005: 116).

1.4.1   Positive effects

When populism is seen as a corrective to the quality of democracy, emphasis is mostly put on the inclusion of marginalized groups of 'the people.' However, there are many different aspects related to this point, some more on the input and other more on the output side of democracy (Easton 1965). For heuristic purposes, we have tried to disentangle the various aspects, realizing perfectly well that they are not always distinguishable in practise.

---

[7] We thank Kurt Weyland for pointing us to the link to Dahl (1971) and Kirk Hawkins for the succinct summary of the argument.

(1) Populism can give voice to groups that do not feel represented by the elites, by putting forward topics relevant for a 'silent majority' (e.g. issues such as immigration in Europe or economic integration in Latin America).

(2) Populism can mobilize excluded sections of society (e.g. 'the underclass'), improving their political integration.

(3) Populism can represent excluded sections of society by implementing policies that they prefer.

(4) Populism can provide an ideological bridge that supports the building of important social and political coalitions, often across class lines, thus providing a key dynamic element in the evolution of party systems and related modes of political representation.

(5) Populism can increase democratic accountability by making issues and policies part of the political realm (rather than the economic or judicial realms).

(6) Populism can bring back the conflictive dimension of politics and thus help revitalize both public opinion and social movements in order to foster the 'democratization of democracy.'

1.4.2   Negative effects

Whereas most positive effects relate to the inclusion of some previously – subjectively or objectively – excluded groups of society, many negative effects mentioned in the literature relate to the marginalization of specific groups of society, the weakening of political institutions, culminating in the undermining of minority rights and protections. Reflecting the main position in the literature, which sees populism as a threat to the quality of democracy, we list the following potential negative effects.

(1) Populism can use the notion and praxis of popular sovereignty to contravene the 'checks and balances' and separation of powers of liberal democracy.

(2) Populism can use the notion and praxis of majority rule to circumvent and ignore minority rights.

(3) Populism can promote the establishment of a new political cleavage (populists vs. non-populists), which impedes the formation of stable political coalitions.

(4) Populism can lead to a moralization of politics, making compromise and consensus extremely difficult (if not impossible).

(5) Populism can foster a plebiscitary transformation of politics, which undermines the legitimacy and power of political institutions (e.g. parties and parliaments) and unelected bodies (e.g. organizations

such as central banks or inspections offices) that are indispensable to 'good governance.'

(6) Ironically, by advocating an opening up of political life to non-elites, populism's majoritarian, anti-elite thrust can easily promote a shrinkage of 'the political' and cause a contraction of the effective democratic space.

1.5   Which circumstances determine the effects of populism?

As we have argued, populism can have positive and negative effects on the quality of democracy. Many of these effects have been documented in empirical studies of populist actors, even if many of these studies used a different definition of populism or did not distinguish between the effects caused by populism and those caused by its 'host ideology.' Still, little has been theorized about the circumstances under which populism can and is used for good rather than evil. In other words, under which circumstances does populism become a corrective rather than a threat for (liberal) democracy?

It makes sense to look first at the two key variables in that relationship: populism and democracy. We divide both into a strong and weak group: the distinctions are between populism in government (strong) and populism in opposition (weak) and between consolidated democracies (strong) and unconsolidated democracies (weak). Certainly, democratic 'consolidation' is another contested concept within the realm of the social sciences. In consonance with O'Donnell (1996), we maintain that the notion of consolidated democracy does not allude to a 'complete' or 'perfect' form of government, but rather to a political regime in which free and fair elections are institutionalized as the mechanism whereby access to political power is determined. This means that consolidated democracies show a great level of variance, since they have different institutional arrangements (e.g. parliamentarian or presidential system), and might be more or less prone to the development of specific liabilities (e.g. corruption, abuse of executive decree, weak accountability, etc.) (Mazzuca 2010: 335–6).

Hence, by using the notion of (un)consolidated democracies, we adhere here to the approach developed by Schedler, who maintains that "[t]he term 'democratic consolidation' should refer to expectations of regime continuity – and to nothing else. Accordingly, the concept of 'consolidated democracy' should describe a regime that relevant observers expect to last well into the future – and nothing else" (1998: 102). Our key suppositions are: (i) populists will be more effective when democracy is weak;

Table 1.1. *Relationship by strength of populism and democracy*

Populism Democracy	Opposition	Government
Consolidated	*The Vlaams Blok/Belang in Belgium (since 1991)*	*FPÖ/BZÖ in Austria (2000–2007)*
	The Reform Party in Canada (1987–2000)	Hugo Chávez in Venezuela (since 1998)
Unconsolidated	*SPR-RSČ in the Czech Republic (1992–1998)*	*Alberto Fujimori in Peru (1990–2000)*
	Andrés Manuel López Obrador in Mexico (2006)	Vladimír Mečiar in Slovakia (1992–8)

or, to put it in another way, the strength of democracy influences the depth of the populism's impact on democracy; (ii) populists will prioritize negative effects in government and positive effects in opposition; in other words, the strength of populism influences the depth of its impact on democracy. This leads us to the following key hypotheses:

> *Hyp 1) Populism in government has stronger effects on democracy than populism in opposition.*
> *Hyp 2) Populism in government has more negative effects on democracy than populism in opposition.*
> *Hyp 3) Populism has stronger effects on unconsolidated democracies than on consolidated democracies.*

On the basis of these two key variables we constructed a two-by-two table that has structured the selection of case studies (see Table 1.1). We have chosen two cases per type of relationship between populism and democracy, always ensuring that one case is from Europe (East or West) and the other from the Americas (North or South). The case studies of the book will analyse empirically the effect of the main populist actor in their country on democracy, guided by the conceptual and theoretical framework of this chapter. We build from the cases with the hypothesized smallest and most positive effects to those with the hypothesized largest and most negative effects.

(1) *Populism in opposition in consolidated democracies.* In this first case liberal democracy is much stronger than populism. We hypothesize that populism will make small positive effects to the quality of democracy, as there is little room for change (including progress). We selected two countries with strong oppositional populist forces to increase the

chances of any effect of the populists. In Chapter 2 Sarah de Lange and Tjitske Akkerman analyse the case of Belgium, with a sizeable *Vlaams Blok/Belang* presence in parliament (i.e. since 1991), while David Laycock focuses on Canada during the height of the Reform Party (1987–2000) in Chapter 3.

(2) *Populism in opposition in unconsolidated democracies.* In this case both populism and democracy are relatively weak. Given that they have no hold on actual power, we hypothesize that populists will be more a corrective than a threat to the quality of democracy. They will focus on criticizing the various problems of the new democracy, including corruption, inefficiency, and exclusion and will push for democratic reforms. Séan Hanley discusses the Czech Republic when the SPR-RSČ was in parliament (1992–8) in Chapter 4, while Kathleen Bruhn analyses the case of Mexico when Andrés Manuel López Obrador challenged for the presidency (2006) in Chapter 5.

(3) *Populism in government in consolidated democracies.* Here, both populism and democracy are strong. We hypothesize that populists will have a moderate either positive or negative effect, as they will be confronted by a resilient liberal democracy. Moreover, it is worth noting that populism's overall impact on the liberal democratic regime will depend on its electoral force of the former, that is, the existence of a majority supporting the populist actors in government, particularly when it comes to undermining the 'checks and balances.' In Chapter 6 Franz Fallend analyses Austria under the Schüssel governments (2000–7), and in Chapter 7 Kenneth Roberts critically assesses the situation of Venezuela under President Chávez (since 1998).[8]

(4) *Populism in government in unconsolidated democracies.* In this last situation populism is believed to have the strongest position vis-à-vis democracy. We hypothesize that populism will be most effective in this situation. However, we also predict the most negative effects, as populism in power leads to polarization and consequently defensive measures from the government, which will threaten the strength or development of liberal democratic institutions and protections. The

---

[8] It is important to note that there is a significant difference in executive power between presidents in a presidential system and (junior) coalition parties in a parliamentary system. In addition, we are of the opinion that Venezuela is a prime example of a consolidated democracy within Latin America: Whereas in the 1960s and 1970s almost every country of the region saw the rise of authoritarian regimes, Venezuela has maintained relatively free and fair elections since 1958. As Philippe Schmitter (2010: 28) has recently argued, "[t]he revival of 'delegative democracy' or 'hyperpresidentialism' in Latin America with the recent spate of regimes imitating that of Hugo Chávez in Venezuela does not seem (to me) to be the result of failed transitions, but rather a reaction to practices of *consolidated* democracies that were excessively collusive (Venezuela) or that were insensitive to the demands of excluded ethnic groups (Bolivia and Ecuador)" (our italics).

cases that we selected for this category are Peru under President Fujimori (1990–2000), discussed by Steve Levitsky and James Loxton in Chapter 8, and Slovakia under Prime Minister Vladimír Mečiar (1992–8), analysed by Kevin Deegan-Krause in Chapter 9.

After having explained the case selection, we can develop a set of more detailed research questions about the ambivalent relationship between populism and liberal democracy. In concrete terms, we propose the following additional hypotheses:

> *Hyp 4) Populism in opposition in consolidated democracies will have modest positive effects on the quality of democracy.*
>
> *Hyp 5) Populism in opposition in unconsolidated democracies will have moderate positive effects on the quality of democracy.*
>
> *Hyp 6) Populism in government in consolidated democracies will have moderate negative effects on the quality of democracy.*
>
> *Hyp 7) Populism in government in unconsolidated democracies will have significant negative effects on the quality of democracy.*

Obviously, there are other circumstances that can influence the nature of populist effects on liberal democracy. However, we do not intend to develop more hypotheses in this introductory chapter, since this would probably generate more confusion than clarity at this stage. In other words, we are aware of the fact that many other factors may determine whether populism works as a threat or a corrective for democracy. Future studies can use the framework developed here and propose additional hypotheses.

Conclusions

In this introductory chapter we have laid out our views on the relationship between populism and democracy, which constitutes the conceptual and theoretical framework of this edited volume. First, we provided definitions of populism, democracy, and liberal democracy. Second, and following from this, we argued that, in theory, populism has a clearly positive relationship to democracy, but an ambivalent relationship to liberal democracy. In other words, populism can be both a corrective and a threat to liberal democracy. Third, we suggested possible positive and negative effects of populism on the quality of existing democracies. And fourth, we hypothesized which conditions influence the *strength* and *type* of the effects.

We have asked the other contributors to the book to accept, at least for this particular endeavour, our definitions and the consequent ambivalent relationship between populism and liberal democracy. This has fostered a coherent and consistent edited volume and ensured that the different individual case studies speak to each other. However, we also very much encouraged constructive critical feedback on the suggested potential effects and on the hypothesized factors affecting them (Sections 1.4 and 1.5), and provided ample space for each contributor to consider additional and alternative effects and factors. In the concluding chapter, we assess the validity of the presented framework and discuss the various critiques and innovations presented in the empirical chapters. We end the volume with some suggestions for future research on the relationship between populism and democracy.

In summary, this introductory chapter does not intend to say the last word on how to examine the ambivalent relationship between populism and democracy. We simply aim to offer a clear and concise framework for analysing the impact of populism on democracy in *empirical* rather than in normative and/or theoretical terms. Accordingly, the approach presented here can be used and complemented by future studies. Given that there is almost no cross-regional research on populism, we hope that this edited volume contributes to opening up the canon on the study of populism and its impact on democracy.

2 Populist parties in Belgium: a case of hegemonic liberal democracy?

Sarah L. de Lange and Tjitske Akkerman

Introduction

Over the past decades populist parties have become increasingly successful in Western Europe. Especially in consensus democracies such as Austria, Belgium, Denmark, the Netherlands, Norway, and Switzerland, left- and right-wing populist parties have managed to attract the support of substantial parts of the population. In some of these countries populist parties have recently joined government coalitions (e.g. the FPÖ in Austria and the LPF in the Netherlands), but in other countries they have not been able to make the transition from pariah to power. Belgium is a prime example of the latter group of countries, because populist parties have never governed in this country.

Several populist parties have emerged in Belgium since the 1980s, of which the Flemish Interest (VB) has been the most successful. The populist radical right party achieved its electoral breakthrough in the local elections in Antwerp in 1988. Three years later it also became an important player in the federal parliament with twelve (out of 150) elected representatives. In recent years the party has been joined in the federal parliament by two other populist parties of right-wing signature: the Flemish List Dedecker (LDD) and the Walloon National Front (FN). The first party is usually qualified as a neoliberal populist party (Pauwels 2010), while the second is mostly included in the family of populist radical right parties (e.g. Art 2011; Carter 2005; Coffé 2005a; Mudde 2007; Norris 2005). Left-wing populist parties have not been represented in the Belgian parliament, although the social democratic Socialist Party. Different (SP.A) has been accused of having populist tendencies (Jagers 2006).

This chapter assesses the effects of the rise of the VB, Belgium's most successful populist party, on the quality of liberal democracy in the country. First, it outlines the emergence of the VB and examines the populist ideology of the party. Second, it investigates if and how the VB constitutes a corrective and/or a threat to Belgian liberal democracy. The chapter demonstrates that the positive *and* the negative effects of the rise of the VB are partly shaped by the fact that the party has been excluded from power by means of a *cordon sanitaire*. In this respect Belgium is a clear case of a hegemonic liberal democracy, in which the influence of a successful populist party on the quality of liberal democracy is limited.

2.1   Populist parties in Belgium

In 1977 a number of prominent politicians left the People's Union (VU) because the Flemish nationalist party had agreed to the Egmond Pact, which arranged the transformation of Belgium into a federal state. Dissatisfied with the compromises that the pact entailed, Lode Claes founded the Flemish People's Party (VVP), while Karel Dillen established the Flemish National Party (VNP). For the elections of December 1978 the two parties entered into an electoral alliance titled Flemish Block (VB), which obtained 1.4 per cent of the vote. Since Dillen was the only candidate elected, he took control over the more radical wing of the VVP and merged it with his VNP. The nascent party continued under the name Flemish Block, a reference to the pre-war Flemish National Block.

Dillen laid down the party ideology in a manifest popularly known as the *Orange Booklet* (*Oranje Boekje*). Therein he presented the three ideological pillars of the VB, namely conservatism, secessionist nationalism, and solidarism, and declared that Flemish independence was the most important goal of the party. However, the ideological appeal of the VB turned out to be very limited in the 1980s. Dillen remained the party's only representative until 1987, when Gerolf Annemans joined him in the federal parliament.

In the early 1980s the VB broadened its ideological profile and enthusiastically embraced nativism and populism. In the 1982 local elections in Antwerp, the party started to campaign on immigration and integration issues and in 1992 it published the infamous seventy-point programme, in which it promoted the return of immigrants to their countries of origin (e.g. Mudde 2000; Spruyt 1995). Moreover, it started to heavily criticize the established parties, claiming that they had betrayed the people. To reinforce the impact of these ideological changes, Dillen recruited a number of young politicians such as Filip Dewinter, Frank Vanhecke, and the already mentioned Annemans to appeal to voters that did not come from the Flemish nationalist milieu.

The changes proved highly successful and in 1988 the VB had its electoral breakthrough in the municipal elections, gaining 17.7 per cent of the vote in Antwerp, the biggest city in Flanders. The party's national

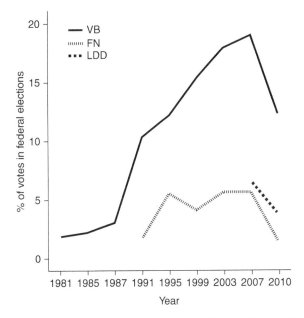

Figure 2.1. The electoral success of populist parties in Belgium, 1981–2010.
Note: Since Belgium has a confederal party system, percentages are calculated on a regional basis. The LDD and VB participate in electoral districts in Brussels and Flanders, while the FN participates in electoral districts in Brussels and Wallonia.
Source: Ministry of Interior.

breakthrough followed on 24 November 1991, often referred to as (the first) Black Sunday, in which it won 9.3 per cent of the vote in the federal elections. In reaction to the breakthrough of the populist radical right party, the established parties erected a *cordon sanitaire*, excluding the VB from power on a priori grounds. Notwithstanding the *cordon sanitaire*, the VB continued to grow in subsequent elections, obtaining 12.2 per cent of the vote in 1995, 15.3 per cent in 1999, 17.1 per cent in 2003, and 19.0 per cent in 2007 (see Figure 2.1).

Shortly after the turn of the century the tables started to turn for the VB. In 2004, after a trial that had taken four years, a judge ruled that the party had "clearly and repeatedly promoted discrimination against foreigners" and it was convicted for breaking the anti-racism law (Bale 2007; Brems 2006). Consequentially, the party changed its name from Vlaams Blok (Flemish Block) to Vlaams Belang (Flemish Interest), a change that many commentators believed to be merely cosmetic. Analyses of the various VB programmes show that no sub-stantive changes have been made since the party changed its name in 2004 (Coffé 2005b; Erk 2005).

Although the VB did fare well in the 2007 elections, tensions started to emerge in the party over the ideological course it should steer. A group of *realos* believed the party should moderate its stances to attract more voters and become an acceptable partner to the established parties, while a group of *fundis* thought that moderation would endanger the electoral success of the party and pleaded in favour of a more radical course. This is, incidentally, a classic dilemma for populist parties (Heinisch 2003; Van Donselaar 1995).

As a consequence of this internal struggle, the VB lost five of its seven-teen seats in the elections of June 2010. The other populist parties on the right, the FN, which had entered parliament in 1991, and the LDD, which emerged on the political scene in 2007, performed equally poorly. The LDD managed to hold on to one seat, occupied by the party's founder Jean-Marie Dedecker, while the FN has disappeared from the federal parliament altogether (see Figure 2.1). The electoral beating the VB has received has made the internal tensions in the party worse and a large number of prominent members of parliament have left the party since the elections, including Karim van Overmeire, Koen Dillen, Francis Van der Eynde, Franck Vanhecke, and Jurgen Ceder. Thus, at the moment the future of the three Belgian populist parties looks rather bleak.

Many scholars have studied the electoral success of the VB and have investigated who votes for the populist radical right party and why. The average voter for the VB is a male (skilled) blue-collar worker, with a low level of formal training and no religious affiliation, and is either rela-tively young (between nineteen and thirty-four) or relatively old (fifty-five or older) (Billiet 1995; Billiet and De Witte 1995 2001; Coffé 2005c; Lubbers et al. 2000; Rink et al. 2009; Swyngedouw and Billiet 2002). In terms of demographic and socio-economic characteristics the average VB voter is thus a typical populist radical right supporter. In the early 1990s the VB recruited its voters mainly from the centre (CVP and VU) and left (SP); in later years voters primarily came from the right (VLD) (De Witte and Scheepers 1997). Until recently VB voters were extremely loyal. Once they had switched from one of the established parties to the populist radical right, they rarely returned. In the most recent elections this has changed, and a substantial number of VB voters has changed allegiances to the LDD (in 2007) or the N-VA (in 2010) (Pauwels 2010). In terms of geographical spread the support for the VB is concentrated in Antwerp and surroundings (Thijssen and De Lange 2005) and, to a lesser extent, in the triangle between Antwerp, Brussels, and Ghent (De

Decker et al. 2005). The party is especially successful in municipalities that (1) have high percentages of Moroccan and Turkish immigrants; (2) have small networks of social organizations; and (3) are relatively wealthy (Coffé et al. 2007; see also Lubbers et al. 2000; Rink et al. 2009).

Voters from these municipalities support the VB because of the attractiveness of the populist radical right party programme. The anti-immigrant proposals of the VB appeal to this group of voters, who have negative attitudes towards immigrants. They are more likely than the voters of other Flemish parties to feel threatened by immigrants, both in the cultural and economic domain. VB voters also feel more strongly about Flemish nationalism than other voters and have lower levels of political efficacy and political trust. However, the vote for the VB can be better qualified as an anti-immigrant vote than a political protest vote (Billiet and De Witte 1995, 2008), as voters are more attracted by the VB's nativism than by the party's populism.

2.2.   The populism of the VB

Many scholars have examined the ideology of the VB in detail (e.g. Gijsels 1992, 1994; Lucardie 2010; Spruyt 1995, 2000; Swyngedouw and Ivaldi 2001). There seems to be widespread agreement that it includes at least three ideological cornerstones: Flemish nationalism (e.g. Breuning and Ishiyama 1998), nativism (e.g. Mudde 1995, 2000), and populism (e.g. Jagers 2006). The three are closely related, as the people feature prominently in each of the ideological components. This is clearly visible in the former party slogan of the VB: *Eigen volk eerst!* (Own people first!).

The VB claims to represent the Flemish people, which it contrasts to (1) the francophone people in Brussels and Wallonia, (2) the asylum seekers and immigrants that have come to Flanders, and (3) the political elite, both on the Flemish and the Walloon side of the language border. In the ideology of the VB the delineation of the people is thus both horizontal (Flemish nationalism and nativism) and vertical (populism).

Jagers (2002, 2006) examined party magazines, programmes, and propaganda published in 2003 and 2004 to determine which populist elements can be detected in the ideology of the party. He concluded that the documents show that the VB is a full-fledged populist party that consistently refers to the Flemish people as both homogeneous and morally just.[1] The Flemish people are said to have common sense and to be

---

[1] Until the late 1980s, the VB can be better qualified as an aristocratic or elitist party (Lucardie 2010: 156–7; Mudde 2000: 112–13; Spruyt 2000: 84–5). In the *Orange Booklet* the party tried to disseminate the "aristocratic idea" that should replace "democratism and the spoiling of parliamentarism."

honest and industrious, something immigrants and the Walloon people are not. According to Jagers (2006: 216), 'The proverbial people of the VB are a homogeneous, undivided and internally congenial group, whose opinions and interests are systematically contrasted with those of other people, and especially those of the establishment.'

Anti-establishment rhetoric is very prominent in the programmes and propaganda of the VB. The political elite consists of politicians belonging to both government and opposition parties and is represented at the subnational, national, and supranational levels. The politicians are described as arrogant, corrupt, egoistic, incompetent, irresponsible, unreliable, and criminal. The VB regularly speaks of deception and electoral fraud and qualifies established politicians as political bandits and swindlers. Interesting, the VB describes the political elite in Flanders in different terms than the political elite in Wallonia. Flemish politicians are depicted as weak and submissive, while francophone politicians are portrayed as cunning and determined. Moreover, the VB is more critical of politicians of the left than the right.

One of the main reasons the VB criticizes the political elite is that it is unresponsive. According to the VB, 'It is a public secret that the positions of the ruling political class – for example those on immigration, drugs, crime and ethical issues – often deviate substantially from those advocated by the people' (VB 2004b). The party also believes that the political elite can remain in power because it is supported by a cultural elite, which populates institutions such as academia, the church, the judiciary, the media, the monarchy, and the trade unions. Together, the cultural and political elites undermine the sovereignty of the people. In the words of the VB, '"Own people first" expresses that power lies with the people and only the people and that it should not be concentrated in a dubious caste of professional politicians in an ivory tower or supranational organization' (VB 2004c). Jagers (2006: 221) therefore concludes that:

> The anti-establishment discourse of the VB, the pariah of Belgian politics, is very dominant. The *leitmotiv* is the notion of a conspiracy, a moral critique that from a well-defined center of power all possible means are being used against the VB and the people. The VB believes that it is struggling with the ruling political class over both ideal and real power.

Although the ideology of the VB is clearly populist, the party has few of the organizational characteristics usually associated with populist parties. Party leader Filip Dewinter is often qualified as charismatic, but his position in the party is contested. He shares his power with Bruno Valkeniers, chair of the party, and Gerolf Annemans, chair of the parliamentary group in the federal parliament. The VB also lacks the movement character that many populist parties have. The party is highly centralized, with decision making power concentrated in the hands of a small party elite, and the level of institutionalization is high. Members have few opportunities to influence candidate lists or party programmes.

2.3 The VB's relationship to liberal democracy

The populism of the VB informs the party's relationship to democracy. The party propagates the idea of a populist democracy in which the *volonté générale* prevails. To realize this type of democracy in Belgium, the VB proposes extensive institutional reforms. It seeks to abolish intermediary institutions, such as the provinces and the senate, and have more state functionaries elected, such as mayors and OCMW council members. Moreover, the VB would like to introduce a binding referendum to give citizens more say in Belgian and Flemish politics. According to the VB, the established parties are hesitant to introduce citizen initiatives or referenda because they are afraid to confront the people. It claims that the established parties fear that these instruments will bring to light the minority position of the political elite and thus undermine the legitimacy of their claim to power (Jagers 2006: 236).

Many commentators, journalists, politicians, and scholars claim that the VB poses a challenge, if not a direct threat, to democracy, because the principles of the populist democracy it seeks to establish conflict with the principles of liberal democracy. They allege that the populist radical right party rejects the *trias politica* and does not respect certain fundamental freedoms and rights enshrined in the Belgian constitution such as the freedom of speech and the right not to be discriminated against on the basis of ethnicity or religious affiliation. Many politicians also use these arguments to defend the *cordon sanitaire* around the VB, stating that 'in its programme and political practice the Vlaams Blok undervalues the fundamental democratic principles and related human constitutional rights' (Geysels 2008: 51).

The VB vehemently rejects these claims. In many documents the party asserts that 'from its foundation the VB has explicitly chosen democracy as the political model' (VB 2004b) and that 'the Vlaams Blok is in favor of the parliamentary democracy, which we understand to be a political system in which the people are governed by elected representatives from their own ranks' (VB 1996). Moreover, the party underlines that:

For us, Flanders should not only be a democracy, it should also be a democracy ruled by law. This entails that the rulers are subject to law (in the broadest sense of the word) and that they are not allowed to make any decisions that go against the constitution or the law. An essential principle of a constitutional democracy is also the separation of the legislative, executive, and judicial powers. (VB 2003)

In its party programmes the VB also claims to respect most constitutional rights such as the freedom of association, the freedom of education, the freedom of speech, the freedom of religion, and the principles of equality and non-discrimination. Moreover, in the VB's declaration of principles adopted in 2004, the party recognizes the European Convention on Human Rights (ECHR) and the right to self-determination of peoples as laid down in article 1 of the International Covenant on Civil and Political Rights (ICCPR).

In fact, the VB has often accused others, most notably the political elite and immigrants, of not obeying the Belgian constitution and the ideas that underpin the *trias politica*. In many publications the party asserts that the established parties do not respect the separation of powers and the constitutional rights of Flemish citizens. Especially after the party was convicted for breaching the anti-racism law, it argued that the established parties had instigated a political process and thereby crossed the line between the executive and the judiciary. In the words of the VB:

Courts are not qualified to judge the programs and propaganda of political parties. It is up to voters to judge these. Dissident opinions, also of those that criticize those in power, nourish the societal debate. (VB 2010)

The process is a classical example of the averting of power. It is a serious violation of the freedom of association and speech, as well as of elementary principle of the separation of powers. (VB 2004b)[2]

The party also attacks non-political actors such as civil society organizations and journalists for trying to limit the constitutional rights of Flemish citizens. According to the VB:

The *Centrum voor Gelijke Kansen en Racismebestrijding* [Center for Equal Opportunities and Fighting Racism] (CGKR) should be disbanded. Under the pretence of the fight against racism this centre curtails the freedom of speech. (VB 2010)

---

[2] In its verdict the Court of Appeal (cited in Brems 2006: 706) addressed these allegations and declared that:[The provision] in no way imposes the tyranny of 'political correctness.' Criticism, even severe criticism, by any group or association and even more by a political party is and remains possible. The public debate is a necessary and essential guarantee of the correct functioning of the democratic institutions. Criticism addressed to the immigrant population of the country is, as such, certainly not prohibited by the law. Problems that may be caused by this part of the population can and must be discussed. Proposals to remedy such problems that are objectively and reasonably justified can without doubt still be formulated. Yet what the provision aims to avoid is 'the profiling of a group or association, albeit a political party, as a group or association [...] that systematically incites to intolerance inspired by racism and xenophobia.'

The VB not only criticizes Belgian cultural and political elites for not respecting the principles of a constitutional and representative democracy, it also violently attacks Islam for disrespecting these principles. The party argues that the Islamic religion does not respect the separation of church and state and it vehemently criticizes Muslim organizations and states for not defending or respecting equal rights (e.g. for men and women) and the freedom of speech (Jagers 2006: 245). In its programme for the 2004 regional elections, the VB declared that 'Not everybody finds it natural that men and women are treated equally, that church and state are separated in our society, that one has the liberty to chose who one wants to marry. We in Flanders do find that natural' (VB 2004b). Given these statements, Jagers (2006: 249) concludes that 'the VB discourse on democracy is explicitly populist, but not anti-constitutional. It is in principle in favor of the rule of law, but the people are sovereign and have the last word about the rights that are judicially enforceable via citizens' initiatives.'

However, some opponents of the VB have argued that these statements are nothing more than hollow phrases. They claim that the populist radical right party only supports liberal democratic principles because it wants to avoid a second indictment for breaking the anti-racism law. Moreover, critics believe the VB does not practice what it preaches. The party has, for example, been criticized for not respecting the freedom of speech of its adversaries, since it has taken legal action against a number of journalists that have published critical works about the party. In 2005, for instance, the party filed a complaint against Eric Goeman and Ron Hermans, two journalists and left-wing activists who had written a highly critical book about former commissioner and VB prominent Johan Demol.

The party has also been accused of blackmailing and threatening the artists that participated in the 0110 concerts against intolerance, which were held in Antwerp, Brussels, and Charleroi in October 2006 (De Cleen 2009; De Cleen and Carpentier 2010). The party website described the concerts as 'a political propaganda tool of the traditional political elites,' arguing that 'it should be clear by now that the entire plan has little or nothing to do with "tolerance" but everything [to do] with an operation orchestrated and paid for by the regime against a successful opposition party.' In an open letter VB leader Dewinter urged artists not to take the stage in any of the participating cities, stating that:

Of course it is a good thing that artists too commit and speak out against intolerance and racism. The perfidious attempt to link racism and intolerance to the Vlaams Belang and to dissuade the voter from voting for Vlaams Belang by creating the impression that popular artists support this point of view, however, is unfair and unacceptable. (VB 2004b)

A number of critics of the VB also point out that the party still defends the idea of an ethnocracy in its programmes and propaganda (Spruyt 2000). Even after the name change to Vlaams Belang in 2004, the VB still argued that 'only in a Flemish state sufficient consensus exists in society about shared norms and values to solve disagreements in a democratic and reasonable way' (VB 2004b). In its declaration of principles, drafted the same year, the VB stated that 'the multicultural mistake should be undone' (VB 2004a) and the party still advocates the repatriation of immigrants that refuse to assimilate. Many of the policy proposals included in VB manifestos are thus at odds with the principle of pluralism, which is strongly anchored in the Belgian constitution. Other policy proposals, especially those to curtail the rights of Muslims in Belgium, potentially conflict with the freedom of religion codified in article 19 of the Belgian constitution.

2.4   The effects of the rise of the VB at the political level

Populist parties fulfil a number of important functions in representative democracies, of which the signaling function is probably the most important. According to Taggart (2002: 75), their rise indicates the 'failings, fundamental or otherwise, in the system of politics.' The absence or presence of populist parties can thus be considered the 'barometer of the health of representative politics' (ibid.). Other scholars have argued that the emergence of populist parties is a consequence of 'the incapacity of traditional parties to provide distinctive forms of identifications around possible alternatives' (Mouffe 2005a: 55) and should therefore be interpreted as a manifestation of the so-called crisis of representation.

The established parties in Belgium have clearly picked up on this signal. Shortly after the breakthrough of the VB, many established parties decided to show voters their willingness to change and become more responsive by transforming their party names and by presenting new, young party leaders. The liberals led the way and changed their party name from the Party for Freedom and Progress (PVV) to Flemish Liberals and Democrats (VLD) in 1992. The change was initiated by Guy Verhofstadt, the newly elected PVV leader who had published his ideas to reform Belgian politics in a series of 'Citizen Manifestos' published between 1989 and 2006.

In the manifestos Verhofstadt stated that pressure groups had too much influence on policy outcomes in Belgium. To reduce the impact of these groups, he proposed to create an 'open debating culture' in which reforms were no longer exclusively discussed in backrooms, but also in the media and parliament. Moreover, Verhofstadt argued in favour of more transparent decision-making processes in Belgium and for more possibilities for citizens to influence policy making. In the 'citizens democracy' he envisioned, citizen initiatives and referenda served as important means to bridge the gap between politicians and voters. Thus, the change from PVV to VLD was not only cosmetic, but also ideological.[3]

The PVV clearly set a trend. Agalev continued under the name Green! (Groen!) in 2003, the Christian People's Party (CVP) became the Christian-Democratic & Flemish (CD&V) in 2001, and the Socialist Party (SP) started to present itself as the SP.A the same year. In the latter party the name change was followed by a period of ideological and organizational re-orientation. In 2003 the SP.A members elected Steve Stevaert, known for his one liners, as the new party leader. Many members hoped Stevaert could stop the electoral demise of the SP.A, which had lost a considerable number of voters to the VB. Stevaert, a former bar owner from Hasselt, believed he could turn the electoral tide by introducing a new form of socialism, sometimes referred to as 'cosy socialism.'

According to many journalists and political commentators Stevaert's socialism had a populist element to it since it focused partly on popular measures such as free public transport. He also modernized the party by creating a more open party structure and rejuvenated the party elite by selecting more female and younger candidates for regional and national elections. However, these measures were insufficient to gain the support of the former SP.A voters who had left the party for the VB.

In addition to these very manifest effects of the rise of the VB, the party also has had a more subtle influence on the established parties. Prior to the rise of the VB, political debates primarily addressed regionalist, religious, and socio-economic issues. The VB has put a number of other issues on the agenda, the most important being immigration and integration and law and order issues, and has obtained issue ownership over these issues.[4] However, the VB has not realized this independently. It has profited greatly from the agenda setting function of the media, which have devoted a lot of attention to the issues of the VB and thereby reinforced the issue ownership of the party (Walgrave and De Swert 2004, 2007). In reaction to the electoral success of the VB, the established parties have increasingly addressed issues like immigration and integration

---

[3] One of the other objectives of the transformation of the PVV was to get rid of the anti-Flemish image of the party. To achieve this, it enlisted a number of politicians from the VU, including Jaak Gabriels and Hugo Coveliers. The latter later left the VLD because he refused to respect the *cordon sanitaire*, and entered into an electoral alliance with the VB.

[4] Contrary to some other populist radical right parties in Western Europe, the VB has been less successful in obtaining issue ownership over the issue of European integration, which remains highly depoliticized in Belgium.

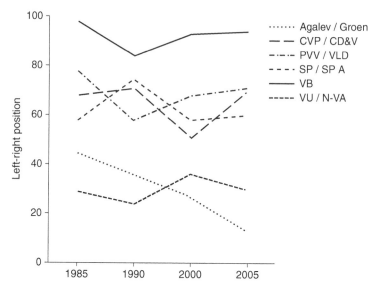

Figure 2.2. Left–right positions of Flemish parties, 1985–2005.
Source: Benoit and Laver (2006), Castles and Mair (1982), Huber and Inglehart (1993), Laver and Hunt (1989), and Lubbers (2001).

or law and order in their campaigns and election manifestos. Expert surveys demonstrate that in recent years the immigration issue has become the second most important issue in Flemish politics. The issue is especially salient for the VB (19.8 on a scale of one to twenty), Green! (16.4), the VLD (13.5), and the SP.A (13.2) (Benoit and Laver 2006).

The electoral success of the VB has not only forced established parties to address these issues, it has also given these parties an incentive to clarify and adjust their positions. It has been demonstrated that many established parties in Western Europe have moved to the right, both on the general left–right dimension and the issue of immigration and integration, in an attempt to address the political dissatisfaction on which populist radical right parties feed and to counter the electoral success of these parties (Bale 2003; Carter 2005; Meguid 2005; Norris 2005; Van Spanje 2010). Figure 2.2 shows that several established parties in Belgium have reacted in a similar fashion to the electoral success of the VB. The CD&V, the N-VA, and the VLD have gradually moved to the right in recent years, slowly closing the gap between the established right and the populist radical right. However, Green! and the SP.A have not sought to counter the electoral success of the VB by copying the stances of the party. Instead, these parties have opted for an adversarial strategy (cf. Meguid 2005), and have moved more to the left on the left–right continuum. Consequentially, polarization has slightly increased as a result of the success of the VB.[5]

Despite the VB's impact on the programmes of the established parties, policy making in Belgium does not carry the mark of the VB. Since the rise of the VB the established parties have stayed away from reforming policies over which the populist radical right party has issue ownership. They have struggled to come to terms with the demands for devolution, institutional reform, and stricter immigration and integration laws voiced by VB politicians and voters. When it comes to questions of devolution, Flemish and Walloon parties do not see eye to eye and the established parties have therefore been unable to reach a policy compromise that arranges for the partition of the administrative and electoral district Brussels-Halle-Vilvoorde, to name only one important issue in this field. Also, in terms of institutional reform, few initiatives have been taken by the established parties. In 1995 the federal parliament passed the Wet op de Volksraadpleging (Law on People's Consultation), which makes it possible for municipalities to organize referenda. However, few municipalities have made use of the law and the number of referenda that has been organized since 1995 remains extremely low (Buelens 2009). Moreover, Belgium is one of the few West European countries in which it is not possible to organize referenda at the regional or national level (Qvortrup 2005). Hence it is difficult to speak of the emergence of plebiscitary politics in Belgium.

Reforms in the field of immigration and integration policy have taken place, but often in a direction opposite to the one advocated by the VB. Today immigration and integration legislation is Belgium is quite liberal, especially when compared to that of other consensus democracies in Western Europe, such as Denmark, the Netherlands, and Switzerland. In the 1980s and 1990s the Belgian established parties pushed through a number of laws generally seen as very progressive. In the early 1980s Belgium abolished the *ius sanguinis* in favour of the less restrictive *ius solis*; in 2000 the Snel Belg Wet (Fast Belgian Law), which makes it possible for asylum seekers and immigrants to obtain Belgian citizenship after five years of legal residence in the country, came into effect; and in 2006 Belgium was one of the first countries in Western Europe to award the right to vote to immigrants from non-EU countries. Moreover, contrary to many other West European countries, Belgian citizenship is not

[5] The increase in polarization is not directly related to the difficulties established parties have experienced in recent years when forming government coalitions. These difficulties stem from conflicts between (individual) Flemish and francophone parties about devolution and the future of the Belgian state.

conditional on passing an integration test. Finally, symbolic measures, which have been highly popular in Denmark and the Netherlands, such as the creation of a minister in charge of immigration and integration affairs, have not yet been taken in Belgium.[6]

One of the main reasons why the influence of the VB on policy making has been restricted lies in the fact that the established parties have treated it as an outcast. Since the electoral breakthrough of the VB in 1989 the established parties have excluded the populist radical right party from power by means of a *cordon sanitaire*. They have agreed not to cooperate with the VB in the electoral arena (no electoral cartels, no joint press conferences or declarations towards the press), in the parliamentary arena (no joint legislative activities or voting agreements, no support for resolutions introduced by the VB), or the executive arena (no governmental coalitions) (Damen 2001). Consequentially, the VB has not been able to realize any of its policy proposals and Belgian democracy does not in any way resemble an ethnocracy or populist democracy.

At the same time, the *cordon sanitaire* has also made the established parties more vulnerable to the anti-establishment attacks of the VB. Since the party is excluded from the executive arena, established parties of the left and right have been forced to cooperate in ideologically heterogeneous 'rainbow coalitions.'[7] In Antwerp, for example, where the VB won 33.5 per cent of the votes in the 2006 local elections, cooperation between the Christian democrats, greens, Flemish nationalists, liberals, and socialists was necessary to form an executive committee and recruit aldermen. The committee, led by socialist mayor Patrick Janssens, included the CD&V, Green!, N-VA, SP.A, and VLD, but controlled only 66.5 per cent of the seats in the council. Many commentators were critical about the composition of the committee since it obfuscated the ideological differences between the established parties and made the VB's claim that the established parties form a cartel more credible.

Moreover, by erecting the *cordon sanitaire*, the established parties have also introduced a moral distinction between the righteous and the sinful in Flemish politics, which is in many ways analogous to the distinction between the pure people and corrupt elite. In other words, the *cordon*

---

[6] To counter the electoral success of the VB the established parties did create a new ministerial position, that of the minister of urban policy in 1995 (De Decker et al. 2005); Local politicians and semi-governmental organizations have enforced their own rules to promote integration in recent years. In 2009, for example, the Raad van het Gemeenschapsonderwijs (Council for Communal Education) has imposed a ban on headscarves in public school.

[7] Geys et al. (2006) have demonstrated that, because of the existence of the *cordon sanitaire*, established parties are less likely to form minimal winning, minimal number, and minimal size coalitions.

sanitaire is an expression of the moralization of Flemish politics, which might lead to self-idealization on the part of the established parties (Mouffe 2005b). Thus, although the *cordon sanitaire* contains the influence of the VB's populism on the quality of democracy in some ways, it also legitimizes and reinforces the discourse of the party.

2.5   The effect of the rise of the VB at the societal level

To properly assess the consequences of the rise of populist parties one also has to consider the impact these parties have on society. After all, the rise of populist parties is not only likely to affect parties and policies, but also the attitudes and behaviour of voters. Populist parties can either channel existing feelings of political distrust and dissatisfaction or reinforce these feelings with their anti-establishment discourse. Existing research suggests the latter effect is generally stronger, with citizens becoming more distrustful once they start voting for populist parties (Bélanger and Aarts 2006; Van der Brug 2003).

However, in the case of the VB there is little evidence that the party fuels anti-establishment sentiments. Figure 2.3 highlights that trust in political institutions in general, and in political parties, parliament, and government in particular, has been on the rise in Belgium since the late 1990s (see also Dekker et al. 2006; Dekker and Van der Meer 2004). From 1997 onwards the percentage of voters that trusts the Belgian and Flemish political institutions has steadily increased, reaching its height in 2001 with forty-three per cent of citizens trusting these institutions. The percentage of Belgian citizens satisfied with democracy has also grown since the late 1990s, with sixty to seventy per cent indicating that they are (very) satisfied with the way Belgian democracy works. Although it is difficult to demonstrate that these increases are in any way related to the rise of the VB, it does show that the rhetoric of the party has made Belgian citizens not more distrusting or dissatisfied, at least not at the aggregate level.

It thus seems that the VB channels existing feelings of distrust and dissatisfaction without intensifying or spreading them. The party functions as a safety valve in Belgian politics, since it makes the discontent of voters visible to the established parties. Belgium is one of the few countries in Europe in which voting is still compulsory and as a consequence voters cannot abstain to show their dissatisfaction with the established parties. Since exit is not an option, they can only voice their concerns by voting for populist parties.

Hooghe et al. (2009) demonstrate that voters that have low political trust are more likely to support the VB, which suggests that they indeed

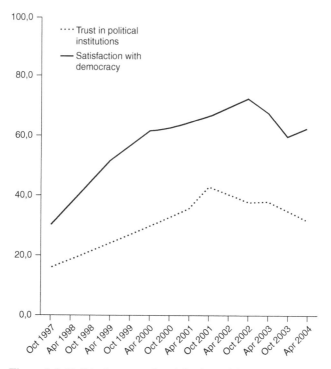

Figure 2.3. Political trust and satisfaction with democracy, 1997–2004.
Source: Eurobarometer 48.0, 51.0, 55.1, 56.2, 57.1,59.1,60.1,61.0
(weighted results)

cast a ballot for the populist party to send a message to the established
parties. They also show that forty-four per cent of voters that have low
political trust claim that they would never vote if compulsory voting were
to be abolished, compared to twenty-four per cent of voters with medium
political trust and ten per cent of voters with high political trust. Some
commentators have therefore concluded that compulsory voting fuels the
success of the VB, as it makes it impossible for disenchanted voters to
abstain. Their claims appear to be supported by simulations that demonstrate that the abolishment of compulsory voting would lead to the under-
representation of lower educated voters (Billiet 2002; De Winter and
Ackaert 1998), who are more likely to support the VB. However, more
detailed analyses (Hooghe et al. 2009; Hooghe and Pelleriaux 1998) highlight that, despite their low political trust, VB supporters are very loyal to
their party and unlikely to abstain when voting is not compulsory.

These observations at the individual level are confirmed by aggregate
analyses. In recent years the Belgian government has ceased to prosecute

citizens that do not participate in elections and turnout has been slowly declining, from ninety-five per cent in 1977 to eighty-seven per cent in 2010. During the same period support for the VB has steadily grown, from 1.1 per cent in 1981 to 12.0 per cent in 2007. The relationship between turnout and support for the VB is thus not a positive, but a negative one (correlation −.724, significant at the .05 level).[8] In other words, the higher the turnout in Belgium, the lower the percentage of votes cast for the VB. Hence, the party does channel feelings of political dissatisfaction, but it does not have a clear mobilization function.

The VB has nevertheless contributed to an increase of political awareness, interest, and participation among a very specific group of citizens in Flemish society. Over the years the party has recruited more than twenty-five thousand members (Quintelier 2008), most of which come from the Flemish nationalist milieu (Art 2008, 2011). A substantial proportion of these new members have not been politically active before they joined the VB. The VB manages to reach out to these citizens by campaigning actively in neighbourhoods in which the established parties are not or no longer present, but also by organizing a wide variety of party activities, such as barbeques, music festivals, and party congresses. These activities often have a popular, if not populist, character. The music festivals, for example, usually feature performances by popular Flemish singers that are representatives of so-called low culture, as opposed to the 'high culture' promoted by the established parties. In Antwerp, the electoral stronghold of the VB, the party has opened a community centre to provide party supporters with a place to meet and interact with party officials (Warmenbol 2010). The capacity of the VB to recruit large numbers of members is impressive, because the membership of established parties in Belgium has declined significantly since the early 1980s (Quintelier 2008).

Although the impact of the VB on society is thus primarily positive, civil society organizations have taken a wide variety of initiatives to counter the alleged negative effects of the rise of the VB, often supported by government subsidies. Most of these initiatives have been designed to 'unmask' the racist agenda of the VB and sensitize citizens to the threat posed by the populist radical right party. Others directly engage with the populist message of the VB, showing that the majority of Flemish citizens do not support the VB. This is, for example, the case of the mass demonstrations organized by VAKA-Hand in Hand (HiH) in 1992, 1994, 1998,

---

[8] The number of blank and invalid votes cast in Belgian elections, often seen as a sign of political dissatisfaction and protest voting, has been declining in recent years as well. It dropped from 8.4 per cent in 1978 to 5.1 per cent in 2007. The decline is, however, unrelated to the success of the VB.

and 2002 and Objectief 479,917, which sought to collect more signatures than votes cast for the VB. According to Detant (2005: 190–1), 'Through mobilizing large numbers HiH wanted to undermine the VB's populist claim that it was "the spokesperson for the silent majority."'[9] The organization sought to demonstrate that the support for the ideas of the VB was limited and that *the* Flemish people do not exist. De Cleen argues that the musicians who organized the 0110 concerts in October 2006 had a similar objective. A wide variety of popular artists were invited to perform during the concerts. De Cleen (2009: 587) contends that 'Through their participation in a concert for tolerance [...] these "people's singers" break the populist link between the VB and "the ordinary Flemish people" they represent.' More generally he believes that 'Such mobilizations of large numbers of people can be considered attempts to counter the VB's populist claim that it is the representative of the people' (De Cleen 2009: 587; see also De Cleen and Carpentier 2010).

Conclusion

In 1969 Ionescu and Gellner noted that 'a Spectre is haunting the world – populism.' Their observation still seems accurate today, especially in Belgium where three populist parties have emerged since the 1980s. The most successful of the three, the VB, has been represented for more than thirty years at the local, regional, and national levels. It can thus be expected that, if the rise of populist parties has an impact on liberal democracies, this can best be observed in Belgium. In its programmes, the VB pledges allegiance to the most important principles of liberal democracy, although the party also promotes a wide range of proposals that would transform Belgium into a populist democracy. However, critics argue that it has a selective reading of many constitutional rights, such as the freedom of speech and the freedom of religion, which it is only willing to respect as long as the people support these rights.[10] The attitude of the VB towards liberal democracy is thus not entirely supportive. At the same time, the influence of the VB on the quality of liberal democracy can be expected to be small, since it has been hypothesized in the introduction of this volume that populist parties will have a smaller

---

[9] The mass demonstrations organized in France after Jean Marie Le Pen reached the second round of the presidential elections in 2002 served a similar purpose (Berezin 2009).

[10] It seems that the conviction of the VB by the Court of Appeal in 2004 can explain the discrepancy between the party's rhetoric, on the one, and its actions, on the other hand. The conviction has made the VB aware of the fact that it should adhere to the principles of democracy, at least on paper.

influence in consolidated democracies than in unconsolidated democracies and that populist parties in opposition will have a smaller influence than populist parties in government (hypotheses 1 and 3).

Analysis of the consequences of the ascent of the VB confirms these expectations. The analysis demonstrates that the influence of the party on the quality of liberal democracy is mainly positive – providing support for hypothesis 2 formulated in the introduction to this volume – but also relatively small. Most significant, the VB channels feelings of discontent and distrust and makes these visible to established parties. In an attempt to decrease these feelings and win back disaffected voters, Belgian parties have reformed their organizations and programmes and become more responsive. However, the established parties have not changed their policy proposals to such an extent that they have become supporters of the idea of a populist democracy.

It appears that the positive effects of the rise of the VB are partly the consequence of the existence of a *cordon sanitaire* in Belgium. The *cordon* assures that the VB is excluded from executives at the local, regional, and national levels and therefore restricts the policy influence of the party. However, it also puts constraints on the established parties, since it limits the extent to which they can alter their positions on the issues raised by the VB (most notably immigration and integration issues). If the CD&V, Green!, N-VA, SP.A, and VLD were to copy the stances of the VB without any reservations, they would delegitimize the *cordon sanitaire*. To make matters more complicated, the *cordon sanitaire* also provides the VB with ammunition in its campaign against the established parties and introduces a friend–foe distinction in Belgian politics that is at odds with the inclusive, pluralist underpinnings of liberal democracy. Thus, the decision of the established parties in Belgium to exclude the VB by means of a *cordon sanitaire* has itself mixed effects on the quality of liberal democracy.

It can nevertheless be concluded that the Belgian case has many of the features of hegemonic liberal democracy. Populist parties are successful in the country, but their rise has not had a pervasive effect on liberal democracy. The quality of the democratic process in Belgium does not seem to suffer greatly from the emergence of populist parties and the negative effects that the emergence of populist parties has had on liberal democracy are offset by positive effects, the most important being an increase in the responsiveness of the established parties, at least in the electoral arena, which has to some extent revitalized Belgian politics.

3   Populism and democracy in Canada's Reform Party

David Laycock

Introduction

Canada's recent political scene has been dramatically altered by three parties of the right in succession: the Reform Party of Canada (RPC), in federal parliamentary opposition between 1993 and 2000; the Canadian Reform and Conservative Alliance (CRCA) or Canadian Alliance (CA), in opposition between 2000 and 2003; and the Conservative Party of Canada (CP), in opposition between 2003 and 2006 and in government since. Only the Reform Party qualifies as a populist party whose initial and sustaining appeal was to 'the people' as against 'the elite.' That the identities of both the people and the elite in Reform Party discourse were strikingly at odds with those understood in much of North American populist history and appeal has been vital to the Reform Party's distinctive role in Canadian politics.

The Reform Party was established in November 1987, selecting Preston Manning as its leader. In retrospect, seen from the vantage point of a national governing Conservative Party with its roots in thirteen years of Reform Party activity, it is easy to say that Reform had an impact on Canadian politics and public life out of proportion to its limited, highly regionalized electoral success. This chapter argues that Reform's success and legacy are due more to its populist character than its conservatism, despite the fact that more conservatism than populism was bequeathed to its successor, the Conservative Party. In addition to addressing the relevant framing hypotheses from this volume's introduction, I will focus on how Reform's populism was blended with conservative themes in an effort to alter Canadian democracy and polarize the party system. Reform's mixed populist/conservative legacy will occasionally be gauged with reference to the continuity of populist themes between the Reform and Conservative Parties.

3.1   The Reform Party in a new party system

The Reform Party had an inauspicious initial experience with national politics in Canada. Formed at a 1987 convention, it obtained 2.1 per cent of the national vote and no seats in the 1988 federal election. In this contest it was reduced to saying 'us too!' in response to most of the governing Progressive Conservatives' major appeals. Its creation in 1987 was largely the work of Preston Manning, an Alberta business consultant and son of a right populist 'third party' premier of Alberta from 1943 to 1968.[1] Manning led and dominated the party from its beginning until it morphed into the Canadian Reform and Conservative Alliance party in 2000.

Dogged persistence, along with its support of the claim that western Canadians had not received the regionalist voice they deserved from the governing Progressive Conservatives, was crucial to the Reform Party's spectacular entry, with 18.7 per cent of the vote and 52 seats, into the Canadian federal party system in the 1993 election. (Flanagan 1995) The Reform Party's early appeal to historic western Canadian griev-ances, in a federal system dominated by Ontario and Québec, was easy to make and eagerly consumed in the four western provinces. Western Canadian populist politics go back to the early twentieth century, fea-turing a quasi-colonial relationship to central Canada, a combination of western-based protest of 'third' parties, and occasionally either strong western provincial leaders or national party leaders as its spokesmen (Carty et al. 2000; Laycock 1990). Despite securing the overwhelming majority of western provinces' parliamentary seats, from 1984 to 1993 the federal Progressive Conservative government failed to show the same concern for western economic interests as it did for those in Ontario and Québec. This government also failed to satisfy right-wing conserva-tives' desires for major tax and social spending cuts and for traditionalist approaches to social issues.

A decisive window of opportunity opened for Preston Manning's new party between 1990 and 1992, as a result of two failed federal gov-ernment attempts at constitutional reform. Both of these were aimed primarily at getting the Québec government to accept and legitimize the major Canadian constitutional overhaul of 1981. The 1992 consti-tutional reform effort also aimed to provide better representation and extended rights to women, aboriginal peoples, and regional interests in a modified senate.

---

[1] Preston Manning co-authored *Political Realignment* in 1967 with his father, the sitting premier, Ernest C. Manning. The book makes a case for a merger of 'social conserva-tives,' including supporters of the provincial and federal Social Credit parties, with the much larger but usually second place Progressive Conservative Party of Canada. There is no reference to the kinds of populist direct democracy proposals that eventually became central to the Reform Party.

The Reform Party stood alone among English Canadian parties in opposing the 1992 Charlottetown Accord, and thus could claim it had been the sole party opposing an all-parliamentary and broader elite consensus on constitutional reform. Reform opposed the Accord in a national referendum campaign on the grounds that it had been constructed behind closed doors by unaccountable political elites and would have given enhanced rights and increased power to native peoples, Québecois nationalists, and 'special interests' such as feminists. Reasons for opposing the 1992 Accord varied across the country and were notably inconsistent between Québec and English Canada (Johnston et al. 1995). Reform was nonetheless the only nationally significant party able to claim that it had been on the side of 'the people' when the Accord failed to obtain majority support across the country.

The 1993 election shattered the coalition upon which Progressive Conservative party success had been built for a decade. Reform gained fifty-two parliamentary seats and the second largest proportion of the national popular vote, seventeen per cent. Reform replaced the Progressive Conservatives as the dominant party in western Canada and as the major opposition to the governing Liberals in English Canada. The dominant party of the right for over a century was reduced to two parliamentary seats.

Despite this dramatic entry into national party competition and the decline of the left populist New Democratic Party in the western provinces and Ontario, Reform found subsequent electoral progress difficult. Its popular support and parliamentary strength barely increased in the 1997 election, thanks to perceptions by voters outside of western Canada that Reform was either too conservative or too narrowly regionalist to merit broader support. Reform's prominent populist regionalism was largely responsible for its dramatic entry into the national party system and for its shared role in the fatal wounding of the previous major party of the right. But this regionalism, and a whiff of conservative 'extremism,'[2] prevented the party from displacing the Progressive Conservatives in Ontario and other English Canadian provinces.

Nonetheless, in the 1997 federal election, the Reform Party won an additional eight seats in Parliament and 'Official Opposition' standing as the second largest party caucus. Reform's 19.4 per cent of the vote came close to doubling that of the New Democratic Party, the largest 'third party' in Parliament since 1935.

---

[2] Many voters in the 1993 and 1997 federal elections identified Reform's views as being too uncomfortably extreme, on social issues, economic policy, or moral issues (see Blais et al. 1999).

3.2   Populist themes in the Reform Party

"The West wants in" was Reform's earliest slogan and expressed its populist regionalism succinctly. For the purposes of staking out a distinct, strategically beneficial political space in the party competition, Reform constructed 'the people' initially as westerners, shut out of the real halls of power in the federal system. For the most part, despite this regionalist appeal, Reform's agenda was typical of post-1980 new-right parties and political discourse throughout the Western world (Betz and Immerfall 1998). After entering Parliament, Reform promoted further decentralization of power to the provinces, fiscal belt tightening through major social and regional development programme cuts, replacement of many social service programmes by private charity work, 'workfare' as an alternative to welfare, elimination of state support for multi-cultural advocacy groups, and elimination of pay equity programmes.

Reform promoted harsher treatment of criminals, juvenile offenders, and 'welfare mothers.' Its criticism of 'old line parties' stressed their allegedly cosy relationships with 'tax-grabbing bureaucratic elites,' and their subsidized friends in women's movement organizations, multiculturalism promotion and aboriginal groups. Reform proposed to address these issues, as well as contentious social/moral issues such as abortion rights, capital punishment, and gay rights, with regular use of the instruments of direct democracy. They promised direct democratic accountability for MPs through 'recall' provisions and legislative enabling of citizens' initiatives. Such direct democracy was to augment a dramatic reduction in the Canadian welfare state and in the attendant scope of organized group participation in public policy development.

For students of comparative populism, this latter feature of the party's agenda may seem contrary to its populist message of returning power to 'ordinary people.' But the contradiction was more apparent than real, since by 1993 Reform had re-defined 'the people' to exclude any constituencies or organizations that sought an expansion of the welfare state, a redistribution of resources from the wealthy to the non-wealthy, or an extension of 'new social citizenship' rights to visible minorities, aboriginal people, women, or gays and lesbians (Laycock 2001: 35–40). The people were to be empowered as individuals by removing mediating institutions and organized group representation in the policy process. As the Reform Party said in a 1992 pamphlet, "in Ottawa, every special interest group counts except one, Canadians" (ibid.: 61).

Like much of the American Tea Party's populist critique, Reform identified the principal culprits as activist governments or parties and groups that enabled such activism. The party identified 'the people' as ordinary, hard-working citizens duped by a coalition of old line parties, special interests and rent-seeking federal government bureaucrats into financing an unfairly redistributive and freedom-denying welfare state. The people had not benefited from these social programmes or from the intrusive state presence because they were hard working, law abiding, and overtaxed, and because they were not members of the special interests.[3] Reform argued that mainstream parties and state bureaucrats favoured immigrants, native peoples, francophone Québecois, and special privilege-seeking women's groups and gays over 'ordinary working people' in the distribution of state resources. This overlay of regionalist, anti-party, anti-state, and anti-minority themes structured the Reform Party's articulation of the classic populist 'people/power-bloc' antagonism.

Reform appeals included heavy doses of party politician and political system bashing. It was an 'anti-system party' (Johnston 2008), opposed not just to the post-war party system, but to this system's cross-party consensus in creating and incrementally extending Canada's modest welfare state. Reform's grassroots supporters had little faith in parliamentary parties or conventional institutions and processes of representative democracy (Archer and Ellis 1994; Clarke et al. 2000; Laycock 2001). Its promotion of direct democracy and extensive efforts to foster suspicion concerning the policy outputs of federal representative democracy were classically 'anti-system.' Such direct democracy promotion also suggested that whenever possible, the general will of the people should direct policy. This 'direct democracy/small state/pure people' versus 'representative democracy/strong state/corrupt elite' antinomy captures a key part of the logic of Reform's populism.

Reform's 1997 election platform called for "a country defined and built by its citizens, rather than by its government." "Social justice" would involve Canadians "working for themselves and their families, instead of for the government" and in devolving previously public obligations to private individuals, families, and unspecified "communities" (RPC 1997: 5, 11). As one would expect in a populist discourse, true citizenship and social justice were presented as antagonistic to the agenda of an 'anti-people' and hence corrupt state. What is distinctive in this populist message, compared to that found in the bulk of twentieth-century North American populism, is that the state is portrayed as acting contrary to the people's interests to the extent that it engages public resources to regulate corporate power and redistribute resources, rather than the reverse.

---

[3] That this is a widespread populist theme, especially in Europe but also the United States, Canada, and Australia is conveyed in Mudde (2004), Kazin (1998), Laycock (2001), and Sawer and Hindess (2004), respectively.

A brief note on the bases of Reform's electoral support provides a clearer sense of how this party blended its populism with efforts to reconstitute Canadian democracy. In the 1993 and 1997 federal elections, the Reform Party made major inroads into working class, farmer, small business, and urban middle class constituencies in Canada's western provinces and significant gains in Ontario, English Canada's largest province. Reform attracted many previous New Democratic Party supporters, including at least one-quarter of English Canadian trade unionists and roughly one-third of low-income voters.

The Reform Party could thus claim relatively broad support from 'non-elites,' especially in its critique of conventional parties and its advocacy of the instruments of direct democracy. Reform had unquestionably re-defined and claimed for the political right the lion's share of the populist ideological space within the Canadian party system. This redefinition and claim had substantial consequences for the future of the Canadian party system and for the public's already declining willingness to confer legitimacy on practices and institutions of parliamentary representation.

Among English Canadian political parties, Reform was the major beneficiary of increasing anti-party sentiment during the 1980s and 1990s (Cross 2002; Gidengil et al. 2001). Trade unionists and low-income Canadians were well represented in the legions of anti-party voters who saw the Reform Party as the most effective electoral medium for an anti-party message. Reform's 'get tough on criminals' message also resonated strongly among less educated voters in Ontario and the western provinces.

By 1993, most moral conservatives in the western provinces, and many in Ontario, had found a political home in the Reform Party. Preston Manning is a lay fundamentalist Christian preacher like his father the Premier. Following the quasi-populist religious right south of the border, Manning's Reform Party promised a referendum on capital punishment, a referendum to re-criminalize abortion, and an active campaign on behalf of traditional family values against the alleged threats posed by gays and feminists. Referenda of this type implicitly signaled a clear demarcation between a virtuous people and urban elites corrupted by various forms of morally suspect thinking.

3.3   Populism in Reform's successors

The new-right core of Reform policy became clearer once the party reconstituted itself as the Canadian Reform and Conservative Alliance in 2000. This metamorphosis aimed to broaden support beyond the western provinces to include centre right voters in Ontario and more urban voters across English Canada. With this re-invention as the 'Alliance,' Reform sacrificed the idea that 'the people' had a western regional identity. The re-invention also sidelined direct democratic remedies to the deficiencies of party politics and representative institutions and virtually eliminated references to western Canadian grievances with central Canadian economic and political power (CA 2000).

This trade-off against Reform's original populist appeal was necessary for a party of the right in Canada to make electoral headway. Three years later, the merger of the federal Canadian Alliance and Progressive Conservative Parties underscored this move away from populist principles and practices even more. Despite this, and undoubtedly to the frustration of many core Reform supporters for whom western regionalism and anti-party, direct democracy populism was the bedrock of their support for Reform, no new more clearly regional or populist party has emerged in federal politics since 2000.

With direct democracy and a populist regionalism jettisoned, a more restrictive but still potently populist anti-elitism was retained in Reform's successor parties. The people were no longer regional, but still pure and homogenous, or at least capable of being pure, and currently all subject to excessive taxation, regulation, and state intrusion. The corollary of the people's suffering under a regime of diminished market freedom was that statist elites were still corrupt – or at least not to be trusted advancing the people's interests. Several examples can illustrate the character of Reform's populist legacy in the current Conservative Party and suggest the attempted transformation of citizens' relations to the Canadian state and each other initiated by Preston Manning's Reform Party. These examples speak directly to the effects that Reform as an oppositional populist party had on subsequent practices of democratic politics in Canada.

Former Manning policy advisor and Reform Party MP Stephen Harper won the leadership of the Conservative Party in 2004 promising "lower taxes for the many, not special subsidies for the few." He asked CP members – and the broader public – to imagine a "country of freedom and rights for ordinary people, taxpayers and families, not just for criminals, political elites and special interests" (Harper 2004: 2). Grouping political elites and special interests with criminals certainly underscores the sense in which the people's enemies are corrupt. In the 2006 federal election campaign, Harper promised to govern for 'mainstream' Canadians and accused other parties of putting the demands of special interests ahead of the needs and values of ordinary working families. The latter are, by definition, virtuous but under assault by special interests, which include feminists, anti-poverty groups, the gay rights movement, native Canadians, and any other ethnic and racial minorities requesting enhanced government programmes. One can easily draw a direct line between the anti-elitist populist dimension of Reform's 1993 and 1997 campaign appeals and these 2004 and 2006 appeals by Conservative leader Harper.

In his first *Speech from the Throne*, Prime Minister Harper characterized citizens as besieged taxpayers whose true wishes had been ignored by special interests, government bureaucrats, and a national government too responsive to both. He presented his childcare policy as the antithesis of a big government, special interest-driven programme. "We're going to provide parents with real choice in childcare (...). The idea here is to help parents pay for childcare that makes the most sense to them – not to some bureaucrat or special interest group in Ottawa" (Harper 2006: 3).

So even when Reform's successor party formed a national government, it continued to campaign against its own bureaucracy as one of the 'special interests' aligned against the people. With considerable prior effort by the Reform Party, the people had been re-defined by the Conservatives as taxpayers. Pre-1970s North American populist depictions of the people as active citizens whose interests might be advanced by a government working to reduce corporate power had been rejected in the Reform discourse and partisan legacy, just as they had been successfully marginalized in the United States.

Our brief look at the Conservative Party leader's use of anti-elitist appeals suggests how difficult it is to untangle populism from the underlying new-right conservatism in the message pioneered by the Reform Party and passed on to the Conservatives. By defining the popular sovereignty-denying elites as state agencies, programmes, and those who support their extension (or maintenance), Reform's populism was simultaneously anti-statist. Democratic remedies that would benefit the people at special interests' expense would thus necessarily involve dismantling the ability of the state to intrude in the natural rhythms of civil society.

Reform's democratic ideal was not just anti-statist, but also pro-market. Democracy was desirable to the extent that it enabled freedom for individuals, and the market order was the mechanism through which freedom was most naturally obtained. This story was filled in with strongly anti-party, anti-interest group representational undertones, such that Reform's ideal democracy would feature no political mediating forces between the people and their free pursuits of individual and family interests. But the antipathy to parties and special interests was at bottom an antipathy to the state which parties and special interests expanded at the expense of 'real freedom,' expressed in what Robert Nozick famously called "capitalist acts between consenting adults" (Nozick 1974: 162).

Arguably, Reform's continued campaign for an elected senate (with equal provincial representation, along American lines) expressed its recognition that if a political zone free from parties and special interests was not a realistic objective, the second best alternative would be to install another, contra-majoritarian but now democratically legitimate – because elected representative – body in Canada's parliament.[4] Such a body could, if made equally legitimate to the House of Commons, block further attempts to expand the state's reach into civil society and initiate occasional reductions in the size and impact of this state.

3.4   Reform's populism and democracy: Testing hypotheses

The Reform Party provided a clear partisan option for voters who felt some combination of alienation as western Canadians, a desire for a more traditionalist Christian perspective on policy matters, a distaste for the modern welfare state, or who were seriously 'anti-party.' To this extent, Reform served the first positive function of populism outlined in this volume's introduction by giving voice to "*groups that do not feel represented by the elites, by putting forward topics that are relevant for a 'silent-majority'*" (positive effect 1). That many in these constituencies felt unrepresented or poorly represented is clear (Archer and Ellis 1994; Clarke et al. 2000). But according to his chief policy advisor during the early to mid 1990s, what Manning often referred to as the 'common sense of the common people' was best understood as 'an artifact of agenda control' by the leader over his party (Flanagan 1995: 27).

In terms of positive populist effects postulated in this volume's introduction, the mobilization and integration of Christian conservatives into a major party certainly counts as an impressive achievement. This constituency was largely apolitical before the Reform Party emerged, but in less than two decades has found a comfortable home in the Conservative Party and a confident voice in the halls of federal government power (Farney 2009). Reform's populism thus in one sense mobilized "*excluded sections of society ... improving their political integration*" (positive effect 2). It is worth emphasizing, however, that this group had voluntarily excluded itself from politics before Preston Manning spoke their language. Christian conservatives in Canada have not been prevented by formal, class, income, or other substantial barriers typically identified by social scientists as accounting for the existence of 'excluded groups.'

---

[4] Canada has retained an appointed senate as a second chamber of its federal parliament since this was constitutionally embedded in the British North America Act of 1867.

Related to these positive effects, Reform "*provided an ideological bridge that supports the building of important social and political coalitions, often across class lines, thus providing a key dynamic element in the evolution of party systems and related modes of political representation*" (positive effect 4). This ideological bridge building, party system transforming role had been performed by earlier Canadian left and right populist parties – the Cooperative Commonwealth Federation, various centre left provincial farmers' parties, and the Social Credit Party in Alberta (Laycock 1990). It is now true, with a different kind of dynamic effect on the national party system: the Reform Party joined most Western countries' populist parties in shifting the range of policy options and centre of political gravity rightwards. Reform initiated a different kind of cross-class alliance, this time between the wealthy and the white, lower middle class or rural population and often non-unionized urban working class.

Reform's distinctively non-ethnic minority constituency was reflected in, and to some degree enhanced by, its early opposition to the inter-party consensus on state-sponsored multi-culturalism, a consensus that had existed in federal politics since the early 1970s. This opposition found expression in an account of 'the people's' identity that appealed to elements of anti-immigrant, anti-aboriginal, and anti-French-Canadian racism. But compared to the racism openly displayed and courted by many European populist parties, the Reform Party's discomfort with multi-culturalism and non-white and/or non-Christian immigration was a minor matter (Laycock 2001: ch. 7).

By the standards of Western European radical right populists, Reform's populism was quite inclusive, as the eventual involvement of visible minority candidates and party activists attested. However, Reform Party voters remained the least supportive of multi-culturalism, non-white immigration, and ethnic minority rights among national parliamentary parties (Clarke et al. 2000; Cross and Young 2002; Gidengil et al. 2001; Laycock 2001: ch. 7). The party nominated and elected several minority ethnic group member MPs, but made no institutional concessions to encouraging internal party diversity (Flanagan 2010).

Nativism was not central to Reform's construction of its narrative of a virtuous people whose national traditions were being undermined by a shadowy, unscrupulous, and self-serving elite. Their narrative of this elemental opposition focused instead on a Hayekian logic in which the people's depredations were explained by an unholy alliance between a bureaucratic, market distorting welfare state on the one hand, and undemocratic parties held hostage by special interests benefiting from these freedom- and prosperity-curtailing market distortions on the other (Laycock 2001, 2005b).

With the exception of pre-1960 French Canadian nationalism, Canadian populisms and populist nationalisms have never seriously posed a threat to minorities. One could easily argue, in fact, that the dominant social democratic expression of English Canadian populism between the 1930s and the early 1990s had been even more supportive of a strong regime of liberal rights and more enthusiastic about the democratic potential of parliamentary government than either of the two larger centrist parties.

This pattern changed with the advent and early years of the Reform Party. Since 1982 Canadian liberal democracy has included elements of constitutionally protected minority group accommodation via 'group-differentiated rights' (Kymlicka 1998, 1996) and a somewhat redistributive welfare state as the basis of meaningful civic equality. So relative to the dominant political practices and political culture Canadians have experienced for over a generation, a Hayekian 'market populism' (Sawer and Laycock 2009) that aims to unravel this regime of individual and social rights poses a threat to the specifically Canadian form of liberal democracy. This suggests, then, a modest Reform party counterfactual to hypothesis 4. But at least in federal-level politics, and consistent with the overall expectation of that hypothesis, pre-Reform Party populism in Canada did not generate much evidence of negative effect 2, that is, that "populism can use the notion and practice of majority rule to circumvent and ignore minority rights." It bears mentioning, however, that the major constraint on the current Conservative government's desire to overturn the achievement of gay marriage rights in Canada, not to mention prevent gay people from teaching in public schools, is the Supreme Court of Canada's expansive interpretation and defence of equality provisions in Canada's Charter of Rights and Freedoms. The Conservative Party's animus against gay rights was directly inherited from the Reform Party.

The Canadian variant of the Westminster system features a higher level of executive dominance of the legislature than that found in other established liberal democratic regimes (Bakvis and Wolinetz 2005). The potential for such dominance can be exploited by a party able to make a populist appeal, operating in a context of widespread popular distrust in politicians and representative institutions (Blais and Gidengil 1991; Howe and Northrup 2000; Nevitte and White 2008). This has been illustrated by Steven Harper's Conservative government, which has demonstrated its contempt for Parliament and minimized government accountability in a variety of ways (Fossum and Laycock 2011; Martin 2010).

There is little substantively populist about minimizing government accountability, except perhaps for the distaste shown for minority positions in Parliament and the larger public. But the selling of policies central to the Harper government's agenda frequently bears populist markings easily traced to the Reform Party. The associated appeals are notably anti-statist, anti-elitist, anti-intellectual, aimed at popular sentiments that are 'tough on crime,' or suspicious of mainstream media or complexity in government. Preston Manning's party pioneered all of these appeals, and though they have a distinctly right-wing orientation, they are populist in the sense that all of them presume, and often explicitly engage, basic antagonisms between various elites and a virtuous, oft-bamboozled people.

The Reform Party also spoke often and insistently about the absence of democratic accountability in a Canadian parliament dominated by 'old line parties.' Arguing that existing party elites and their special interest associates had consistently ignored the people's will on everything from capital punishment to abortion rights to constitutional deals that would entrench Québec's veto power in the federal system, Reform advocated referendums, initiatives, and recall procedures. These were to provide citizens with the means of holding politicians accountable, or, when this became too frustrating, of exercising elite-trumping 'end runs' around party politicians.

Reform also proposed an alternative, quasi-delegate representational theory, in which the policy preferences of members of parliament would be directed by their constituents. It advocated expanding the number of parliamentary 'free votes' not subject to party line discipline so that constituents could hold their MPs accountable without mediation by parliamentary parties, and a host of less significant democratic reforms. (Barney and Laycock 1999; Laycock 2001). The party even held several experiments in 'push button populism,' in which party members within specific constituencies were encouraged to register their preferences regarding policy options supported by Reform, with the idea that these local policy referenda would be converted into legislators' support for the winning options (Barney 1996).[5]

In 2005 Preston Manning established the Manning Centre for Building Democracy in Calgary. Given his past pronouncements on letting the 'common sense of the common people' prevail, one might expect that this centre would host the development of more thoughtful approaches

[5] However, the internal practice of decision making within the party was at odds with this public invocation of popular wills over legislative deals. Preston Manning's senior policy advisor from 1992–5 contended that Manning and his inner circle choreographed Reform Party 'Assemblies' and so dominated the party structure that what appeared to most activists as member direction of policy development was a carefully staged illusion (Flanagan 1995, 2010). The appearance and felt experience of Reform Party member control was belied by the reality of organizationally designed leader domination and manipulation of party policy development (Barney 1996; Laycock 2001).

to using direct democracy to harness the sovereign will. Instead, the Manning Centre's Web site states that its mission is to "equip the next generation of political leaders, particularly those who share our conservative values, with the ideas, skills, and networks necessary to serve the best interests of Canadians," in a "free and democratic Canada where conservative principles are well articulated, understood, and implemented" (Manning Centre 2010: 12). Manning's centre is essentially a training shop and networking instrument for Conservative political operatives. The once vaunted principles of popular democracy now warrant just one vague phrase in the centre's first 'State of the Conservative Movement in Canada' report, and receive no attention in the discussion of how to build Canada's 'conservative infrastructure' (Manning Centre 2010). Now that the Conservative Party is the best organized, best financed, and most strategically adept of the national parties (Flanagan, 2010), and is running the least transparent and most tightly controlled administration in Canadian history (Martin 2010), Manning's interest in direct democracy has been set aside. In short, the Reform legacy of advocating supra-representational measures for registering the people's will has come up noticeably short, at least in national politics.

Provincially there has been a somewhat different legacy. British Columbia is the only province in which Reform-style enthusiasm for direct democracy has been legislatively enabled and practiced, with a 2005–6 'Citizens' Assembly on Electoral Reform' and a 2010 citizens' initiative successfully demanding a referendum on the adoption of a sales tax (Warren and Pearse 2008; Meissner 2010).

Manning's use of populist appeals was not simply manipulative. His sense of Canada's democratic deficit, not just in national politics but also in provincial relations with the federal government, was effectively articulated and genuinely felt. It can also be true, however, that well-considered strategic considerations (Flanagan 1995) also shaped Manning's adroit use of western Canadian 'popular democratic traditions' (Laclau 1977) to court a receptive constituency and provide an effective opening for a new party of the right in Canada. There is ample evidence that a large western Canadian constituency antagonistic to 'old line' parties, suspicious of the federal government, and keen on direct democracy was ready and waiting for an option like Manning's in 1986 and enthusiastic about seeing it transform national politics (Archer and Ellis 1994; Clarke et al. 2000; Gidengil et al. 1998).

Canada has a rich history of early- to mid-twentieth century populism. While it was always anti-elitist, and often anti-party, only a small element of it – the Social Credit element into which Manning was born – was deeply anti-political in plebiscitarian fashion (Laycock 1990, ch. 5). This raises populism's fifth negative effect, as postulated in the introductory chapter: "*Populism can foster a plebiscitary transformation of politics, which undermines the legitimacy and power of political institutions (e.g. parties and parliaments) and unelected bodies (e.g. organizations such as central banks or inspections offices) that are indispensable to 'good governance.'*"

To what extent was this an element of Reform Party practice? In an earlier article, Darin Barney and I argued that:

Reform occupie[d] a position squarely within the plebiscitarian space created by public disenchantment with traditional representative structures. Reformers point[ed] to organized interests and failing brokerage parties as the cause of 'ordinary Canadians' opting out of participation in the party system, and press[ed] for integration of plebiscitary instruments into Canadian governance practices.... [Reform] place[d] heavy emphasis on the sense in which preferences registered in this manner are analogous to preference signaling in markets. Participation modeled on market exchanges between isolated individuals accords with the party's commitment to a minimalist public life, in which the role of mediating institutions and organizations is consciously devalued. (Laycock and Barney 1999: 322–3)

The same kind of distrust of mediating institutions, especially of the courts interpreting Canada's Charter of Rights and Freedoms, was expressed by Reform intellectuals and Manning himself (Laycock 2005b). In each case, the policy directions sought by Reform's Charter critics involved dismantling the kinds of social rights protections and business activity regulations that Reform leaders saw as anathema to the proper functioning of natural market forces.

By the early 1990s, Reform leaders, activists, and intellectuals had become convinced that the Canadian judiciary had entered into a cosy conspiracy with a well-mobilized coalition of special interests – native people, feminists, multi-culturalism advocates, and gay rights advocates – in whose interests high court judges interpreted the Charter's equality provisions. So Reform added the Supreme Court and 'equality-seeker' litigants in Charter-focused court cases to its list of illegitimate actors stifling popular sovereignty. In 1996 a Reform Party task force on the Charter proposed eliminating both the affirmative action enabling section 15.2 of the Charter and section 27, which specifies that the Charter shall be interpreted in a manner consistent with the country's multi-cultural character (RPC 1996b). Subsequent writing by Reform Party-allied intellectuals framed a critique of the 'Court party' in majoritarian, anti-elitist terms that denied the democratic legitimacy of any 'special rights' for minorities and accused their advocates and accomplices in academia, political parties, and the courts of undermining the will of the people (Knopff and Morton 2000; Morton 1998).

What is the legacy of Reform's plebiscitarian populist appeals and proposals? As noted previously, the Conservatives do not promote direct democratic instruments. However, Harper's party and government continue to express distrust in the courts, federal regulatory agencies, and Parliament itself. Harper's use of the Prime Minister's Office to undermine parliamentary committee work through his MPs' 'dirty tricks' (Martin 2010) suggests a plebiscitarian dismissal of normal parliamentary policy development processes. And Harper's two early prorogations of Parliament, in 2009 and 2010, both effectively denied that Parliament had the right to hold the government to account. The implication that parliament itself is an obstacle to true democracy suggests clear plebiscitarian tendencies.

Consideration of the assumptions and system-critiquing meaning of Reform's suspicion of Canadian representative institutions points to a direct line between Reform and the current Conservative government in this regard. The Conservative Party has abandoned the populist contrarepresentational mechanisms of plebiscitarian politics but retained the underlying rationale for such end runs around representative institutions. That Manning and other Reform party notables have offered no criticism of this substitution suggests that they cared more about the conservative ends, not the anti-elitist, anti-party populist means to these ends. Reform's populism was thus unquestionably 'thin-centered,' with much of its ideological core found in the nostrums of the contemporary North American new right. But an often strategic deployment of this populism was nonetheless crucial to Reform's entry into, and ultimate impact on, the Canadian party system.

Reform Party populism garnered much of its public appeal on the basis of its clarion call for democratic accountability and the dethroning of entrenched elites (Archer and Ellis 1994; Clarke et al. 2000; Flanagan 1995; Laycock 2001). And there is no question that the wedge politics practiced by the governing Conservatives since 2006 has emphasized the 'conflictive dimension' of politics. But is this a repudiation or a logical extension of the Reform Party's efforts to foster alternatives to established ways of doing politics in Canada?

By triggering a dramatic transformation of the Canadian party system, the Reform Party did in one sense 'revitalize both public opinion and social movements' while proclaiming its intentions to 'foster the "democratization of democracy"' (positive effect 6). As noted earlier, Reform did provide a political vehicle for organizations and ideological tendencies that had found at best a lukewarm reception in the centrist, media-voter-seeking Progressive Conservative Party. Neither free market fundamentalists nor Christian fundamentalists had made decisive inroads into the key circles of power in this centrist party (Farney 2009).

It is also true that the Reform Party put social advocacy groups keen to extend welfare state programmes and protections increasingly on the defensive during the 1990s. There is no question that this 'brought back the conflictive dimension' in Canadian politics (positive effect 6) or at least enhanced it along a new and policy-consequential axis. This was complemented by a notable shift to the right in Canadian print media (Martin 2010), increased funding for and legitimacy of free market think tanks, pursuit of right-wing agendas by Progressive Conservative administrations in several key English Canadian provinces (Ibbitson 1997; Laird 1998; Laycock 2001), and the incumbent Liberal government's extended efforts to eliminate federal deficits and debt. All of these developments enhanced conflictive politics.

Whether Reform played a positive role in 'revitalizing public opinion' is a matter of ideological preference, with those on the right thinking so and those on the centre left and left thinking not. This judgement is linked to whether one considers 'vitalization' of economic and social conservative movement organizations and a 'de-vitalization' of left-wing social movement organizations supportive of a 'democratization of democracy.' Here, standards of democratization vary tremendously, but employing those utilized in this volume's introduction will be helpful.

Procedurally, did Reform have any effect on citizens' power to evaluate governments' support for citizens' equal freedoms and formal equality? It would be hard to make a case either way, though one might suggest that the undertones of plebiscitarianism in Reform's populism provide increased legitimacy for attacks on the state's efforts to facilitate more equal citizen power in this regard. To the extent that Reform condemned the involvement of 'special interests' in public life, and identified any and all supporters of redistributive policies as special interests, they were aiming to diminish the effective political agency of citizens for whom these were desirable ends. So we can suggest at least a somewhat negative score on this procedural dimension.

In terms of the *content* criterion of democratization, even though the party wished to 'de-fund' and remove the previously mentioned 'special interests' from policy making processes, there is no evidence that Reform intended to undermine the legal foundations of their members' political liberties or formal equality. Some commentators have argued that the Conservative Party's move to eliminate public subsidies for political parties in 2011 (previously $2.00 per federal election vote) indirectly undermines citizen's formal equality (Conacher 2011). But more direct moves against civic equality are highly unlikely. Canada is simply too mature a democracy, with too deeply entrenched a democratic political culture, for such moves to be initiated by serious political actors.

In terms of a more demanding definition of democracy, however, Reform contributed to undermining the legitimacy of liberal democratic governance in the eyes of Canadians. In Canada, as elsewhere, there is widespread citizen disenchantment with conventional liberal democratic representative institutions (Nevitte and White 2008). The logic of Reform's effort to stimulate further de-legitimization of key Canadian governing institutions was similar to that found on the political right in the United States, where undermining trust and confidence in government has been essential to what celebrated conservative strategist Grover Norquist has called the 'starve the beast' strategy.[6]

The beast in question is an activist, regulatory, and service providing state. Starving it entails driving down revenues that finance such state activities by precipitously cutting taxes (Hacker and Pierson 2010). Making the case for ever lower taxes requires a continual campaign to convince citizens that politicians and their parties are corrupt, that proponents of any kind of government activism are either undeserving or on the take, that government programmes deliver poor value relative to private sector alternatives, and that, consequently, lower taxes will mean greater freedom and more prosperity for all. Calling the representative political processes that have facilitated 'high' taxes into question is a necessary part of this broader message.

The point here is that when a thin-centred populism is attached to a new-right core ideology, de-legitimization of existing representative institutions and processes is not just a consequence of the ideological marriage, but a key linchpin in its success. This is revealed in the basic definitions of 'the people' and 'the elite' in this type of populism, arrayed on either side of such a welfare state. Remove the specificity of these definitions and the logic of right populism unravels; buttress these images of the people and the elite, and the odds of its political success are greatly enhanced. In either case, public legitimacy for basic representative democratic processes is very much in play.

Reform's leaders wished to remove many previous political decisions about resource allocation from the sphere of political determination and return them to the marketplace. Reform offered representative institutions a kind of second rate legitimacy relative to market mechanisms so long as they did not overstep the natural boundary between politics and markets.

As we have seen, the Reform Party secured its entry into the centre of Canadian party competition and parliamentary debate largely by

---

[6] See http://en.wikipedia.org/wiki/Grover_Norquist; http://en.wikipedia.org/wiki/Starve-the-beast.

opposing the political establishment's consensus on proposals for constitutional reform, and it continued to harness and expand popular distaste with 'old line parties' throughout its short but effective political life. Its rapid accession to the rank of major opposition party in English Canada was a key factor in the fragmentation of Canada's party system after 1993 (Carty, Cross, and Young 2000).

With its Westminster parliamentary system and fused executive and legislature, the Canadian political system's checks and balances come from federalism and the judiciary, especially insofar as it interprets the legislative reach of the Charter of Rights and Freedoms. The Reform Party consistently opposed the Charter's provisions for 'group-differentiated rights,' especially as they apply to native peoples, women, and gays and lesbians (Laycock 2005b). Insofar as their invocation of popular sovereignty took on plebiscitarian dimensions, Reform advocated extension of popular sovereignty at the expense of a deliberative Parliament and a judiciary upholding a complex constitutional equality that included support for group-differentiated rights.

The plebiscitarian aspects of Reform Party theory and practice did not change the political game such that either competing party felt obliged to follow suit or that the legitimacy of non-partisan government institutions has been decisively undermined in favour of plebiscitarian instruments exercised by strong leaders. Canada is not Venezuela, nor does it risk becoming comparable. Nonetheless, the plebiscitarian talk of Reform, followed by similar actions of the Conservative Party in power, have degraded democratic accountability and the overall quality of democratic representation in Canada (Fossum and Laycock 2011).

The Reform Party wished to re-define Canadian public life by substantially contracting group pluralistic modes of decision making in policy spheres concerned with distributional issues. In their view, too many groups had taken the promise of pluralistic politics in a welfare state setting too seriously, with the result that a bloated, overly intrusive, inefficient, and taxpayer disabling state had emerged. It is thus not surprising that in the Reform Party appeal there was a good ideological fit between promotion of 'special interest free' direct democracy and criticism of the welfare state, its advocates, and institutional delivery structures. Direct democracy was intended to help sideline such distorting instruments of the people's 'real will' to produce policies consistent with this real will.

But despite the good ideological fit between Reform's promotion of direct democracy and its attack on the welfare state with its 'special interest' beneficiaries, direct democracy was rapidly edged out of the Canadian Alliance's spotlight by other themes and has remained unambiguously at the margins of the Conservative Party.

Finally, we should note the connection between Reform's plebiscitarian approach to politics and the shrinkage of pluralistic, meaningfully inclusive politics in Canada. Plebiscitarian politics is about forcing a reduction of the inevitable complexity and pluralism of political life through a simple, often highly polarized package of 'us versus them' option sets. Reform's plebiscitarian appeal was such that even when the appearance of participatory politics disappeared within the successor Conservative Party, the anti-elite, anti-party appeal associated with the earlier plebiscitarianism could be retained and put to effective use. As the introductory chapter proposed, populist anti-elitism, plebiscitarian undermining of elected institutions and contraction of effective democratic space are linked in certain settings. Their linkage and combined negative effect has not been as dramatic or problematic for liberal democratic politics in Canada as in most other countries discussed in this volume. But this legacy of Reform Party populism is, nonetheless, significant.

Conclusion

This chapter has analysed the populism of the Reform Party of Canada and its impact on Canadian democracy over the past generation. The populist appeals described here were ideologically consistent with and supportive of Reform's broader new-right ideological objectives and demonstrated the particular power of this blend in a North American setting. But we saw, as well, that some elements of these populist appeals are dispensable, since Reform's successor, the Conservative Party, had no difficulty adopting a plebiscitarian approach to political engagement while abandoning the direct democracy elements of anti-elite appeals central to Reform populism.

The Reform Party did not practice the rhetorical exclusion or threats to minority rights sought by recent European populist parties. Lacking the racist element so central to these parties, Reform's populism was nonetheless initially notably exclusionist with respect to indigenous peoples (i.e. members of the 'First Nations') and even Québecois when compared to other Canadian parties. But Reform's primary concern was mounting a challenge to the welfare state and new forms of 'social citizenship' or group-differentiated rights, not to the basic institutional and cultural foundations of liberal democracy, Canadian style. To have gone beyond that would have consigned the Reform Party to Canada's political fringe.

In Canada, as in the United States, populism – or at least a heavy dose of populist appeals – is a necessary but not a sufficient condition of conservative success.[7] But more than in the United States, Canadian conservatives over the last generation have needed a compelling populist appeal to overcome many voters' suspicions of the corporate elites identified by earlier populists. This appeal was also a necessary condition of successful Canadian and American conservative parties, because all parties must utilize the egalitarian ethos that underlies centrist and centre left politics. A regionalist appeal for western Canadian equality with central Canada, and presentation of direct democratic measures as ways of circumventing the elite-dominated swamps of old-party bargaining, were crucial to Reform's successful engagement with this egalitarian ethos.

In such a situation, strategic deployment of populism in ways that speak to both 'popular democratic traditions' and contemporary concerns with the democratic deficit is vital to a new political force on the right. Messages emphasizing social or ethnic exclusion cannot hope to attain partisan success easily in Canada, with its long experience with multi-culturalism. By 2000, it was clear that right-wing populists had to increasingly speak the language of inclusion with a multi-cultural accent. This is demonstrated most clearly now in the Conservative Party's extensive and increasingly successful efforts since 2006 to win over the leadership of immigrant communities across urban Canada. Conservatives do so on the valid assumption that recruiting the large ethnic minority vote is the key to their majority government, following two generations in which the Liberal Party owned the overwhelming majority of 'ethnic' votes (Friesen 2010; Friesen and Ibbitson 2010). Their achievement of a majority government in the May 2011 federal election, leveraged by major gains in heavily 'multi-cultural' ridings in Ontario and British Columbia, seems to bear out the wisdom of this strategy.

The picture of the Reform Party that emerges from the foregoing analysis provides us with a keener sense of how populism in opposition in North America works at a time of conservative political resurgence and widespread citizen disaffection with 'politics as usual.' We have seen that the Reform Party leveraged the basic populist antagonism between 'the people' and 'the elite' to direct citizen frustration at groups that have sought protection from the welfare state. Compared to other cases considered in this volume, it should be stressed that Reform's efforts in this regard threatened neither constitutional protections for minorities nor polyarchical institutions and processes. Reform's populism was hostile to pluralistic inclusion of organized group interests in welfare state policy

---

[7] In the early- to mid-twentieth century, populism was also a necessary but not sufficient condition of social democratic party success in Canada (see Laycock 1990: ch. 4).

development, but not hostile to either pluralism or democratic inclusion per se. It aimed to shrink an enlarged, extensively mediated democratic space of policy deliberation, thus enabling citizens to register and mediate more of their preferences in the marketplace while allowing them to register their policy preferences directly – and outside what they saw as a corrupt space of state-sponsored 'special interest' bargaining – in initiative, referenda, and recall votes.

Before it was transformed into the Canadian Conservative and Reform Alliance then merged to form the Conservative Party, the Reform Party was largely unable to realize its distinctly populist objectives. Direct democracy remained marginal to Canadian public life, western Canadian provinces were denied the reformed (elected) Senate that Reform had championed, and Canadian politics continued to be characterized by group interest bargaining through parties and Parliament. But the longer term effects of the party's combination of populism and conservatism are far from trivial. The Reform Party triggered a transformation of the federal party system, mobilized new (but not previously excluded) religious groups, began construction of new political alliances, added potent fuel to the flames of citizens' suspicion of governments and established parties, and laid the foundations of political success for a party far more conservative than most commentators would have thought possible two decades ago.

Reform also encouraged considerable public suspicion over the scope of women's, gay, and aboriginal group rights, and did more than any other political force to prevent a constitutional reform that would have enhanced minority rights and Québec provincial government powers. There is little doubt that Reform aimed to polarize Canadian politics and the party system, initially by disturbing the partisan consensus on matters of multi-culturalism and women's rights, and continually on the broad issues of support for the welfare state. And Reform unquestionably polarized Canadian politics by injecting a fragmenting, populist cleavage into the party competition. In doing so, the party promoted plebiscitarian approaches to governance that hastened the decline of legitimacy Canadians attribute to their representative institutions, and campaigned to 'shrink democratic space in Canada' in ways later pursued by the current Canadian government.

The threads connecting Reform Party advocacy and Conservative Party governance support hypothesis 1, that "populism in government has stronger effects on democracy than populism in opposition." However, the Conservative Party and government's roots in Reform also offer a revealing test case for tracing the long-term effects of a populism that moves from the political margin to a dominant position in the party system. Finally, though making such a case has not been the purpose of this chapter, evidence presented here also suggests that these stronger effects of government populism are also negative for Canadian democracy, *pace* hypothesis 2.

This list of Reform Party populist effects on Canadian democracy includes few items as negatively consequential as other authors of this volume have discovered in relation to their populist cases. Nonetheless, the list adds up to an impressive cumulative impact for a party that contested only four federal elections and elected all but one of its MPs within one region of Canada. The Reform Party is gone, but by no means forgotten as a key cause of change in twenty-first-century Canadian democratic politics.

4 The Czech Republicans 1990–1998: a populist outsider in a consolidating democracy

Seán Hanley

Introduction

The Association for the Republic-Republican Party of Czechoslovakia (SPR-RSČ) was a small, radical, right populist party in the Czech Republic politically successful for much of the 1990s. The Republicans were represented in the Czech parliament between 1992 and 1998, but their support subsequently declined and the party lost parliamentary representation and then rapidly fragmented. Radical right forces in the Czech Republic have since failed to unite and, despite high-profile and provocative bursts of activism, have remained electorally and political marginal.

In this chapter, I examine the SPR-RSČ as a case study of party-based oppositional outsider populism in a consolidating democracy. Having first traced the origins and development of the party, I then examine the populist nature of its radical right appeals in the 1990s and the implicit understanding of democracy these contained. I conclude by evaluating the Republicans' impact on the development of Czech democracy and assessing the extent to which it has left a legacy in contemporary Czech politics.

4.1   The rise and fall of the SPR-RSČ

Miroslav Sládek and a group of associates formed the SPR-RSČ in December 1989 as a radical right-wing party; the group formally registered as a political party in February 1990. The SPR-RSČ apparently originated as one of a plethora of small, anti-communist groups founded in late 1989 during the course of Czechoslovakia's Velvet Revolution which styled themselves 'right-wing' and 'Republican'; the latter an allusion to both U.S. Republicans and the conservative inter-war Czechoslovak Agrarians, who officially named themselves the Republican Party. Neither Sládek, who worked as a low-ranking official for the Czech censor's office, nor other founders of the SPR-RSČ were politically active before 1989. None seem to have been Communist Party members or to have had contacts with dissidents or the less visible 'grey zone' of opposition-minded technocrats that emerged in the 1980s. The SPR-RSČ was quickly marked by Sládek's egocentric, dominant personality and his radical outspoken statements, which led to a rapid breakdown in attempts to co-operate with similar small groupings. Sládek's group thus contested the 1990 Czech and Czechoslovak elections outside the main alliance of small new anti-communist groupings, the Conservative Party-Free Bloc (KS-SB).[1]

The SPR-RSČ initially profiled itself as a respectable right-wing, nationalist, anti-communist party critical of Czechoslovakia's new president, dissident playwright Václav Havel, and his Civic Forum movement for not becoming 'a platform for electoral struggle against the communists' (SPR-RSČ 1990: 1). However, chauvinistic and authoritarian elements, such as support for a strong presidency and hostility to African and Vietnamese guest workers, are detectable in the party's earliest programmatic documents and, even more so, in Sládek's statements and speeches. In the June 1990 Czech and Czechoslovak parliamentary elections both KS-SB and SPR-RSČ's joint electoral list with the tiny All People's Democratic Party (VLDS) received negligible support, each gaining just over one per cent in the Czech lands and winning deputies in neither the Czech nor Czechoslovak federal parliaments.

In the course of 1990 Sládek's party developed a distinct brand of right-wing politics combining disruptive activism with ultra-radical, conspiracy-minded anti-communism and a pallet of anti-elite, chauvinistic, and racist anti-Roma themes. It used its newly founded weekly *Republika* (*Republic*) to promote conspiracy theories that the Velvet Revolution had been staged as a result of secret agreements between communist and dissident elites. The SPR-RSČ also received considerable publicity from protest demonstrations it organized against this 'conspiracy' during President George H. W. Bush's visit to Prague in November 1990. Banners in English, held by party activists and visible in media coverage of the event, read 'President Bush – You Are Talking To Communists.' Independent reports spoke of an estimated 2,000–3,000 Sládek supporters attending protest demonstrations organized to coincide with the visit (*Republika*, 26 November 1990; *Svobodné slovo*, 19 November 1990).

---

[1] Although the SPR-RSČ fielded candidates in both the Czech lands and Slovakia before the breakup of the Czechoslovak federation in 1993, it was in essence a purely Czech-based organization and its support in Slovakia was always negligible.

In addition to anti-communism, the SPR-RSČ took up an eclectic mix of issues designed to draw rapid popular support. It called for larger social benefits and increased public services; greater law and order; less bureaucracy and state intervention; the re-incorporation of Transcarpathia (ceded to the USSR in 1945) into Czechoslovakia[2]; the defence of Czech national interests against the West (and, in particular, alleged German and Sudeten German revanchism); and tough measures against the Roma minority as a (supposed) source of crime and disorder, the racism for which the party became best known.[3] Beginning in the spring of 1991, the party's extreme and outrageous rhetoric, provocative and well-publicized demonstrations, and continual public campaigning in rallies and open air meetings addressed by Sládek had mobilized enough support to create a small national organization and growing electoral support.[4]

In June 1992, benefitting from the fluid and uncertain political environment created by the breakup of Civic Forum into separate parties, the launching of economic reforms, and the Czech-Slovak tensions over the redesign of the Czechoslovak federation, the SPR-RSČ made an electoral breakthrough, polling just over six per cent of the Czech vote in parliamentary elections and gaining representation in the Czechoslovak Federal Assembly and the Czech parliament (see Table 4.1).

The Republicans' parliamentary faction quickly fragmented; nine of the SPR-RSČ's fourteen federal deputies, elected in 1992, broke with the party. However, this represented only a limited setback for the party, as the SPR-RSČ was largely inactive in the legislative process, preferring instead to continue its strategy of outrageous headline grabbing protest stunts.[5]

Republican representatives thus repeatedly came into conflict with the police and the courts, usually in connection with laws on inciting racial

---

[2] The region is also known as Sub-Carpathian Ukraine and Ruthenia.

[3] Some analysts suggest that the Republicans toned down anti-Roma and anti-foreign rhetoric before the 1992 elections to focus on criticizing government corruption and the failure to fight crime (e.g. Pehe 1991).

[4] The party also received supportive publicity from newly established sensationalist tabloids such as *Špigl* and *Expres*.

[5] Such events included the blocking of the main highway between Prague and Bratislava by SPR-RSČ members in 1993; regular SPR-RSČ rallies in Prague's Wenceslas Square on 28 October, the anniversary of Czechoslovak independence; the disruption of a commemoration in 1994 at the site of the Terezín (Theresienstadt) concentration camp, where German representatives were present; and the nationwide distribution in 1995 of leaflets alleging a conspiracy between the Czech and German governments to return the Sudetenland to Germany. Sládek was also nominated by his party as a presidential candidate in 1992, 1993, and 1998, using the special parliamentary sessions that elected the Czechoslovak (and later Czech) president as a platform to make inflammatorily phrased attacks on establishment politicians.

Table 4.1. *Support for SPR-RSČ in elections to the Czechoslovak Federal Assembly, 1990–1992**

	Chamber of the People (lower house)			Chamber of Nations (upper house)		
Year	# votes	% votes	# seats**	# votes	% votes	# seats
1990	67,781	0.94	0	72,155	1.00	0
1992	420,848	6.48	8	413,459	6.37	6

* Representation in the Czechoslovak Federal Assembly was based upon separate polls in the Czech Republic and Slovakia. This table only includes the support in the Czech Republic.

** For the Czech Republic, 101 deputies were elected to the Chamber of the People in 1990 (99 in 1992), and 75 deputies to the Chamber of Nations. In total (with the inclusion of deputies from Slovakia) 150 deputies sat in each Chamber.

Source: Czech Electoral Commission website www.volby.cz.

hatred and public order offences: Sládek, for example, faced prosecution for his 1997 remarks that the only thing Czechs should regret about their relationship with the Germans is that they did not kill more of them during the Second World War (Mareš 2003: 196–7). The greater access to the media it enjoyed as a parliamentary party, and the platform afforded by parliament itself, enabled the SPR-RSČ to amplify its message and build on its initial success. In the 1996 Czech parliamentary elections, the party gained over eight per cent of the vote, increasing its representation in the Czech parliament from fourteen to eighteen deputies (see Table 4.2).

However, in early parliamentary elections in June 1998, despite having performed strongly two years earlier and having mounted a costly and apparently effective billboard campaign, the Republicans saw a dramatic decline in support and unexpectedly failed to re-enter the Czech parliament. Exit polling had suggested that, unlike in earlier years, the party had failed to win over significant numbers of first-time voters and that many younger, less educated male voters, who had previously supported the Republicans, turned in 1998 to the Czech Social Democrats (ČSSD), who offered a more credible and professional solution to the economic issues of pressing concern to such groups (Kreidl and Vlachová 2000). The party was also undermined by revelations about Sládek's management of the party, notably his nepotistic placement of his partner (later his second wife) and relatives on the party's electoral list in 1996 and the apparent misuse of party funds to finance his own lifestyle (Tácha 1998). The latter accusation seems to have been especially damaging electorally,

Table 4.2. *Support for SPR-RSČ and successors in elections to the Czech parliament, 1990–2010**

Year	# votes	% votes	# seats (of 200)
1990	72,048	1.00	0
1992	387,026	5.98	14
1996	485,072	8.01	18
1998	232,965	3.90	0
2002**	46,325	0.97	0
2006	not contested	not contested	–
2010***	1,193	0.03	0

* Elections in 1990 and 1992 were for the Czech National Council, subsequent elections for the Chamber of Deputies.
** Miroslav Sládek Republicans (RMS).
*** Re-founded SPR-RSČ. Electoral lists in three of fourteen districts.
Source: Czech Electoral Commission Web site www.volby.cz.

given the party's regular attacks on established politicians as corrupt and self-seeking.

Faced with this sharp electoral reversal, the SPR-RSČ was rapidly undermined by organizational instabilities stemming from its culture of activism, charismatic leadership, and lack of functional formal party structures. The party was essentially a loose network of local groups linked to a national leadership dominated by Sládek, who ran it through a clique of trusted associates, friends, and relatives (Cerqueirová 1999: 59–78). Sládek's personal dominance of the party had already led to repeated factional conflicts and several waves of defections[6] which accelerated after the debacle of the 1998 parliamentary elections and subsequent further declines in support in regional elections in 2000.

After the party declared bankruptcy in 2001 because it could not pay employees, remaining members regrouped in a new, smaller successor organization: the Miroslav Sládek Republicans (RMS). However, the RMS's electoral impact was negligible and the organization declined into a political rump, which was a relatively minor player even on the Czech Republic's small radical right scene. In succeeding years other radical

[6] After the initial departure of moderates alienated by Sládek's radicalism in early 1990, the Radical Republican Party (RRS) broke away after the 1990 elections and joined with other ex-SPR-RSČ members (including two Republican deputies) who had left Sládek's party in 1992 and 1995 to form the Party of Republican and National Democratic Unity (SRNDJ), later re-named the Patriotic Republican Party (VRS). VRS was joined by a further large group from SPR-RSČ in 1998 (Mareš 2003: 190–9, 225–38).

right parties have made a similarly insignificant electoral impact in the Czech Republic.

4.2　The SPR-RSČ as a populist radical right party

Although central and east European parties sit uncomfortably within comparative typologies derived from the west European experience, the Republicans fit comfortably within the category of radical right populist party, understood as a combination of populism and nativism, social authoritarianism, and scepticism towards liberal democracy (Mudde 2007). The SPR-RSČ's nativism was expressed in an ethnically exclusive, xenophobic vision of the Czechoslovak (and later Czech) state defined by anti-Roma racism, anti-German nationalism, and rejection of membership in international organizations, including NATO and the EU. Its authoritarianism was expressed in demands for law and order and support for tougher punishments for criminals, including the restoration of the death penalty. In almost all cases, issues of crime and disorder were ethnicized and explained as part of the 'Gypsy problem' or put into a populist idiom and discussed in terms of the crime and corruption of elites. However, unlike Czech neo-fascist and neo-Nazi groupuscules, the SPR-RSČ was not opposed to representative democracy on principle; rather, like a number of mainstream parties, it wished to supplement liberal democracy with elements of direct citizen participation.

By the mid-1990s the Republicans had come to see themselves as part of a Europe wide family of 'radical right' parties which, they believed, were a response to the wider 'moral crisis of the democratic system' plagued by corruption, crime, immigration, the 'dictatorship of money,' and the inability of governing coalitions to resolve the problems of ordinary people (Sládek 1995: 73–4). The party enjoyed close relations with France's Front National (FN), participating in several events organized by the first incarnation of the FN-sponsored EURONAT grouping.

The SPR-RSČ ideology combined this radical right outlook with populist discourse containing all three key core characteristics outlined in the first chapter of this volume: (1) a view of society as divided into two homogenous and hostile groups – a corrupt, self-serving elite and a morally unsullied people; (2) an understanding of such divisions as predominantly *moral*, that is based on character and self-chosen conduct; and (3) a conception of the proper purpose of politics as the expression of social and national unity and its defence against threatening external forces or corrupt internal minorities. The Republicans' specific construction of these elements was essentially framed in terms of a radical anti-communist ideology of regime change.

4.2.1   'Ordinary people' versus corrupt (crypto-)communist elites

The Republicans saw themselves as representing hardworking, previously unpoliticized 'ordinary people,' who had been neglected and overlooked by privileged elite groups, including the communist nomenklatura and the dissident intelligentsia alike. Early in 1990 Sládek summed up this view, speaking of his party as a defender of

> ordinary people, who are the salt of the earth, they work, they look after families, they were here through the most difficult of times and had to rely only on their miserable wages. They didn't emigrate; neither did anyone support them in a professional career. It is they who make up this country. They should therefore have the opportunity to influence this country's future (...) And not merely to watch passively as power is taken over. (SPR-RSČ 1990: 1)

As this statement described elite-mass relations during communism and the transition from communism, the Republicans thus unsurprisingly viewed Czechoslovakia's post-1989 political institutions as essentially a continuation of the old regime: a 'new totalitarianism,' outwardly reformed, but basically continuous with the former communist nomenklatura in their use of a media monopoly to maintain an ideological façade of pluralism as means of exercising social control for self-seeking reasons (SPR-RSČ 1990: 1–2). As Sládek explained, the new political parties had

> very small to tiny memberships, but their leaderships have an excess of financial resources and unlimited access to the media (...) now fully in the hands of this new totalitarianism. (...) These parties identify with different political currents, not for programmatic reasons, but for reasons of personal advancement [z prospěchářských důvodů], because they think that this or that current will enable them to continue their sweet inactivity at the expense of the majority of citizens. (Sládek 1992: 89)

The party partly explained the elite collusion through conspiracy theories, actively promoting the work of Miroslav Dolejší, a political prisoner in the 1950s who was re-imprisoned on politically motivated charges in the 1970s and the 1980s. He claimed that dissidents had been a secret reserve of loyal Communist Party members, created in 1969–70, whom the regime had only pretended to persecute and that, consequently, the 1989 Velvet Revolution had been the product of a secret agreement between Reagan and Gorbachev in 1987 and staged jointly by the KGB and the CIA. However, the party also used the more widely accepted argument, influential on both the radical anti-communist right and among mainstream right-wing elements in Civic Forum, that the reform communist politics of many dissidents in the 1960s gave them an unacceptable ideological and political affinity with ex-nomenklatura elites. Such arguments, although they could be formulated subtly, quickly became reduced to a straightforward equation of dissidents and communists and were generally used by the Republicans in this form (Hanley 2008: 164–6).

The Velvet Revolution and all subsequent developments were explained within this framework of elite manipulation as staged and manipulated by a powerful, sinister establishment operating behind a façade of democracy. The creation of a party system, the division of Czechoslovakia, coupon privatization and increasing social inequality were all viewed as products of the conspiracies against the people by an alliance of communist elites and crypto-communist dissidents. As an unsigned article in *Republika* (16–22 November 1992) discussing the imminent division of Czechoslovakia put it:

I have the impression that everything was planned beforehand (similarly to the Velvet Revolution) and that the Czech and Slovak nations have been deceived, abused and violated by a foreign power working with its domestic lackeys (*přisluhovačů*).

The Republicans' most original contribution to this radical anti-communist discourse of elite collusion and manipulation was, as stated in the words of Sládek cited previously, to link domestic elites with external threats and foreign interests. For the SPR-RSČ such threats stemmed mainly from the danger of economic and geo-political domination by Germany and, to a lesser extent, Austria; particularly from Sudeten German claims for recompense for the mass 'transfer' of ethnic Germans from Czechoslovakia in 1945–6.

4.2.2　Moral politics

The SPR-RSČ construction of collusive communist and crypto-communist elites was not framed purely in terms of their (supposed) shared origins or ideological affinities. Drawing on the common understanding, implicit in much dissident discourse, of communism as primarily a *moral* phenomenon (i.e. a form of evil), rather than a social or historical one, the Republicans framed the distinction between the people and the elite as a *moral* one, between the decent and hardworking majority and a corrupt and indolent minority using its monopoly on political power dishonestly to enrich itself in the privatization process, both directly and by serving foreign interests.[7]

---

[7] This view often shaded into a more deeply anti-political view: Politics was, as Sládek once put it, a dark tunnel in which the only light by which people could orient themselves, as they fumbled their way along, was the Republican Party and its goals (1992: 90).

The Republicans had a highly personalized, moralistic view of politics, which explained the failings of political institutions in terms of establishment politicians' personal corruption and turpitude. By contrast, unlike dissident and communist elites – who, the Republicans argued, were interlinked and co-responsible for the inequities of both past and present (SPR-RSČ 1990: 1–2) – the SPR-RSČ stressed that they were 'new faces' with a 'clean record.' Unsurprising, the party's discourses about the type of political change it wished to bring about were replete with references to moral renewal, purging, and purification. Its internal culture of continual activist mobilization, intended to build a distinct ethos of unity and self-sacrifice (Sládek 1992: 90), also highlighted the party's moralization of politics.

In contrast to the 'decency' and popular base of the SPR-RSČ, Civic Forum and its various successor parties were depicted as vehicles for corruption, personal enrichment, and elite manipulation by ex-communist functionaries, dissidents, and former black marketeers, which required 'purging' (e.g. *Republika*, 20–26 January 1992, 14–20 September 1992) because they had money and power but no roots among the people. In the Republican view Czechoslovakia's new liberal democratic and liberal market institutions were not simply phony and inauthentic, but the product of *deliberate* deceit by ruling elites, further evidencing their moral turpitude. This was, in the Republican view, true not simply of pretended differences between communists and dissidents or between mainstream parties of left and right, but also of seemingly more impersonal economic processes. Sládek thus argued that growing social inequalities resulting from economic reform were a *deliberate* action intended by elites to depoliticize and control discontent through poverty, rather than an indirect consequence of marketization (Sládek 1995: 104).

4.2.3   *Defending the national community*

Although notionally in favour of liberal rights and political pluralism, and certainly of private property, the Republicans viewed Czechoslovak (and later Czech) society as an organic community, united by strong ethnic and historical bonds, whose cohesion, distinctness, freedom, and – over the longer term – very survival were threatened by a range of external and internal threats consciously and unconsciously unleashed by elites. These included such diverse phenomena as growing economic inequality, family breakdown, declining birth rates, rising crime, consumer culture, and European integration. The task of the Republican movement, Sládek (1992: 27–9) explained, was to counteract such centrifugal and disintegrative forces and to channel the expression of the 'will of the nation' (*vůle národa*). Consequently, the proper relationship between state and society could be understood in collectivist and paternalist terms: The role of the state was to care for the people and guarantee popular well-being as a means of preserving the nation. In Sládek's view, ensuring such security for the people 'is not the right, but the duty of the state, if it is to have any reason for its existence' (Sládek 1995: 23).

4.2.4   The Republicans' understanding of democracy

In the 1990s the Czech Republic saw an extensive public and political debate about the most appropriate model of democracy. In outline, it opposed those who favoured a liberal, majoritarian model based on bipolar competition between professionalized, ideologically well-defined parties of left and right, to those supporting a more consensus-based model with greater scope for organized interests, direct citizen participation, and civil society to play a role in decision making. The best known representatives of the two views were Prime Minister (now president) Václav Klaus and the Czechoslovak (1989–92) and later Czech (1993–2003) president Václav Havel, respectively. However, the consensus vision was broadly shared across the political centre and centre left of Czech politics, albeit with a greater emphasis on traditional corporatist arrangements by the Social Democrats and Christian Democrats (see Machonin 1996: 31–43; Pithart and Klaus 1996; Potůček 1999).

Situating the Republicans in such debates and identifying the party's broader understanding of democracy is problematic, however. First, the Republicans showed limited interest in policy or programme development and, in contrast to radical right parties in some other European states, the party was not supported by a distinct right-wing nationalist intelligentsia milieu, which might have formulated a more coherent and elaborate ideal of democracy. SPR-RSČ programmes are thus typically short, one-page lists of demands intended to highlight themes to voters, while Sládek's own speeches and writing, the most extensive source for understanding the party's ideology, are often repetitive, rambling, and loaded with invective and hyperbole. Neither source engaged explicitly or coherently with contemporary Czech debates about models of democracy.

Second, the Republicans were regarded by mainstream politicians, journalists, and intellectuals as an extremist pariah party; their views were not taken seriously and were therefore largely ignored. Sládek, who bore a close physical resemblance to British comedian Rowan Atkinson, was widely dismissed by opponents as a disruptive 'Mr Bean' figure.

Third, and perhaps most significant, the Republicans' discourses on democracy were confused because, unlike most Czech political parties with the exception of the hard-line communists, they did not consider post-1989 Czechoslovakia and the Czech Republic to be a democracy, but saw outward pluralism simply as a façade for a new form of authoritarianism. The Republicans thus rejected the idea that there was a meaningful democratic competition, considering other parties mere vehicles for corrupt elites (Sládek 1992: 90). Sládek spoke of 'pretend new parties and (...) a fictitious political spectrum in Czechoslovakia. (...) Its goal is to confuse voters in Czechoslovakia and create the impression that there is a multi-party system in Czechoslovakia' (Sládek 1992: 71). The Republicans' pronouncements on democracy are thus often simultaneously concerned with *democratization* – how to bring about a genuinely democratic system – and with what form such genuine democracy might take.

The Republicans' positions nevertheless have an underlying coherence and logic, which amounts to an implicit strategy of transformation to an illiberal form of democracy and market society (Machonin 1996: 31–43). The party's primary role, as they saw it, was to 'do battle with the current establishment' (*Republika*, 26 June–9 July 1992) to 'intervene to save the nation from destruction' (Sládek 1995: 4) by bringing about genuine revolutionary regime change of the kind that Civic Forum had pretended to carry out in November 1989. The Republicans saw their party as a dynamic campaigning vehicle whose main task was to mobilize members and supporters through continuous demonstrations, public meetings, and rallies very much in the way that Havel's OF had done during the Velvet Revolution.

The Republicans' proposals for the type of democracy they would introduce in a reformed political system are somewhat sketchy and incoherent. Proposed institutional reforms include voters' right to recall legislators, proportional representation with no formal threshold, decentralization of power to the level of the commune, the restoration of the fourfold provincial structure of inter-war Czechoslovakia, and a reduction of central government to a mere seven ministries (Sládek 1992: 30, 65, 70, 1995: 43–8). All were, however, claimed by the party to empower ordinary people against corrupt professional politicians or to enable popular control over elites.

Insofar as it is possible to identify any more general underlying model in Republican pronouncements, it appears that the party saw democracy very largely as a simple mechanism for creating accountability between rulers and ruled, which could operate to bring about the revolutionary displacement of discredited rulers. As Sládek (1995: 104) put it, 'In a functional democracy elections represent a mechanism not dissimilar to a revolution.' The role of parties was simply one of continual mobilization and campaigning. In Sládek's words, 'For a political party the election campaign starts the same day that the previous elections end. Otherwise it isn't a political party, but a group of layabouts (*spolek lenochů*)' (1992: 236). However, other more contentious forms of mobilization could also be justified. Sládek even went so far as to claim, on one occasion, that 'It would be easy and understandable and fully in accordance with the Bill of Rights and Freedoms [in the Czech Constitution] to bring about the removal of illegitimate authorities using any means, including violence' (1995: 72).

4.3   The Republicans and Czech democracy

The Czech Republic rapidly and successfully consolidated democracy after the fall of communism. Unlike Slovakia, the country suffered few serious repercussions to its democratic development following the negotiated breakup of the Czechoslovak federation at the end of 1992. However, the quality of Czech democracy, and in particular the quality of elite-mass linkage, has been persistently called into question. The broad Civic Forum movement, which came to power during the November–December 1989 Velvet Revolution, soon faced criticism over the representativeness of its leadership structures and the real mandate of its ex-dissident leaders. However, the Forum's breakup in 1990–1 and rapid replacement with conventionally organized parties, which then became dominant actors in the political process, raised further questions.

Although stable, formally democratic in their internal organization and capable of articulating clear programmatic positions to voters, Czech parties' generally low memberships made them closed organizations, vulnerable to the informal influence of vested interests. Moreover, the rapid consolidation of the Civic Democratic Party (ODS), which formed from the right wing of OF in 1991, and the fragmented state of the Czech centre left enabled incumbent centre right parties to politicize public administration and turn a blind eye to corruption for much of the 1990s. While the emergence of the Social Democrats (ČSSD) as the dominant party of the centre left towards the end of the decade brought more equal competition between left and right, it also led to a series of close electoral contests, which failed to produce clear majority governments. The resulting pragmatic co-operation between major parties of centre left and centre right was then seen by critics as generating a collusive, clientelistic pattern of party politics, which denied voter choice and further blocked citizen participation and civil society development (see Green and Leff 1997; Hanley 2008; Kitschelt et al. 1999; Pehe 2010; Roberts 2003; Vachudová 2008).

4.3.1   *Positive effects on democracy?*

How did the Czech Republicans fit into this pattern of democratic development? As Rovira Kaltwasser and Mudde suggest in Chapter 1, populists can, in some circumstances, play the role of a democratic corrective by acting as a channel for previously unexpressed interests and issues. This, however, presupposes either that they have a degree of electoral support sufficient to make an effective claim on power or, failing this, that they enjoy sufficient acceptance and co-operation from established parties to enter the coalition making game. The SPR-RSČ lacked both significant electoral support and minimal levels of acceptance by other political actors.

Although willing to share a television studio with SPR-RSČ representatives, from the outset other parties (including the hard-line communists) treated the SPR-RSČ as an extremist pariah party. All other parties considered the SPR-RSČ unacceptable as a potential coalition partner at the national and local levels, and the Republicans, for their part, seem to have had little interest in gaining office. However, although the Republicans' rhetorical suggestions of direct action and persistent racism led some to wonder whether there were grounds for banning the party as an anti-democratic grouping (e.g. Fabrý 1997),[8] there was little discussion about formalizing the effective *cordon sanitaire*.

This reflected the fact that much debate about the Republicans, and extremist parties more generally in the Czech Republic, was subsumed into the more politically salient and controversial question of the status of the Communist Party. The main successor to the former ruling party in the Czech lands, the Communist Party of Bohemia and Moravia (KSČM), was an organizationally well entrenched and well supported organization,[9] but was regarded by mainstream parties as an extreme and

---

[8] A 1991 law (amended in 2001) forbids the propagation of movements that "demonstrably tend towards the suppression of human rights and freedoms or espouse ethnic, racial, religious or class hatred." On the legal background see 'Zákaz propagace komunismu,' *Revue Politika* 2/2005, available at http://www.cdk.cz/rp/clanky/243/zakaz-propagace-komunismu (accessed 25 November 2010).

[9] Between 1990 and 1998 the KSČM's electoral support ranged from ten to fourteen per cent. In 1998 its membership was an estimated one hundred and twenty thousand. SPR-RSČ membership records were chaotic and its claimed membership of fifty thousand clearly inflated. A realistic estimate based on candidates fielded in the 1994 local elections would suggest a membership of perhaps five thousand to ten thousand.

undemocratic force that posed a significant challenge for Czech democracy. KSČM was subject to a series of legal and political challenges by right-wing and liberal politicians during the 1990s, while no serious attempts were mounted to ban the smaller, and more ideologically inchoate, SPR-RSČ.

Given the existence of lustration legislation, barring individual high-ranking former communists from many forms of public office, though not elected office (Williams 2003), the mainstream parties were content to maintain an informal but openly stated *cordon* against the KSČM. The one exception was the Czech Social Democrats (ČSSD), who passed a formal congress resolution in 1995 forbidding co-operation with the communists or other 'extremist parties.' The resolution named a series of 'extremist parties' alongside the KSČM, including the SPR-RSČ. However, characteristic of such debates, the Republicans' inclusion served principally to blur the contentious issue of co-operation with the KSČM, which sharply divided the ČSSD (Kopeček 2008).

The *cordon sanitaire* around the SPR-RSČ – and the party's own lack of interest in programmatic issues or gaining office through coalition making politics – meant that it had no policy influence or indirect leverage on other parties. Even the Republicans' existence as a parliamentary party had limited relevance: Until 1996 liberal and centre right governments enjoyed clear parliamentary majorities in the Czech lands. Only with the inconclusive parliamentary elections of 1996 did the parliamentary presence of the Republicans (and the communists), as uncoalitionable parties, have an influence on political outcomes, contributing to the formation of a minority centre right government with Social Democratic support. However, the continuation of this pattern of deadlock in several subsequent elections following the political demise of the Republicans in 1998 suggests that the SPR-RSČ was one among many contributing factors.

Nor can it be argued, viewed from the perspective of political mobilization, that the Republicans played a 'bridging' role by facilitating cross-class politics: As in other post-communist central and eastern European nations, politics in the Czech Republic in the early 1990s was not based on rigid historically based class blocs, which a populist movement might bridge.[10] Nor, arguably, did the Republicans expand the political realm in post-communist transition politics. Most, if not all, aspects of economy, state, and society were already politicized and subject to political

---

[10] Communist societies lacked a conventional class structure. The concept of class was discredited and overshadowed by the focus on democratization and social transformation. Moreover, the post-1989 social structure was in flux, resulting in a transition politics that was already highly dynamic and 'cross-class.'

debate and political decision making about how they should be transformed into autonomous, non-political systems.

The Republican phenomenon did give voice to topics and groups that did not find a voice in the mainstream post-transition discourse of elites associated with OF: radical anti-communism, anti-German nationalism, and anti-Roma racism (the 'Gypsy problem'). They also politically mobilized and engaged a certain segment of Czech society – young, poorly educated, predominantly male – which might otherwise have been politically disengaged. In a more underlying sense, the party's nationalism, authoritarianism, and commitment to economic statism and a large communist-era welfare state also provided a means for many voters to express their support for the values and policies of the former communist regime while in their own minds radically disavowing it. To some extent, especially in 1990–1, the Republicans could also be credited with introducing – or at least alerting the Czech public to – the fact that democratic politics entailed conflict and competition, not (just) consensus.

Many of the statements in the preceding paragraph must, however, be markedly qualified. The SPR-RSČ was, in many cases, far from the only outsider vehicle for expressing such public sentiments, 'silent majority' issues elites did not wish to acknowledge. Radical anti-communist views emerged in the public arena very quickly through more establishment oriented groupings such as the Confederation of Political Prisoners (KPV), the Club of Committed Independents (KAN) and, most notably, in the splits in OF itself that propelled Klaus to the OF chairmanship in October 1990 and led to the foundation of the centre right ODS the following year. With the waning of ODS anti-communism, always more rhetorical than real, new parties – such as the Democratic Union (DEU) and Right Bloc (PB), founded in 1994 and 1996, respectively – offered additional vehicles for right-wing radical anti-communism devoid of the SPR-RSČ's racism and etatistic economic remedies. Anti-German nationalism, very similar in tone and focus to that of the Republicans, was strongly expressed by the KSČM.

The only 'silent majority' issue SPR-RSČ was unique in voicing was the 'Gypsy Problem': a belief that Roma were an undeserving, criminal minority generating a range of social problems against which punitive and repressive policies should be targeted – a sentiment prevalent across large parts of Czech society (e.g. Fawn 2001). However, the Republicans' obvious extremism and lack of intellectual and programmatic sophistication made the party a highly ineffective champion of such issues. The SPR-RSČ's culture of extremism and paranoia, which served to mobilize members, also cut the party off from broader Czech society, making it, in the words of former leading Republican, a 'microcosm' (*Lidové noviny*, 18 June 1998) and 'a sect, which abhorred everything and everyone around it' (Tácha 1998). The net impact of its activities was arguably to produce a closing of ranks among other parties and confirm the taboo status of its illiberal nationalist and racist views.

4.3.2   Negative effects?

The SPR-RSČ's negative effects on Czech democracy are somewhat easier to enumerate, although here too its relative weakness and isolation limited their scope. In fact, it would almost certainly be an exaggeration to speak of them as ever being in any sense a threat to Czech democracy or democratization. The Republican vision was certainly one that overwhelmingly stressed popular sovereignty and was devoid of any liberal concern for check and balances, minority rights, or the rule of law. However, the party's lack of power and influence left it in no position to circumvent such rights in practice. Indeed, as various court cases involving the party and its leaders show, legal provisions protecting the rights of others were often enforced *against* them.

The Republicans' moralistic and radical discourse demonizing and abusing political opponents and rejecting the legitimacy of the political system did little to foster a culture of dialogue or consensus in Czech public life. However, as suggested previously, the Republicans did arguably help cement a form of establishment consensus among mainstream parties to affirm liberal norms regarding the (non-) ethnic character of the Czech state and the civic character of Czech nationalism and national identity. Liberal understandings of Czech nationalism were, however, sufficiently strong and embedded (Auer 2003) that it is unlikely that the Republican challenge, even if it had been less self-defeatingly crude and extreme, would have opened up political space for conservative ethnonationalist themes.

Overall, the role played by the SPR-RSČ broadly conforms to the expectations that weak populist forces in an unconsolidated, new democracy will play the role of a corrective than a threat to democracy. However, the SPR-RSČ's political isolation and lack of political and intellectual credibility left it poorly equipped to make any meaningful critique of the socio-economic exclusion, alienation, and disempowerment of some groups in post-communist Czech society or the corruption that increasingly marred post-communist transformation (Reed 1996).

4.3.3   The Republicans' outsider populism: Causes and context

The case of the SPR-RSČ is broadly in step with the hypotheses advanced in the first chapter about wider contexts, which determine the impact of populism on democracy, although it also raises some questions. For example, the Republicans' nationalist, anti-communist, and welfarist ideology led the party to radical positions rejecting the legitimacy of Czech democracy and advocating the possible use of violence which – although never acted upon and containing strong elements of hyperbole and farce – were potentially threatening to democracy had the party won greater mass support.

However, the threat was a weak one, given the generally high levels of legitimacy enjoyed by the political establishment of ex-dissidents and technocrats swept to power by the November 1989 Velvet Revolution and elected in a landslide victory in free elections in 1990. At the same time the openness of Czech party electoral politics following the disintegration of Civic Forum in 1991 may also have been a braking factor on the SPR-RSČ. Although it provided opportunities for growing and allowed the Republicans to establish a hegemonic position on the extreme right, it faced a range of other parties and groups articulating an anti-establishment and/or anti-communist message.

4.4   Legacies of the SPR-RSČ

The SPR-RSČ has left few strong discernable legacies in Czech politics. Despite a brief personal comeback in local politics in 2003–4, during which he became mayor of a small borough on the outskirts of Brno, Sládek appears to be a marginal, semi-retired figure, now widely derided even on the Czech radical right for his political failures (*Mladá fronta Dnes*, 19 March 2006). Most other leading members of the SPR-RSČ of the 1990s seem to have left politics, although former rank-and-file Republicans have reportedly remained active at the grassroots level in a variety of parties and movements; the most notable being the former editor of *Republika*, Andrea Cerqueirová, now a prominent campaigning journalist writing on lesbian and feminist issues.

Some younger activists in the Republicans of Miroslav Sládek (RMS) have, however, remained active on the Czech far right: Tomáš Vandas, the former RMS secretary, was the leader of the Workers' Party (DS), which he formed in 2003, currently the most heavily supported radical right organization in the Czech Republic. However, the DS seemed to have largely moved away from Sládek's populist radical right 'Republicanism' (*republikánstí*), in favour of a more overtly neo-fascist style. The group stresses street and sub-cultural politics rather than election campaigning to reach out to the masses of discontented voters. The DS's aggressive protests in areas with high concentrations of Roma and its paramilitary style parades, which have gained it considerable publicity, appear closer to the strategy of Hungary's Jobbik than to the Republican model of the 1990s developed by Sládek.[11] Indeed, the radicalism of the DS led to its formal banning for unconstitutional anti-democratic extremism in February 2010, a fate the Republicans easily escaped.

The Republicans also appear to have left little ideological legacy. Shortly after the political collapse of the Republicans in 1998–9, the centre right ODS of Klaus started to explore anti-German nationalism – albeit in different, and usually more measured, terms than the SPR-RSČ – as part of a realignment towards 'national interests' and a more explicit defence of Czech statehood against the alleged encroachment of Germany and the EU. However, although the demise of the SPR-RSČ arguably diminished the taboo on overtly expressed Czech nationalism, closer examination of the ODS trajectory reveals that its 'nationalist turn' owed more to internal development and debates than to any external influences (Hanley 2008: 180–5). Indeed, even the few fringe elements linked to ODS, which have sought to develop a more ethnically based conservative-nationalist form of right-wing politics, such as the Young Right group, have drawn on foreign models or the historical 'integral nationalist' National Democratic tradition of the inter-war period rather than on the legacy of Sládek and his party (Hanley 2007).

Similarly, no party, with the exception of other far right groups, has ever taken up the Republicans' harsh approach to the Roma minority; although Czech public opinion continues to be largely hostile to Roma (*Czech Daily Monitor*, 13 May 2010) and some local politicians from mainstream parties, running for the Czech senate or in municipal elections, have campaigned against Roma in thinly disguised form, often winning landslide victories. Some politicians from the Public Affairs (VV) party, which entered the Czech parliament in May 2010 after an unexpected meteoric rise, have similarly advocated tough measures against anti-social behaviour in housing estates where large numbers of Roma live, even going so far as to advocate the use of citizen patrols. However, no such tendencies are detectable within the position of VV as a whole, whose highly successful political strategy combined anti-establishment populist rhetoric denouncing established parties as corrupt 'political dinosaurs' with calls for market-oriented reforms and greater use of direct democracy (VV 2010).

Perhaps the closest equivalent to Sládek's Republicanism found in contemporary Czech politics can be detected in the left-wing Euroskeptic Sovereignty bloc, led by former newsreader and former independent

---

[11] The Workers' Party (DS) has a limited electoral base: It polled 1.07 per cent in the 2009 European elections and, under a slightly different label, 1.14 per cent in the 2010 parliamentary elections.

MEP Jana Bobošíková. Although its rhetoric is not anti-communist, Bobošíková's party – an amalgamation of independent groupings and fringe parties formed in 2009 – has an economically interventionist, nationalist, and Euroskeptic programme framed in populist terms as a critique of an indolent and corrupt elite with surprising echoes of Sládek and the SPR-RSČ of the 1990s.[12] Like the SPR-RSČ, Sovereignty is heavily dependent on a high-profile, charismatic leader, although Bobošíková projects an image combining professionalism, toughness, and femininity very different from that of Sládek.[13] However, once again no direct linkages with the old SPR-RSČ are traceable, suggesting, at most, that the same structural conditions that helped shape the Republicans may have endured and influenced the development of other populist parties.

Conclusions

The SPR-RSČ was a radical right populist outsider, whose populism was strongly shaped by the transitional context of early democratization in which it emerged. Key to the party's populism was a blurred distinction between a socially unifying politics of revolutionary regime change and conventional democratic competition between parties. The Republicans' populist discourse and understandings of democracy were thus strongly shaped by a radical anti-communist view of transition from communism as incomplete, unjust, and manipulated. The impacts of the party on Czech democracy are broadly those anticipated of a non-incumbent outsider populist party. However, such impacts – both positive and negative – were limited by the party's relatively low electoral base, short life span, isolation from the liberal democratic mainstream of Czech party political and political discourse, and inability to formulate a more programmatically coherent and intellectually sophisticated radical right populist discourse.

As Dvořáková (1991) has suggested, the Republicans are best understood as a product, albeit it an unusual product, of a broader Czech anti-political tradition with cultural and political roots in the nineteenth century, which views professionalized political elites and state institutions as inherently inauthentic and corrupt and stresses the need for a moral politics backed and brought about by citizen mobilization and

---

[12] See Bobošíková's speech, launching her party's election programme, in which she denounced the EU for "pseudo-humanist and so-called politically correct waffle about human rights and minorities" (Bobošíková 2010).

[13] The party, whose full name is Sovereignty – the Jana Bobošíková Bloc, polled 4.26 per cent in the 2009 European elections and 3.67 per cent in the Czech 2010 parliamentary elections.

self-organization (e.g. Belohradský 1992: 31–4). Such anti-political traditions can be seen as shaping the political outlooks of numerous other actors in post-1989 Czech politics, including President Havel and other ex-dissident politicians, the many local independents' groupings still active in Czech electoral politics, the civic protest movements such the 'Thank You, Time to Go' initiative that erupted in November 1999 to protest against established parties' perceived clientelism (Dvořáková 2003), as well as newer, anti-establishment parties such as Public Affairs.

5   "To hell with your corrupt institutions!": AMLO and populism in Mexico

Kathleen Bruhn

Introduction

Mexico is a particularly interesting case to study the effects of populism on unconsolidated democracies, because it straddles in some ways two quadrants of the framework laid out by the editors. The 2006 presidential campaign of Andrés Manuel López Obrador (or AMLO) featured a populist rhetorical approach and his outsider campaign left him in the opposition. The chapter focuses primarily on this experience, as the editors designed, and analyzes hypothesis 5, that "populism in opposition in unconsolidated democracies will have moderate positive effects on the quality of democracy.". However, just prior to the 2006 campaign – from 2000 to 2005 – López Obrador governed Mexico City. Holding constant the individual politician, party, and time period, we can therefore compare the impact of his populist style in different roles: governing versus opposition. Finally, López Obrador's party, the Party of the Democratic Revolution (PRD), incorporated many elements of populism in its appeals prior to the rise of López Obrador, under its previous leader Cuauhtémoc Cárdenas. We can thus look beyond the particularities of 2006 for patterns of behaviour across time and across presidential campaigns.

While the body of the chapter explores the populist aspects of López Obrador's campaign in greater detail, it may be useful for those not familiar with Mexico to first clarify its status as a new, unconsolidated democracy. In contrast to most other cases of Third Wave democratization in Latin America, Mexico's transition did not involve a major constitutional break. After the formation of the ruling Institutional Revolutionary Party (PRI) in 1929, Mexico never experienced a military coup, and the transition took place slowly over a period of about a decade, without altering the basic constitutional framework in place since 1917. The PRI, which had hegemonic control and governed undemocratically for seventy years, continued to exist and in fact governed the majority of Mexico's states and held large numbers of seats in the legislature even after losing the presidency in 2000. Partly for this reason, there are many aspects of democracy in Mexico that remain incompletely reformed. The 1990s reforms which finally permitted democratic competition at the national level were not always copied at the state or municipal level.

Moreover, the 2006 election would expose the extent to which a significant percentage of the Mexican population believed that these reforms failed to establish adequate conditions for democracy – and indeed would feed their suspicions. When Andrés Manuel López Obrador lost by a mere two hundred and forty thousand votes out of more than forty-one million cast – less than one per cent – he denounced the results as fraud, mounted massive protests, and refused to accept the official winner, Felipe Calderón of the National Action Party (PAN), as the legitimate president (http://www.ife.org.mx/documentos/RESELEC/SICEEF/principal.html). The bulk of his political party supported him. But concern about the institutional foundations of democracy extended well beyond disappointed AMLO supporters. According to one 2008 survey sponsored by the Mexican government, sixty-two per cent of respondents openly disagreed with the statement, 'elections in our country are clean' (www.encup.gob.mx). It thus seems fair to categorize Mexico as an unconsolidated democracy in the sense that the existing rules of democratic competition are not yet universally accepted, adhered to, and defended by all actors.

The chapter is divided into four sections. First, it examines the primary case: Andrés Manuel López Obrador's use of populist rhetoric in the 2006 presidential campaign and its effects on the quality of democracy in Mexico. The second section compares this experience to the López Obrador government in Mexico City. The third section examines the relationship between AMLO and his party, as one of the distinctive features of the Mexican case is the existence of a pre-existing party incompletely controlled by the populist leader. This feature may mediate the impact of populism on democracy. The chapter concludes with an analysis of the longer term effects of the 2006 campaign.

5.1 The 2006 presidential campaign: "For the Good of All – the Poor First"

The 2006 presidential campaign was notoriously ugly, polarized, and polarizing. López Obrador – or, as he liked to refer to himself, the 'little ray of hope' for the poor – emphasized populist themes in many of his campaign speeches and focused on inclusion of the marginalized in his platform. His campaign slogan, "For the Good of All, the Poor First," exemplifies the populist dynamic. The goals of this section are, first, to analyze the role that populist rhetoric played in producing a polarized campaign, despite little evidence of polarization at the mass level (Bruhn and Greene 2007). Second, it discusses whether leftist ideology led to polarization rather than populism alone. Finally, it discusses whether López Obrador's campaign had 'moderate positive effects' on democracy as hypothesized or whether on the contrary it posed a threat to democratic institutions, as some observers of the election's aftermath suggested.

When López Obrador resigned his position as mayor of Mexico City in 2005 in order to run for president, he was one of the most popular mayors in Mexico City's history, with an approval rating over eighty per cent (Murphy 2006). Despite a corruption scandal involving his chief political operative and an ultimately fruitless effort by the PAN government under President Vicente Fox to disqualify him from becoming a presidential candidate, the formal campaign started with López Obrador in possession of a commanding lead in the polls. In his own mind, he had already won. While mayor, he had worked hard to build a cross-class alliance, blending populist rhetoric and programmes targeted at the poor with public works projects to please the middle class (such as expansion of the freeway system). He even worked closely with one of Mexico's richest men, Carlos Hank González, in an ambitious plan to revitalize the city's historic centre. Running on this reputation, he strove to present a moderate public image, especially at the start of the campaign.

However, even the 'moderate' AMLO focused on the need to include marginalized Mexico, left behind in the race to adopt neoliberal reforms. This emphasis is evident in his personal electoral platform, the 'Fifty Commitments to Recover National Pride.' The first five commitments refer to the 'historic debt that we have with the indigenous communities,' the right to a pension for the elderly (a group he targeted as mayor), scholarships for poor and handicapped students, free health care for all, and an increase in the minimum wage (López Obrador 2005a: 1). Thus, before discussing macroeconomic stability, his platform focused on the needs of marginalized groups. Moreover, he referred to his future presidency as that of a 'responsible politician (…) a man of state, not the leader of a party, faction or group' (López Obrador 2005a: 6) – he would represent the entire Mexican people, not a single party. Further, in presenting his Fifty Commitments, he described the goal of his 'citizen movement' as 'a true purification of public life' (López Obrador 2005a).

Nevertheless, taken as a whole, his platform is surprisingly moderate. I coded both his platform and the platform issued by the PRD coalition[1]

---

[1] This coalition also included the Workers' Party (PT) and Convergence.

using the methodology developed by the Comparative Manifestoes Project and based on content analysis.[2] According to the left-right scale developed by Budge and Robertson (1987),[3] the positions taken by López Obrador put him squarely in the centre of the political spectrum and substantially to the right of his own party's platform. With respect to economic issues, López Obrador's emphasis on markets over state intervention places him to the right of the PRI as well as the PRD. Government efficiency was his top priority; it ranked fourth in the PAN platform. Though he rejected NAFTA's elimination of protection for the vulnerable corn and bean sectors and opposed privatization of the electricity sector, his programme stopped well short of calling for a reversal of neoliberal reform. Furthermore, apart from a few caustic references to ex-presidents of Mexico who became inexplicably rich, his platform refrained from the Manichean opposition of corrupt elite to pure masses, as did most of his televised ads.

However, broader analysis of his campaign rhetoric reveals greater deployment of populist themes. The analysis draws on an archive of speeches and interviews collected by the Mexican NGO Lupa Ciudadana for all of the major candidates in the 2006 presidential campaign (www.lupaciudadana.com.mx). Randomly selected speeches were analyzed according to a rubric containing ten topics either directly mentioned in the editors' definition of populism or implied by it.[4] Thus, the rubric focuses on references to a morally superior people, demands for its sovereignty, denunciation of a corrupt elite, characterization of politics as a good versus evil struggle between these two groups (Manicheanism), and alignment of the candidate on the side of the people.

---

[2] Coders assign each sentence in a platform to one of fifty-six common categories, according to the sense of that sentence (or part of a sentence, if it contains multiple ideas). The data is expressed in percentage terms as the relative emphasis for each category with respect to the length of the platform. Coded sentences can be grouped according to issue areas ('domains') or summed together to create scales on specific dimensions (e.g. left-right placement). The Left-Right scale developed by Budge and Robertson (1987) on the basis of the European party platforms includes thirteen 'right emphasis' items and thirteen 'left emphasis' items from the list of categories. To enhance the comparability of the data, I obtained the full code books and training manuals from the Comparative Manifestoes Project and passed their intercoder reliability test. In the initial phases of coding, I received assistance and advice from Dr Andrea Volkens as I came across problems. I wish to thank the Comparative Manifestoes Project and Dr Volkens in particular for their generous assistance.

[3] The percentage of platform sentences emphasizing 'left' issues is subtracted from the percentage of platform sentences emphasizing 'right' issues; negative scores indicate positions to the left and positive scores positions to the right.

[4] Every fifth document listed by Lupa Ciudadana was selected: a total of eighty-one speeches, thirty-four interviews, and four 'other' documents (e.g. a public letter to Calderón). Most of the speeches were delivered in the context of campaign rallies, though a few (nine out of eighty-one) were speeches to specific audiences (e.g. business leaders).

Table 5.1. *Populist themes in the discourse of Andrés Manuel López Obrador (Mean number of references per document)*

	In plaza speeches	All other documents
	N = 72	N = 47
References to the good, morally superior 'people'	**4.82**	1.28
Demands for enhanced popular sovereignty	.44	.21
Identification of the candidate with 'the people'	1.54	.49
Claims to represent an 'unheard' voiceless group	.15	.04
Portrayal of the candidate's qualifications in moral terms	1.19	.26
References to existence of a corrupt elite who runs things	**3.61**	1.04
Suspicion of or rejection of established institutions	.67	.13
Need for purification and transformation of public life	2.42	.87
Support for plebiscitary decision making	0	.09
Characterization of politics in conflictual/Manichean terms	1.9	.57

The most obvious result of the analysis is a sharp and consistent divide between the kind of rhetoric employed in AMLO's contacts with mass media and the rhetoric he employed in campaign rallies to fire up his supporters. Populist discourse was reserved primarily for the latter. If one compares these plaza speeches to all other documents, there are strong and statistically significant differences between them, with plaza speeches much more likely to emphasize populist themes (see Table 5.1). Highlighted in bold, the two most common themes were appeals to 'the people' and contrasts between 'the people' as inherently good/wise versus a corrupt elite.

These populist references formed part of his main stump speech, delivered with variations in many different towns across Mexico. With respect to the central theme of the struggle between a good and honest people and a corrupt elite, for example:

What we have to do therefore is unite the people, this is the struggle of the whole people of Mexico to defend its interests, against a band that has perpetuated itself in power and has carried our country to ruin, that's how clear things are. (López Obrador 2006b)

Those at the very top (*de mero arriba*) do not want to let go of power ... they cannot be satisfied, they want to continue devouring the country, but enough already, now it's the people's turn; it is time now for the people to govern our country, for the people to benefit. (López Obrador 2006e)

Power and money will never be able [to overcome] the dignity and moral character of our people, that is what we are going to demonstrate on July 2 [election day]. (López Obrador 2006f)

We must convince those from below of the PRI and PAN because the quarrel is not with them, they are just as hopeful and just as beaten down as the majority of the people, the differences we have are with those from above and not the people from below. (López Obrador 2006d)

Or, more simply, as he stated in one of his first public speeches accepting the PRD candidacy: 'Arriba los de abajo, abajo los de arriba,' which translates, awkwardly, to, 'up with those from below, down with those on top' (López Obrador 2005c).[5]

With respect to the question of AMLO's critical attitude towards Mexico's existing democratic institutions, the signs are more subtle, but present, even at the start of the presidential campaign. There are many references in his stump speech to 'the corrupt and outdated institutions that have the people oppressed,' and to the need for a 'true purification of public life' (López Obrador 2005b, 2005c). Even before the election results led him to claim electoral fraud, he expressed doubts about the state of democracy in Mexico, arguing, for example, that 'we must continue to press for all of the changes that are necessary, it is necessary of course that there be democracy in the municipal governments, but it is necessary also that there should be democracy in the state governments and democracy at the federal level' (López Obrador 2006a). He said, with some truth, that:

los de arriba, the elitists, say that we do not respect the state of law, they keep invoking every little while the state of law, legality, the law is the law, but that is a farce, what we want is that there should be true legality in our country, that we do not just jail those who do not have the means to buy their innocence, that the law be applied equally. (López Obrador 2006b)

Moreover, as he had when campaigning for mayor of Mexico City, he promised to hold a referendum three years into his six-year term to determine whether the people felt he should stay, an extra-legal procedure that he actually carried out after he became mayor (he won easily).

López Obrador devoted the bulk of his plaza speeches not to vague rhetoric, however, but to specific programmatic pledges intended to clarify how 'the people' would benefit from his presidency, such as promises to extend a food pension to the elderly, scholarships for the poor, health care for all, subsidies for farmers left 'abandoned' by NAFTA, and more public universities so that all youth would have the chance to study. His pledges focused on helping the marginalized, those left out by neoliberal economic policies, and those historically abandoned to their fate, such as the indigenous. He spoke frequently about the importance of addressing

---

[5] He would later soften this formulation to 'arriba los de abajo, abajo los corruptos,' to counter PAN claims that he meant to take property away from the middle class.

the needs of the poor, arguing that it was impossible for Mexico to continue to live in a 'sea of inequality (…) not just for humanitarian reasons, which would be more than sufficient (…) but [because] we will not be able to have tranquility, or public security, or governability if there continues to be so much social and economic inequality in our country' (López Obrador 2006g).

In and of themselves, promises to address social needs are not necessarily populist. To some extent, all politicians in Mexico have to concern themselves with the poor. Mexico *is* a deeply unequal country, and a significant proportion of the population lives in poverty. López Obrador himself complained, in response to accusations that he was a dangerous populist, that, 'the little that goes to the people they call populism, paternalism, the vast amounts they give to a few, to the bankers, that they call [economic] stimulus or rescue, to hell with that trick' (López Obrador 2005d).

However, López Obrador's promises were distinctively populist in two senses. First, he most often extended benefits as a right, rather than using means tested methods of determining who should receive benefits; *all* elderly adults, not just poor adults, should receive a government food subsidy, for example. The Mexican right (and in fact, some moderate left governments in Latin America, such as the Concertación in Chile) extended welfare benefits based on selective criteria to the most needy only. Second, López Obrador argued that he could raise all the money needed to pay for his social programmes by attacking the privileges [his words] of the elites: making the rich pay taxes instead of evading them through influence, cutting the salaries of top government officials, and eliminating corruption and nepotism.

Nevertheless, López Obrador's populism does not, by itself, explain the polarization of the 2006 campaign. He kept his wilder rhetoric for the plazas, appeared regularly on mass media in a suit and acting sensibly, made public promises that he would not bust the budget, and appealed to the middle class and 'responsible, legitimate' businessmen. So why did the campaign become so polarized? Two factors stand out. First, and most important, the PAN – not the PRD or López Obrador – decided to go negative in March 2006, a scant three months before the election, because the PAN candidate trailed badly in the polls and had made up no ground in the three months since the start of the campaign. Regardless of López Obrador's rhetoric, Calderón's campaign team was politically motivated to paint him (as they did) as a danger to Mexico.

But AMLO's populist rhetoric made it a little too easy. Footage from plaza rallies, which López Obrador did not use in his own ads, provided colourful evidence of his more fiery tendencies. In the most notorious episode, frustrated by President Fox's open support for the PAN candidate (against Mexican electoral law), he warned him to 'stop squawking and shut up (*callate chachalaca*)' (Flores-Macias 2009: 204). The phrase referred to a noisy tropical bird, the *chachalaca*, which to the great delight of his audiences he soon started physically producing at rallies, as he repeated the allusion to Fox (and other PAN members) as *chachalacas*. Beware, the PAN ads warned: Behind the moderate mayor of Mexico City beats the heart of the radical who led protest marches and occupied oil wells in Tabasco. Voters who saw calling the president a *chachalaca* as disrespectful were more likely to switch their preference from López Obrador to Calderón over the course of the campaign (Flores-Macias 2009: 204).

The PAN's negative campaign worked, in part, because López Obrador did little or nothing in response, claiming in true populist fashion that the PRD did not have the money for slick ad campaigns (only partly true: the PRD, like all Mexican parties, receives generous public financing though it could not draw on the deep pockets of the PAN's business supporters), and that he relied on the wisdom of the people to see through the PAN's lies. This assurance became part of his stump speech: '[T]hey [the elites] want to convince the people as if the people were stupid. The people is not stupid. Stupid is he who thinks the people is stupid. The people realize everything that is happening' (López Obrador 2006h).

When López Obrador finally agreed that a change in strategy was necessary, he attacked Calderón with charges of corruption and claimed that he represented only the big money interests that controlled Mexico, repeating a populist trope. Nevertheless, after a brief spike in March, when the negative campaign began, populist themes in his discourse declined steadily through June, until the results of the election brought them back with a vengeance (see Figure 5.1).

The second reason the election became so polarized is the genuine and profound policy difference between the PAN and the PRD, especially at the elite level (Bruhn and Greene 2007). Regardless of how López Obrador framed his policies rhetorically, they would have appeared disastrous to the PAN, and vice versa. Never before had the two leading presidential candidates come from the parties on the ends of the ideological spectrum; rather, the party to beat had always been the centrist PRI. In the end, López Obrador lost because the PAN portrayed him as a radical, too risky for Mexico. But populist rhetoric did not bring this fate upon him. It merely fed the fire.

Where we really see the impact of populism is in López Obrador's reaction to his defeat. Again, *any* candidate who loses a presidential election by less than one per cent of the vote may be tempted to challenge the results, all the more so in a context like Mexico where electoral fraud

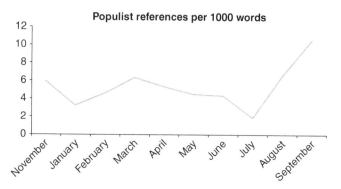

Figure 5.1. Intensity of populist discourse over time.

Note: Because the number and length of documents varied by month, the calculations presented here divide the total number of populist references in all of the documents dated by month by the total number of words in all documents dated in the same month. The vertical axis represents references per thousand words.

has been common. However, where Al Gore, and even Cárdenas, shrank from pushing their claims too vigorously despite legitimate questions over the validity of the results, López Obrador sought to overturn the election not on the basis of solid proof of irregularities, but on the basis that the 'people' *could not* have lost an election to the 'elite.' As he said a number of times, even before the election, 'the victory of the right is morally impossible' (López Obrador 2006g).[6] Thus, there must have been a conspiracy. His self-titled book about the 2006 election, *The Mafia Stole the Presidency from Us* (2007), suggests as much.

There were a lot of fellow conspiracy theorists within the PRD. Many of its activists started off in clandestine movements, others faced PRI repression and intimidation after 1988, and the entire party had suffered from repeated electoral frauds at the national and local levels. All of this produced scepticism about election fairness. Even before the election, PRD candidates and voters were significantly more likely than supporters of other parties to doubt that the elections would be free and fair (Bruhn and Greene 2009: 120–1; Camp 2009: 49).[7]

[6] Paraphrasing nineteenth-century Mexican president Benito Juárez, who made the comment with reference to the inevitable victory of the Mexican Liberals over the Conservatives, who governed Mexico through Emperor Maximilian and his French troops.

[7] I have personally witnessed party strategists in post-electoral meetings (not in 2006) admitting that their own numbers showed they had lost, but still insisting that 'somehow' they must have been cheated.

López Obrador's response went beyond the usual perfunctory protests, however. In July, immediately after the election, measured calls for a recount ('vote by vote') were accompanied by very limited use of populist rhetoric (see Figure 5.1). After the Federal Electoral Institute officially ratified Calderón's victory, López Obrador began to escalate both his rhetoric and his actions. In August, to put pressure on the electoral court to rule in favour of his appeal, he began a series of protests, culminating in the occupation of Mexico City's main square (the Zócalo), and the blockage for months of Paseo de la Reforma, a major street at the heart of Mexico City's financial district, the address of the U.S. Embassy, and the most direct route between the presidential residence and the presidential offices on the Zócalo. It was, therefore, a symbolically significant occupation and a vivid demonstration of the PRD's ability to disrupt life in the capital city. Yet with most Mexico City residents viewing López Obrador's claims as overblown, what would at best have been a justifiable inconvenience was seen instead as an unjustifiable nuisance.

After the electoral courts rejected the PRD's demands for a recount, in September, came the highest level of populist rhetoric (see Figure 5.1). López Obrador joined his supporters camping out in the Zócalo. In a speech on 31 August, as his party prepared to block President Fox from delivering his state of the union address before the congress (for only the third time in 180 years), he famously told those asking him to accept Calderón's victory, 'to hell with your corrupt institutions' (Aviles 2006). A few days later, he elaborated: 'Is not the Presidency of the Republic (...) in the hands of a small group that benefits from the current economic policy that has carried the country to ruin and maintains the majority of Mexicans in poverty? These are the institutions they ask us to respect?' Instead, he proposed a new constitutional convention, 'so that the institutions effectively are of the people and for the people,' denounced the 'usurpation of the presidency,' and called for measures to 'rescue the Republic (...) from a small group of the privileged who have taken over institutions and hold them hostage' so that 'power and money do not triumph over the morality and dignity of the people, as happens today' (Becerril and Mendez 2006).

On 20 November 2006, he accepted the 'people's mandate,' given in a series of plebiscitary assemblies he led in the Zócalo, to become the 'Legitimate President of Mexico,' taking the oath of office, donning a presidential sash, and announcing the formation of a shadow government. He threatened to prevent Calderón from taking the oath of office and asked newly elected PRD legislators not to take their seats in the Congress. Anyone who challenged his strategy publicly, most notably

Cuauhtémoc Cárdenas, was vilified as a traitor (see, for example, Cruz González 2006).

In short, if López Obrador failed to create a constitutional crisis, it was not for lack of trying. The shallowness of his commitment to liberal democratic institutions (and that of many of his supporters) was plain. What mattered more than following existing rules and procedures, which they saw as deeply corrupt and flawed, was achieving a victory for the people, which meant the presidency for López Obrador.

Important, populism in the case of López Obrador in Mexico posed a threat to democracy even in opposition, or perhaps *because* he was forced to remain in opposition. However, he was not in a position to do as much harm standing outside the National Palace as he might have sitting inside it. Moreover, the threat was mitigated by two factors. First, outside the PRD, too few people believed his claims of fraud. Public rejection of his claims and tactics meant that he ultimately harmed, not democratic institutions, but the PRD. Support for the PRD fell from 29 per cent of the legislative vote in 2006 to a dismal 12.2 per cent in the 2009 midterm elections, less than in any national election since its first as a party (www. ife.org.mx). Second, he could not count on the unreserved support of his own party. The PRD prevented Calderón from taking the oath of office in front of the congress, but PRD legislators took their seats and behaved, for the most part, as responsible members of congress. The chapter will return to this point in section three.

However, López Obrador's populist campaign proved a corrective as well as a threat. Calderón's initial reaction to his narrow victory was to shift his emphasis somewhat from his campaign theme (jobs) towards López Obrador's theme: the poor first. On 6 September, shortly after the Federal Electoral Tribunal declared him president-elect, Calderón made a speech declaring that he would make poverty his number one priority (Enriquez 2006b). George Grayson, author of a biography critical of López Obrador, suggested that, 'The messianic Andrés Manuel López Obrador has done a great service to his people (...) He has put the fear of God in Mexico's pampered elite, who live well, pay relatively little in taxes, neglect the poor, and spend anemic amounts on healthcare and education for the masses' (Enriquez 2006a).

Although Calderón's war on drug cartels has attracted more attention, his administration did expand programmes serving the poor. From 2000 to 2006, under Fox, spending on one such programme, Oportunidades (Opportunities), increased by an average of 4 billion pesos per year (*c.* \$325 million); under Calderón, spending on the same programme increased by 4.8 billion pesos per year. Moreover, although the number of families served grew by only two hundred thousand in the first three years of his term, the number of families served in rural areas, where poverty is concentrated in Mexico, actually decreased, while the number of families served in vote-rich urban centres increased. Calderón more than doubled spending on public health insurance (Seguro Popular). In his first three years, he more than quintupled the amount spent on the food subsidy programme (Apoyo Alimentario), from 332 million pesos in 2006 to 1.8 billion pesos in 2009. He increased federal spending on a subsidized milk programme (Leche Liconsa) and expanded programmes for the indigenous, Mexico's poorest citizens. He created a subsidy for housing and established daycare centres for working mothers. While at least some of these increases would have occurred with or without López Obrador, he certainly helped fuel political will to increase funding targeted at audiences that voted for AMLO in 2006.[8]

5.2   Populism in power: Andrés Manuel López Obrador as mayor of Mexico City

AMLO in power proved more of a corrective than a threat to democracy, though elements of both aspects of populism are again evident. There is evidence of a casual attitude towards laws and institutions, starting with a plebiscite in his third year to determine whether he should remain in office. The 'revocable mandate' was an attempt to create a direct connection between the leader and the people, at the margin of both the PRD and Mexican law (the mayor's term is six years). While in office, he held plebiscites on various issues, like whether to adopt daylight savings time or raise the price of a subway ticket. Democratic in appearance, these plebiscites nonetheless lacked the force of law and bypassed the Legislative Assembly of the Federal District (ALDF).

A second example, often pointed to by his critics, was the construction of an access road to a hospital. A prior municipal government had expropriated the land, but the owner filed suit and courts ordered construction suspended. Although he eventually complied, López Obrador initially went ahead with construction, arguing that the lawsuit amounted to extortion (the owner demanded 'exorbitant' compensation). His actions exposed him to criminal liability for defying a court order. Like all public officials in Mexico, López Obrador enjoyed immunity from prosecution for acts carried out as part of his public duties. However, President Fox requested that congress strip him of this protection, which it did in April 2005. Even had he been acquitted, the existence of pending criminal

---

[8] Spending data is taken from Calderón's *Third Informe* at http://www.informe.gob.mx/anexo_estadistico/pdf/2_3.pdf.

charges would have disqualified him from running for president. López Obrador argued that the charges were politically motivated and called for demonstrations that ultimately forced the PAN to back down. Yet López Obrador's claim that legal rulings could be ignored if they were 'unjust' was troubling to many who looked for clues to how he might behave as president.

Third, even as he built a strong record of social programmes serving the poor and marginalized, he tended to create new programmes under his own direction. He personally decided which groups to benefit, rather than through public or legislative debate, and continuation of the programmes was at least implicitly conditional upon the PRD remaining in power.

Nevertheless, the programmes were popular and served many people whose needs had been neglected in the past. The milk subsidy programme reached thirty-four per cent of people in Mexico City by 2002. As of 2007, the government listed 1.3 million direct beneficiaries (Méndez and Valor 2002). He gave scholarships and food baskets to poor families. He created free public high schools (Prepas Populares) in fourteen of Mexico City's sixteen administrative sub-divisions – a significant outreach in a country where high school attendance is usually reserved for those who can pay for private schools.[9] Moreover, he established a new university, the Autonomous University of the Federal District, with admission granted by lottery rather than examinations.

One of his most popular programmes was the Program of Food Assistance, a monthly coupon available to all Mexico City residents over the age of sixty-five regardless of income, and redeemable for food at any supermarket. Outreach specialists went door to door to sign up eligible residents. By 2005, the majority of Mexico City residents participated in the programme themselves or had a family member who did. Although not a large sum, the stipend was popular among the elderly, who often felt themselves a burden on their families, and it kept some older citizens from going hungry. In a 2002 poll, fifty-two per cent of all people over seventy were receiving the stipend and among this group, approval of the mayor was eighty-three per cent, versus seventy per cent overall (Méndez and Valor 2002).

Even programmes designed to benefit the middle class had some positive repercussions for the poor. The two most publicized public works projects were the construction of a second freeway level to ease traffic congestion and the revitalization of the historic downtown. One estimate suggests that these projects created over six hundred and fifty thousand

---

[9] Taken from http://www.df.gob.mx/wb/gdf/escuelas_preparatorias_del_gobierno_del_distrito_f (accessed 20 July 2010).

new jobs, contributing to a growth rate in Mexico City that was twice the national average (Grayson 2006: 221).

López Obrador financed these programmes in part by borrowing, although since Mexico City budgets must be approved by the national legislature it was hardly the orgy of spending that PAN campaign ads later suggested. To lower spending, he and his senior officials took a pay cut, and he eliminated many political appointment positions. During the 2006 campaign, López Obrador claimed that he could finance new social programmes as president simply by cutting government waste. However, Mayor López Obrador also employed a third mechanism to finance social spending: re-directing money designated for less visible projects, such as maintenance of the city's aging water supply system, apparently using executive discretion (confidential interviews with city budget officials, 2006). The parallels to populist presidents who governed by executive decree are evident.

Still, on the whole López Obrador did little damage to the institutions of Mexico City. The PRD candidate for mayor in 2006 easily won election. López Obrador remained popular enough that when he endorsed a non-PRD candidate for delegation chief (head of one of Mexico City's administrative sub-divisions), he beat the PRD candidate in a delegation where the PRD had never lost. Most of the time, he followed rules and allowed institutions to function. He created programmes to address unmet needs of the poor and marginalized. Journalism flourished; indeed, López Obrador was famous for his near-daily press conferences – 1,316 of them between 31 May 2001 and 10 April 2005, missing only ninety-one days – though he typically held them at 6:15 in the morning, when he judged he had an alertness advantage over most reporters (Grayson 2006: 185). He toned down his populist rhetoric, worked with rich businessmen, and governed mostly from the centre.

Given his later behaviour, why was López Obrador such a restrained populist in power and such a radical one in opposition? The theory that he simply went crazy after he lost the election is unprovable and does not fit some of the evidence. He was quite restrained in July, as he sought to overturn the official results through legal appeals. Only when these appeals failed did he turn to the streets. In the previous twenty years, similar protest strategies had – at least at times – resulted in the resignation of questioned governors and mayors. He may simply have misjudged popular support for his claims, as he misjudged the strength of popular support prior to the election itself.

A second theory proposes that López Obrador's actions after the election reflect rational calculations. The clear distinction between his discourse in the mass media and his discourse in plazas suggests that, no matter what he personally believed, he strategically used populist discourse. This in turn argues that he chose to restrain himself while mayor for strategic reasons. Two factors seem particularly important. First, he wanted to be president much more than he wanted to be mayor, and he knew that a radical reputation would frighten voters. One of the keys to the PRD's electoral gains after his election as party president in 1996 was a conscious effort on his part to reshape the PRD's public image as a contentious and disorderly party. So as mayor, he held himself in check (mostly). However, when he lost the presidency, he personally had little to lose by challenging the results, especially since he could not count on receiving his party's presidential nomination again in 2012. He would have to spend the next six years out of office, out of the spotlight, while potential rivals governed Mexico City or other states. Getting himself declared 'Legitimate President of Mexico' might keep him in the public eye. The fact that his party was not his personal vehicle may in this instance have encouraged more risky behaviour.

Second, he could more easily afford to restrain himself as mayor because of the strength of the PRD in the city. His party governed most of the *delegaciones* (nine of sixteen from 2000 to 2003 and thirteen of sixteen from 2003 to 2005) and had an outright majority in the Legislative Assembly in the second half of his term (www.iedf.org.mx). This suggests that the electoral strength of populism, and the extent to which it controls formal institutions, may affect the extent to which populists are tempted to bypass these institutions in order to achieve their goals.

Finally, he simply could not do much damage as mayor because of the difference in scale between the powers of a mayor – even in such an important city – and the powers of a president. As mayor, López Obrador did not control macroeconomic policy, did not have unrestricted authority to contract debt, and did not have the same ability to punish political enemies that he might have had as president. His authority was at least partly checked by the federal government. Populism at a sub-national level may thus be more beneficial than populism at a national level.

5.3   López Obrador and the PRD: Leftist populism in Mexico

Many of the populists described in this book created their own political parties, personalistic organizations designed to provide a vehicle for the leaders' political campaigns. López Obrador, by contrast, won the nomination of an established party, nearly twenty years old at the time of his nomination. This fact would influence his actions and options as a populist leader.

The PRD has been prone to backing populists for several reasons. In the first place, its roots in the left wing of the long-ruling Revolutionary Institutional Party (PRI) give it an historical connection to one of Latin America's iconic populists, Lázaro Cárdenas. The key leader in the formation of the PRD in 1989 was Lázaro's son, Cuauhtémoc, and he brought out of the PRI many people associated with the *cardenista* wing, including López Obrador. His rhetoric was so similar to his father's, analysts suggested, that 'the candidacy of Cuauhtémoc Cárdenas demonstrates the contemporary power of the populist discourse, neglected by successive technocratic administrations' (Castro Rea et al. 1990: 276). The early base of the PRD was attracted to this discourse.

Second, conditions in Mexico in 1988 were ripe for the emergence of a populist leader. As Freidenberg notes, 'marginalization and socioeconomic exclusion are ideal scenarios for the emergence of populism' (2007: 45). Despite a revolution, a hegemonic party that claimed to represent the demands of the working class and peasants, and thirty years of significant economic development (1940 to 1970), Mexico remained a profoundly unequal society. According to one estimate, in 1984 the richest twenty per cent of the population captured nearly half of all income, while the poorest twenty per cent got less than five per cent (Alarcón González 1994: 87). Moreover, during the 1980s the trend moved in the wrong direction. Beginning in 1981, Mexico experienced a deep economic crisis that eroded real wages and standards of living. The crisis constrained the capacity of the state to deliver material goods to its supporters or to maintain subsidies of such staples as tortillas, oil, and bread. Mexico's poor, by some accounts close to half of the population (Levy and Bruhn 2006: 13), were increasingly excluded rhetorically and materially by the ruling party, creating space for a new alternative that addressed precisely these concerns.

Finally, the new PRD faced a long-ruling hegemonic party, whose control of the political system facilitated the rhetorical division of the world into the pure masses and the corrupt political elite. To use the terms of social movement theory, populism provided an appealing master frame for understanding the problems of the contemporary political system. The PRI had been in power since its foundation in 1929, had never lost a presidential election or governor's race, never controlled less than two-thirds of the lower chamber of congress, and never lost a contested senate seat. No other party could be blamed for deficiencies in government performance.

It was, in addition, quite literally and visibly corrupt. Former presidents and other high officials amassed mysterious fortunes during their time in office. Materials purchased for use by government employees were diverted by union leaders and sold on the black market. Police took bribes. Elections were stolen when necessary, using such blatant fraud that Mexico acquired a whole vocabulary to describe specific tactics, from the "taco" (a roll of ballots stuffed together into a ballot box) to the "pregnant urn" (a ballot box that arrived already filled with ballots). The corrupt elite was easy to identify: the PRI. The pure people were the masses who suffered under austerity and economic crisis. Hence, the populist *cardenista* discourse argued that the poor had been punished at the expense of the rich and the political elite – they had paid the costs of structural adjustment for debts that did not benefit them.

Andrés Manuel López Obrador was recruited by Cárdenas in this context to become the new party's candidate for governor in López Obrador's home state of Tabasco. Prior to 1988, he served as a middle rank PRI functionary in Tabasco and at the National Consumer's Institute. His introduction to politics grew out of his work as state coordinator of the National Indigenous Institute, where he championed the cause of the poor and insisted in living in a hut similar to those of the indigenous (Grayson 2006: 34). He found *cardenismo* appealing, though he did not resign from the PRI until after the 1988 presidential election, when he agreed to run for governor.

His rise within the party was based upon Cárdenas's patronage, his organizational success in Tabasco, and his use of protest.[10] When he lost his 1988 gubernatorial bid, he denounced the results as fraud and refused to negotiate the 'people's will.' In the next six years he spearheaded civil resistance campaigns over various issues, including a successful and nationally publicized series of demonstrations, marches, and sit-ins at oil wells, protesting environmental damage by the national oil company PEMEX; he would use some of the payouts to help build the Tabasco PRD. In 1994, he ran again for governor, lost, and again claimed fraud. With the support of his increasingly well-organized Tabasco base, he launched a 'March for Democracy' from Tabasco to Mexico City, demanding that the national government overturn the official results. Again, he refused to negotiate. As he announced, 'They think that our struggle is based on personal ambitions, that it is enough to offer us good-sized bones (...) They are wrong. Our struggle is for legality and democracy, for new elections' (Grayson 2007: 85). The March for Democracy brought López Obrador national attention and contributed to Cárdenas' endorsement of him as the party president in 1996.

---

[10] Tabasco was one of the few states where the PRD increased its vote over 1988, from 20 per cent in 1988 to 31.7 per cent in 1994. The 1994 results come from www.ife.org.mx; the 1988 results come from IFE 1991: 11.

In these early battles López Obrador demonstrated patterns of behaviour that would later mark both his term as mayor and his 2006 presidential campaign. Populist rhetoric, opposing the corrupt politicians to the humble servant of the masses (himself), was attached to a personalistic style of leadership, confrontational and mobilizational politics, and clientelistic tactics to build the party base. His brand of populism did build party institutions in Tabasco, with one catch: He remained in control of these institutions through allies, even as he relinquished formal institutional control, mirroring the pattern at the national level with Cárdenas. Thus, party institutions did not acquire autonomy from their principal *caudillos*.

On the national level, however, López Obrador did not enjoy the same autonomy from party institutions. The PRD is a notoriously factionalized party, cobbled together from dozens of movements, parties, and proto-parties. Even Cárdenas could not control them all, and over time, the factions became increasingly institutionalized. In 2006, AMLO was at the height of his institutional control of the party. As president of the party from 1996 to 1999, then mayor of Mexico City, he placed his own clients at the top of the national leadership, including the party president in 2006, Leonel Cota Montaño. Nevertheless, his presidential campaign manager was Jesus Ortega, a rival who had just challenged (unsuccessfully) López Obrador's preferred candidate for mayor of Mexico City in the party's primary elections. Essentially, Ortega's hiring was meant to appease an important party faction that López Obrador did not control.

López Obrador's tenuous position may have encouraged him to pursue a maximalist strategy after the 2006 election.[11] His power could only weaken over time because PRD statutes forbid re-election of party leaders; his allies were bound to cycle out (in fact, Jesus Ortega subsequently took over as the president of the PRD). At the same time, his incomplete control of the party doomed this strategy to failure. Within Mexico City, the political machine he had built as mayor could be counted on to support his calls for demonstrations, but outside Mexico City other local party leaders and PRD legislators did not follow his lead. If he could have kept the PRD out of the 2006–9 congress, fully a quarter of the legislature would have been missing, provoking a legitimacy crisis that might have forced Calderón's resignation. In this instance, AMLO's relationship with the party both encouraged bad behaviour and limited its effects.

This, in turn, raises another important question. To what extent did López Obrador's actions reflect the inclinations of any populist, and to

[11] I thank Kurt Weyland for this important suggestion.

what extent did they reflect his own idiosyncrasies? A brief comparison between López Obrador and the PRD's other charismatic populist leader, Cuauhtémoc Cárdenas, suggests that personality does matter. Like López Obrador, Cárdenas nearly won a presidential election, was president of the PRD, and was mayor of Mexico City (though only for two years). Although Cárdenas felt himself no less wronged by the official results of the 1988 presidential election than López Obrador in 2006 (and with more reason), he chose not to escalate post-electoral conflict. Of course, López Obrador had a more effective organization than Cárdenas's loose multi-party coalition in 1988, faced a more tolerant federal government (in the PAN) than Cárdenas (in the PRI), and controlled Mexico City's police force. AMLO therefore could hold protests with considerably less risk and more effectiveness.

But there are differences of temperament as well. When Cárdenas led protests, as he often did in the early years of the PRD, he took a measured approach, lining up his allies, watching his words, and often acting as a mediator/statesman rather than a rabble-rousing firebrand. He was more frequently urged to be bolder than to restrain himself, something López Obrador's aides could not claim and often lamented privately. This does not mean that López Obrador was incapable of being pragmatic, or that Cárdenas was incapable of taking an impractical stance on moral grounds; both men were comfortable with confrontations portrayed in absolute moral terms and both men were pragmatic enough to have governed Mexico City effectively. Yet the contrast suggests that the consequences of populism depend at least in part on the personal qualities of the populist leader.

In power, both men made efforts to redirect government attention to the poor, as much because of their shared ideological position as because of populism per se. Both men adopted a more restrained populist rhetoric while in office, compared to their speeches as candidates and party leaders. Cárdenas, like López Obrador, planned to run for president at the end of his mayoral term, controlled a majority of the Legislative Assembly, and had even more limited authority than López Obrador, since Mexico City was still making its own democratic transition away from decades of appointed mayors. Thus, the same factors that I argue motivated López Obrador to govern mostly institutionally were also present in the case of Cárdenas.

A more troubling similarity between the two cases is that neither man made much of an effort to create new institutional channels for popular participation, along the lines of the participatory budgeting programmes created by the Workers' Party (PT) in Brazil. Social welfare policies were directed *at* the poor, by the government, with little popular input. Both men were charismatic leaders who attracted loyalty through their personal characteristics, different though the two men are, and both failed to construct party institutions autonomous from their own leadership. Whether by design or accident, they preferred instead to rely on networks of personal allies. A telling point: Neither man, as a presidential candidate, allowed the party much influence over campaign decisions. In 2006, López Obrador refused even to participate in assemblies held by the PRD to debate the content of its electoral platform, reportedly on the grounds that 'that is your business, not mine' (Bruhn 2009: 171). Later, he issued a personal platform not vetted by the party.

The relationship between established political parties and populist leaders therefore seems contradictory. On the one hand, these populist leaders tended to marginalize party institutions, and did little to build new institutional mechanisms that they did not control. On the other hand, party members accepted or demanded populist rhetoric and confrontational behaviour. In the (unlikely) event that López Obrador had refused to lead protests after the 2006 election, his credibility within the PRD would have suffered. Even after the obviously disastrous effects of his strategy on the PRD vote in the 2009 midterm elections, as of 29 August 2010, a poll by the conservative newspaper *Reforma* (29 August 2010) found that sixty-one per cent of PRD supporters (*perredistas*) preferred AMLO as the party's candidate for president in 2012 compared to seventeen per cent for his main rival, the current mayor of Mexico City.

5.4   Lasting effects?

At first blush, López Obrador's populist discourse seems to have left few lasting marks. Confidence in the Federal Electoral Institute (IFE) remained high. According to the Survey on Political Culture and Citizen Practices (ENCUP), in 2008, the IFE ranked among the top three most respected institutions (www.encup.gob.mx), together with the army and the church, with seventy-one per cent of respondents expressing 'some' or 'a lot' of confidence in the IFE. Popular ranking of the IFE on a 0–10 scale, with 10 indicating the highest opinion, was an average of 7.3 shortly before the 2009 midterm elections (Consulta Mitofsky 2010), slightly higher than the 7.1 detected by the ENCUP in 2005. Moreover, in 2005, forty-two per cent of respondents thought Mexico was a democracy. In 2008, half did.

The PRD, on the other hand, suffered a serious blow, suggesting that populist discourse did not strike a deeply responsive chord. In 2006, seventeen per cent of the population identified with the PRD. In 2007, just thirteen per cent did. In 2010, the average hovered around ten per cent (Consulta Mitofsky, 2010). Thirty-eight per cent of the population expressed 'rejection' (*rechazo*) of the PRD, versus thirty per cent in 2006. Only nineteen per cent expressed rejection of the PRI in 2010, a remarkable recovery for the once detested ruling party (Consulta Mitofsky 2010).

Moreover, perceptions of Calderón as the legitimate president improved. One year after the election, just over fifty per cent of the population thought that Calderón won; thirty per cent thought AMLO won; and the rest did not know. By 2008, the percentage of those who thought Calderón won had increased to fifty-seven per cent. Majorities of PRI, PAN, and independent voters all thought Calderón won. Only PRD members remained convinced of their candidate's victory; ninety-two per cent said there was fraud in 2006 versus forty-one per cent of PRI supporters and thirty-one per cent of independents (Consulta Mitofsky 2008).

From a more pessimistic point of view, however, two facts stand out. First, there are sharp differences among Mexicans with respect to the 2006 election, the IFE, and democracy itself. *Perredistas* have become increasingly alienated from politics. In order to placate the PRD after the 2006 elections, the congress replaced six of the nine IFE councillors and increased the powers of the IFE to monitor and punish negative media campaigns. But the reforms did little or nothing to restore the confidence of *perredistas* in the electoral process: Eighteen per cent thought they would make things better, eighteen per cent thought they would make things worse, and the rest thought things would remain the same (Consulta Mitofsky 2007). Overall, 11.7 per cent of *perredistas* thought the 2009 elections would be very clean, compared to 37 per cent of PAN supporters. A hefty forty-two per cent of *perredistas* thought the elections would be 'not at all' clean or that there would definitely be fraud.

Second, and more alarming, independents are nearly as alienated and distrusting of political institutions as *perredistas*. Those who declared no party affiliation were as likely as *perredistas* to doubt that elections would be very clean, though a smaller percentage expected outright fraud. Overall, sixty-six per cent of those who expected the elections to be dirty said they would definitely not vote ('if elections were held today'), with plans of abstention highest among those with no party identity; *perredistas*, though the most likely of any *party identifiers* to abstain, still mostly planned to vote (Consulta Mitofsky 2007).

Simple statistical tests on the 2008 ENCUP data confirm that *perredistas* were significantly less likely than members of other parties to express confidence in the IFE, to agree that Mexico was a democracy, to believe that elections would be clean, or to think that democracy would improve during Calderón's term.[12] Independents were slightly more likely to have confidence in the IFE than *perredistas* and to think that democracy would improve under Calderón, but they were actually *less* likely than *perredistas* to agree that elections in Mexico were clean or to classify Mexico as a democracy. Since roughly thirty per cent of Mexicans declare no party sympathy, their suspicion of democratic institutions is quite problematic.[13]

Overall, only one out of five citizens (twenty-one per cent) thought the 2009 elections would be very clean. The 2008 ENCUP found a similar level of distrust: Sixty-two per cent of respondents disagreed with the statement, 'elections in our country are clean' (www.encup.gob.mx). Though an ample majority had at least 'some' confidence in the IFE, only a little over a third had 'a lot' of confidence in the IFE, most of them PAN supporters. Between independents and *perredistas*, forty per cent of the population has serious doubts about existing democratic institutions. While these levels do not reach the depths displayed in Peru or Venezuela as their party systems were collapsing, they may be an early warning that patience with Mexico's institutions is waning.

Lack of confidence in elections and disgust with existing political parties contributed to the formation of a movement in favour of abstention and deliberate ballot spoiling in the 2009 elections; the null vote actually came in fourth at 5.4 per cent (Ackerman 2009: 69; www.ife.org.mx). In fact, the abstention rate of fifty-five per cent, added to the null vote, meant that over sixty per cent of eligible voters did not cast a valid vote in 2009, more than in any national election since 1988.

To be sure, these troubling trends to some extent precede the 2006 election. In 2005, PRD sympathizers and independents also had significantly less confidence in the IFE than members of other parties, and were less likely to say that Mexico was a democracy. Among these two groups, however, things deteriorated after 2006. In 2005, roughly ten per cent of *perredistas* and eleven per cent of independents had little or no confidence in the IFE. In 2008, forty-two per cent of *perredistas* and thirty-three per cent of independents had little or no confidence in the IFE.[14] In 2005, thirty-eight per cent of independents and forty-two per

---

[12] Using bivariate comparisons of means with chi-squared tests.
[13] Based on data from the Mexico 2006 Panel Study, at http://web.mit.edu/polisci/research/mexico06/Results.html.
[14] Because the question about confidence in the IFE was asked in a slightly different way in 2005, it is difficult to compare the two years directly. In 2005, respondents were asked to 'grade' the IFE on a scale of zero to ten, with zero indicating the lowest possible grade and ten indicating the highest. If answers ranging from zero to four are considered 'little or no confidence,' the result is the figure indicated.

cent of *perredistas* said that Mexico was not a democracy. In 2008, fifty per cent of both independents and *perredistas* said that Mexico was not a democracy (www.encup.gob.mx). It is hard to discount the impact of the 2006 election, and López Obrador's painting of it as a conspiracy by the rich, in producing such dramatically negative opinion shifts among these specific groups.

Conclusion

This chapter has suggested that populism can threaten the quality of democracy in opposition as well as in power. Indeed, AMLO's conspiracy theories and moral portrayal of political conflict probably did more damage to confidence in democratic institutions than he caused when he governed Mexico City. Yet in both periods, populism carried with it rewards as well as risks. The marginalized populations that AMLO sought to represent were taken into account to a greater extent, but disregard for existing laws – muted while he was mayor and amplified in opposition – was present when he governed Mexico City and again during his 2006 campaign. This argument contradicts to some extent the suggestion of hypothesis 1 that populism in government has stronger effects on democracy than populism in opposition, and the argument of hypothesis 5 that populism in opposition, even in weak democracies, should have modest positive effects.

However, the chapter also points to the relevance of three additional factors that may mediate the extent to which populist discourse poses a threat to democratic quality, whether in or out of government. First, to what extent do populists enjoy broad electoral support? During AMLO's Mexico City administration, the fact that he legally controlled many institutions (the local legislature and the *delegaciones* in particular) meant that he rarely needed to confront these institutions, although he did bypass them. More important, the *lack* of support for his claims after the 2006 election limited his ability to provoke a more serious legitimacy crisis.

Second, what legal authority does the populist enjoy? The limited powers of a mayor meant that AMLO had far fewer negative effects than he might have had as president; instead, his drive to include 'the people' as beneficiaries of government policies resulted in improved quality of life for many. Another way of asking this question is, to what extent does the populist confront an organized and powerful opposition? The fact that AMLO's party did not control the national government when he was mayor led him to face many external checks on his power.

Third, does the populist control the political party with which he or she is associated? Well-organized parties can be useful to populists, but only if they remain thoroughly under the thumb of the populist leader. The fact that López Obrador did not fully control the PRD may have led him to engage in risky behaviour, but also limited the institutional damage this behaviour caused. In fact, since López Obrador would have challenged the results of the election even if he *had* fully controlled the PRD, the existence of an at least partially autonomous party probably helped more than it hurt. Populism is more dangerous when it is unrestrained internally, when the party is not capable of checking populist leaders within its ranks.

These mediating factors suggest, in turn, that populism is most likely to function as a corrective when it is checked either externally or internally. Embedded in all of the editors' hypotheses is an unspoken calculation of relative power between populist and non-populist actors. Populism in government is expected to have stronger effects on democracy than populism in opposition because populism in government has more power and more popular support. Populism is expected to have stronger effects in weak and unconsolidated democracies because institutions enjoy less legitimacy and are less capable of limiting the exercise of popular majoritarian sovereignty that populism explicitly endorses. In a sense, liberal democracy – founded on the principle of checks and balances and on the argument that majoritarianism must be limited – meshes best with the representative thrust of populism when populism faces limits on its power, formal or informal. This chapter suggests that other factors can check the worst tendencies of populism besides whether it governs and whether it faces strong democratic institutions: in particular, whether it develops within an established political party, and whether it faces limits based on the federalist division of authority. One could imagine, for instance, a populist president restrained by strong governors (for example, perhaps Argentina) as well as the reverse (AMLO in Mexico City checked by the national government).

However, when a populist leader enjoys broad popular support, occupies a position with significant legal authority (such as president), and controls a political party that lacks the ability to limit his/her excesses, the political system is particularly vulnerable to a final factor: the personality of the populist leader. In its comparison of Cárdenas and López Obrador, this chapter also suggests that the personality of the populist leaders matters. The thin-centred nature of populist ideology lends itself to a personalistic style of politics. To the extent that populism operates at the margin of political institutions, it may increase a country's vulnerability to the occasional populist lunatic. Yet it also makes populist politics inherently unpredictable: Populist parties are vulnerable to rapidly shifting evaluations of the populist leader. They may be particularly prone to sudden surges and equally sudden collapses, as opposed to programmatic parties that appeal for votes based on ideological proximity to voters or on institutional ties to major social groups.

Appendix: Elaboration of the Populist Rubric

References to the good, morally superior 'people'

For example, references to *el pueblo*, versus references to *ciudadanos* – i.e. collective versus individual characterizations of the represented. Descriptions of 'the people' as inherently good/wise/morally superior.

Demands for enhanced popular sovereignty

For example, demands for *soberania popular* or *la voluntad del pueblo* versus appeals to specific interest groups (unemployed, peasants, etc) or claims that "the people" (rather than a majority) approve of something

Identification of the candidate with 'the people'

For example, by non-verbal means (use of popular dress, idiom, etc.), claims that "I am just like you," or references by the candidate to himself as the embodiment of a mass movement or the will of the people.

Claims to represent an 'unheard' voiceless group

Portrayal of the candidate's qualifications in moral terms

For example, the candidate is qualified to be elected as the most moral candidate versus appeals on the grounds of competence or ideology

References to existence of a corrupt elite who runs things

This category comes from the volume's definition of populism: arguments that there is a cohesive and small group of powerful elites who oppose the people's interests; inclusion of one's opponent(s) as part of this elite.

Suspicion of and/or rejection of established institutions

Need for purification and transformation of public life

That is, rather than calling for "reforms," arguments that there is a need for a complete transformation of politics as usual, a need for a major change in the way politics operates, transfer of sovereignty from government to the people, transformation of the social order, need for purification of public life, or revolution.

Support for plebiscitary decision making

For example, calls for public referendums and or other plebiscitary mechanisms.

Characterization of politics in conflictual/Manichean terms

Especially conveyed in moralistic terms as a struggle between good (the people) and evil (the power elite).

Evaluation of the stakes of political conflict in life or death terms.

6   Populism in government: the case of Austria (2000–2007)

Franz Fallend

Introduction

The Freedom Party of Austria (FPÖ) is one of the most successful right-wing populist parties in Europe. After Jörg Haider was elected party chairman in 1986, the party's strength rose gradually until 1999, when it reached 26.9 per cent of the votes in the national elections and became the second strongest party for the first time during the Second Republic (since 1945). Coalition negotiations between the strongest party, the Social Democratic Party of Austria (SPÖ) and the Christian Democratic Austrian People's Party (ÖVP), which had governed together since 1987, failed. Thus, the ÖVP invited the FPÖ to build the first right-wing coalition in Austria to date, which assumed office in February 2000. In January 2007, however, Austria returned to its favourite government type of the post-war period, a 'grand coalition' between the SPÖ and the ÖVP.[1]

The seven years in which the right-wing populists participated in the federal government were marked by a polarization of inter-party competition between the government block (ÖVP-FPÖ) and the opposition block (SPÖ-Greens), intensive conflicts about the neoliberal policies of the government, and internal turmoil in the FPÖ. As a result of its failure to live up to the expectations of its rank-and-file members and its voters, unsatisfied party functionaries (inspired by Haider) launched a rebellion against the federal party leadership and government team, which precipitated the collapse of the first ÖVP-FPÖ coalition in 2002. In the ensuing general elections the party fell to ten per cent of the votes. The ÖVP nevertheless renewed its coalition with the FPÖ after the elections. In April 2005 the unresolved intra-party discrepancies between the FPÖ's populist, vote-seeking roots and its aspirations to show governing fitness surfaced once again and finally led to the breakaway of a new

---

[1] In the sixty-seven years since 1945, Austria has been ruled by SPÖ-ÖVP coalitions for no less than thirty-nine years (from 1945 to 1947, also including the communists).

Table 6.1. *Elections to the national parliament (lower house, Nationalrat)*

| Year of election[b] | Political Parties[a] | | | | | |
	Greens	Social Democrats	People's Party	Freedom Party	Alliance	Liberals
1983		47.7	43.2	5.0		
1986	4.8	43.1	41.3	9.7		
1990	4.8	42.8	32.1	16.1		
1994	7.3	34.9	27.7	22.5		6.0
1995	4.8	38.1	28.3	21.9		5.5
1999	7.4	33.2	26.9	26.9		
2002	9.5	36.5	42.3	10.0[c]		
2006	11.1	35.3	34.3	11.0	4.1	
2008	10.4	29.3	26.0	17.5	10.7	

[a] The parties are ordered along the left-right dimension. The grey cells indicate the parties forming the government after the respective elections.

[b] Legislative and government periods do not always correspond exactly in Austria. General elections often take place at the end of the calendar year; that is why most new governments only take office at the beginning of the following year (this was, for example, the case in 1987, 1996, 2000, 2003, and 2007).

[c] The second ÖVP-FPÖ cabinet lasted only until April 2005, when the BZÖ formally replaced the FPÖ as the ÖVP's coalition partner without new elections being called.

Source: Federal Ministry of the Interior.

party, the Alliance for the Future of Austria (BZÖ). Federal Chancellor Wolfgang Schüssel (ÖVP) continued the coalition with the more pragmatic BZÖ (chaired, somewhat ironically, by Haider in the beginning), while the FPÖ returned to opposition and resumed its former strategy of vote maximization and relentless criticisms of government. In the general elections of 2006, both right-wing populist parties together gained 15.1 per cent of the votes; in the premature elections two years later this went up to a stunning 28.2 per cent (see Table 6.1).[2]

In Carinthia, one of the nine Austrian provinces, the FPÖ fared even better. In 1999, it replaced the SPÖ as strongest party, with 42.0 per cent of the votes. This was the first time after 1945 that the FPÖ reached the first place in a province. Haider was elected provincial governor, a

[2] However, the relations between the two parties were strained, and their leaders denied any intentions to cooperate or unify – until the end of 2009 when the (federal) FPÖ and the BZÖ organization of Carinthia (by far the strongest provincial organization within the party) joined forces, following the model of the Christian Democratic Union (CDU) and the Christian Social Union (CSU) in Germany.

position he held until his death in 2008.[3] Though limited by two coalition partners (SPÖ and ÖVP), he was in a favourable position to implement his 'Carinthian model.' In 2004 and 2009, his party (first FPÖ, then BZÖ) defended its lead, with 42.6 and 44.9 per cent of the votes, respectively.

Obviously, the FPÖ and its breakaway, the BZÖ, have had a significant effect on the Austrian party system and government composition in recent years. The impact of these two right-wing populist parties on the public discourse and their entrance into government, however, also raise the question of whether they were more a corrective or a threat to the quality of Austrian democracy. This question seems all the more relevant as the 'old' (pre-1986) FPÖ had once been the reservoir of former Nazis, and as the relationship of the 'new,' right-wing populist FPÖ to Austria's past has time and again caused intensive public debates. In fact, from the beginning of Haider's chairmanship in 1986 until 2000, the FPÖ was regarded by many – political opponents, representatives of civil society, journalists, scientists, intellectuals, and so forth – as unfit to govern or as undemocratic or illiberal. In their eyes, the acceptance of the FPÖ as coalition partner in 2000 represented the breach of a political taboo, with unforeseeable consequences for the quality of democracy in Austria. The impact of the FPÖ/BZÖ on the quality of democracy seems also worth studying in Carinthia, where the party was stronger than at the national level and therefore had a greater potential to influence democracy.

The existence and extent of – positive as well as negative – effects of populism on the quality of democracy is dependent upon further circumstances, above all on the degree of consolidation of democracy in a country and on the position of the populist party in the system (in government or in opposition). In this respect, Austria was selected as a case of populism in power in a consolidated democracy, and the following analysis will focus on the period in which the (right-wing) populist parties (the FPÖ and the BZÖ, respectively) took part in the federal government (from 2000 to 2007). Regarding Carinthia, the FPÖ participated in the provincial government before 1999, but only then did it take over the leading position. According to the framework for analysis laid out in Chapter 1 (see in particular hypothesis 3), it can be hypothesized that (right-wing) populists, although strong, will only have a moderate effect on the quality of democracy in a resilient liberal democracy like Austria. More specifically, the assumption, also formulated in the introduction,

[3] Haider had served as provincial governor of Carinthia before, from 1989 to 1991. However, when he praised the 'proper employment policy of the Third Reich' during a parliamentary debate, he was removed from office by a vote of no confidence.

that (right-wing) populist parties would strengthen political participation yet weaken public contestation will be investigated for the case of Austria. The investigation will be primarily empirical, not normative, based on the positive and negative effects of populist parties on the quality of democracy, as hypothesized in the introductory chapter.

The analysis will be structured as follows: Section 6.1 gives an overview of the historical development of the FPÖ. The next section examines the ideology and 'populist' character of the FPÖ. It includes a description of the party's political strategies prior to entering government in 2000. Sections 6.3 and 6.4 deal with the two cabinets in which the FPÖ (later the BZÖ) participated (2000–3 and 2003–7). The cabinets are treated separately, as we assume that the impact of the right-wing populists on the quality of democracy is to a great extent dependent on their political strength within the coalition, which was very different in the two periods (see Table 6.1). Section 6.5 takes a look at the developments in Carinthia, followed by a short conclusion.

6.1   The early history of the FPÖ

Government participation of the FPÖ in 2000 was controversial because of both Austria's and the party's own history. In 1945, after the end of World War II and the National Socialist 'Third Reich,' the three Austrian 'anti-fascist' parties, the ÖVP, the SPÖ, and the small Austrian Communist Party (KPÖ), established the Second Republic. Former Nazi functionaries and party members were disenfranchised for the first general elections of 1945. As a consequence, the League of Independents (VdU) was founded, which rallied ex-Nazis as well as liberal critics of the clientelistic politics of the ÖVP-SPÖ federal government and its nationalization policies. The League, which denounced the de-Nazification measures as a violation of individual, political, and economic rights, won 11.7 per cent and 10.9 per cent in the general elections of 1949 and 1953, respectively. In 1955, after the German national wing had obtained predominance in the party, it opposed the State Treaty, which restored Austria's independence after ten years of occupation by the Allied Powers. This was the beginning of the end of the League, which dissolved in the same year (Morrow 2000: 41–2; Riedlsperger 1998: 28).

Its successor, the FPÖ, founded in 1956, was treated as a pariah and excluded from government participation because of its continuing Nazi affiliation (its first two party chairmen were former Nazis). In addition, Austria's economic success story and its consociational political culture, expressed by 'grand coalitions' between the ÖVP and the SPÖ (until 1966) and corporatism (the so-called social partnership), prevented the FPÖ from playing an important role. Until 1983 it never won more than 7.7 per cent (1959) of the votes in general elections. Permanent struggles between the (larger) German national and the (smaller) liberal wing characterized the party's history until the 1980s. At the end of the 1960s the party leadership strived to move towards the political centre. In 1970–1 it supported a minority government led by SPÖ party chairman Bruno Kreisky in return for a reform of the electoral system which favoured smaller parties. A further step towards recognition was the liberally minded party programme of 1973 (Morrow 2000: 43–4; Riedlsperger 1998: 28–32).

Finally, in 1983, the FPÖ was accepted as coalition partner by the SPÖ, which after thirteen years of one-party government had lost its absolute majority. However, government participation did not turn out well for the FPÖ, which was hardly able to put a stamp on government policy. After losses in provincial elections, it was likely that the party would even miss the threshold for parliamentary representation in the next general elections. As a consequence, in 1986, a member of the provincial government of Carinthia, Jörg Haider, who had emerged as the spokesman of the right-wing FPÖ grassroots, defeated the liberal vice chancellor and party chairman, Norbert Steger, in a crucial vote at a party congress and replaced him as party chairman (Morrow 2000: 45–7).

6.2   Party ideology, vote- and office-seeking strategies

The 'new' FPÖ after 1986, starting with Haider's election as party chairman, has been classified by most political scientists as right-wing populist (e.g. Luther 2006a; Müller 2002; Plasser and Ulram 2000). Some experts, however, have continued to place the party into the extreme right-wing camp, hinting at the integration of old as well as neo-Nazis (e.g. Bailer-Galanda and Neugebauer 1996). In fact, while Haider publicly tried to distance himself from National Socialism, initially his inner circle was dominated by German national rightists who had supported his election as chairman (Morrow 2000: 49). However, as Mouffe argues, while there is 'no doubt that an aspect of the FPÖ's rhetoric was (...) aimed at rallying the nostalgics of the Third Reich,' it would be 'a serious mistake to overemphasize this element and to attribute the FPÖ's success to it' (2005a: 63–4).

If we take a closer look, the development of the FPÖ in the period before its entrance into government can be divided into three phases. In the first phase, lasting approximately until the end of the 1980s, Haider transformed the FPÖ into a protest party against the SPÖ-ÖVP coalition. He 'actively mobilised the themes of popular sovereignty and freedom of choice in order to articulate the growing resistance to the bureaucratic and authoritarian way in which the country was governed by the consociational elites' (Mouffe 2005a: 62). Exploiting many political scandals, the party's goal was 'to convince the public that Austrians were sustaining a corrupt and wasteful system that catered exclusively to the special interests of political insiders' (Heinisch 2008: 80; see also Plasser and Ulram 2000: 226–7). Direct democratic instruments were used for permanent campaigning. With their signatures, FPÖ MPs, for example, started six of the altogether thirteen people's initiatives (*Volksbegehren*) between 1986 and 1999.

At the beginning of the 1990s the FPÖ entered a second phase. The ambition to renew the political system was replaced by a more radical opposition to it, and the party tried particularly to address so-called modernization losers. Immigration, in Austria usually referred to as the 'foreigner question,' the fight against criminality, and anti-EU agitation were added to the issue profile. Around the mid 1990s, a third phase can be observed: Renouncing its German national roots and former neoliberal concepts, the FPÖ upheld national (Austrian) values, law and order, and welfare state chauvinism in order to fight against the dangers of globalization, European integration, and immigration. 'Austria first' was the slogan of a highly controversial people's initiative in 1993, directed against the rights of foreigners. In its party programme of 1997, the FPÖ committed itself to 'a Christianity that defends its values' against Islamic fundamentalism, aggressive capitalism, and consumerism (FPÖ 1997: 13). Political opponents reproached the party for leading a cultural war (*Kulturkampf*) against open society and the liberal constitutional state (Plasser and Ulram 2000: 226–7; Riedlsperger 1998: 32–4).

To what degree the FPÖ can be classified as populist depends on the definition of the term. According to the definition adopted in this book (see Chapter 1), the FPÖ was clearly populist, above all in its first phase (1986 to 1991–2), while the anti-elite and pro-democracy reform position was complemented with an anti-immigration and anti-EU position in the second phase (1992 to 1995–6) and with a pro-Austrian, welfare chauvinistic, and anti-Muslim position in the third phase (1996 to 1999).

In spite of new accentuations in the election campaigns, the FPÖ maintained its plans of democratic reform. During the campaign for the 1994 general elections, Haider stated provocatively that the 'Second Republic' should be replaced by a 'Third Republic.' According to this concept, the offices of the (directly elected) federal president and the federal chancellor should be merged and direct democratic instruments should be strengthened. Haider officially dropped the concept when it

Table 6.2. *Voting motives of FPÖ supporters (1990–1999)*

	FPÖ supporters in %			
Motives to vote for the FPÖ	1990	1994	1995	1999
1. Only the FPÖ seriously combats scandals and privileges	62	68	79	65
2. The party takes the right position in the foreigner question	39	49	51	47
3. The party strives to be economical and combats the abuse of welfare	n.a.	n.a.	52	n.a.
4. Because the party combats the power of the parties and for more citizen rights	n.a.	45	n.a.	n.a.
5. The party brings the 'wind of change'	n.a.	n.a.	n.a.	63
6. To teach the coalition parties a lesson	44	39	32	36
7. The party best represents my interests	26	34	34	48
8. The personality of Jörg Haider	42	39	38	40

Note: Fixed answers, multiple responses possible. The wording of the statements varies somewhat between the surveys.
Source: Müller (2002: 170).

led to accusations that he planned to establish a kind of 'Führership' (Riedlsperger 1998: 37).

However, the 1997 party programme, valid until the party split in 2005, declared a 'democracy and constitutional reform to renew the republic' to be the party's 'most noble task,' and its contents were not all too different from the values espoused by the 'Third Republic.' In the new 'Free Republic' the major executive organs (federal president, provincial governors, and mayors) were to be directly elected. The federal president was to be a member, though not explicitly head, of government; the federal chancellor was not mentioned. 'Party omnipotence' should be reduced, like the position of social partnership, as 'ancillary government.' In addition, the programme wanted 'plebiscitary participation rights' expanded; specifically, it demanded to submit government programmes, major public contracts, and subsidies to consultative referenda (FPÖ 1997: 21–5). Thus, in the FPÖ's ideal democracy, popular sovereignty is increased – the proposal to have the government members elected by parliament in proportion to the parties' strengths did not fit well, however. Admittedly, the concept of the 'Free Republic' was laid down on paper, but hardly ever transformed into political initiatives.

The electoral (vote-seeking) strategies of the FPÖ were reflected in the primary voting motives of its electorate (see Table 6.2). If we take items

1, 4, and 6 as indicators, we can see that a major group of the voters obviously saw the FPÖ as a populist party. Müller (2002: 157–8) argues that the electoral success of the FPÖ was inextricably linked to the Austrian *partitocracia* of the SPÖ and the ÖVP, which governed the country in cartel-like coalitions from 1987 until 2000 and produced noticeably little more than inertia, compromises discredited by foregoing infighting between the coalition partners, and patronage.

Likewise, Mouffe (2005a: 54–6) states that a lack of alternatives and influence on the elites alienated many voters and contributed to the rise of right-wing populism in many European countries. In her eyes, the SPÖ-ÖVP coalitions and social partnership 'led to the blocking of the system' and were 'to allow a gifted demagogue like Jörg Haider to articulate the diverse forms of resentment against the governing coalition and its bureaucratic machine, in the name of "democracy" and "liberty"' (ibid.: 60–1). However, this is only part of the story. As opinion surveys carried out in 1998 revealed, FPÖ supporters had mixed motives: Twenty-seven per cent of them could be regarded as 'system-disenchanted right-wingers,' twenty-one per cent as 'welfare state chauvinists' – the shares of these groups in the whole population were ten and fourteen per cent, respectively (Plasser and Ulram 2000: 236–7).

In the electoral arena, the FPÖ was very successful. However, by radically opposing the established political actors and their consensual style of politics, the party disqualified itself as a serious coalition partner, in any case for the SPÖ, Greens, and Liberals (Müller 2000a: 94–5). The political concept expressing this exclusion was formulated by influential ÖVP politician Andreas Khol in 1994.[4] According to his definition, Haider's FPÖ stood outside the 'constitutional arch' (*Verfassungsbogen*) and should therefore be denied 'governing fitness' (*Regierungsfähigkeit*). Khol (1996) demanded that the FPÖ, to be acceptable as coalition partner, renounce its goals of a 'cultural revolution' and a 'Third Republic,' declare its support for 'social partnership' and the European Union, and unambiguously condemn Nazism (see also Fallend 2004b: 122–3). The official politics of exclusion (*Ausgrenzung*), however, reinforced the FPÖ's populist appeal, as it allowed the party to present itself as a victim of the political establishment (Mouffe 2005a: 64). On the other hand, a vast majority of the voters did not want to see the FPÖ in government. In 1995, sixty-three per cent of Austrians preferred a continuation of the 'grand coalition' while only nineteen per cent favoured a ÖVP-FPÖ coalition (Plasser and Ulram 1995: 513).

---

[4] Khol was leader of the parliamentary group of the ÖVP from 1994 to 2002 and president of the lower house of parliament, the Nationalrat, from 2002 to 2006.

In the eyes of the FPÖ leadership, its vote-seeking strategies were not an end in itself, but paved the way to holding office. According to Luther (2008: 106–7), the FPÖ leadership had already decided in 1994 to seek to enter government if it were to obtain enough votes in the next general elections that the inevitably following electoral losses would not catapult it into an existential crisis. Khol (2010: 384) argues that Haider took his concept of the 'constitutional arch' as a working programme in order to prepare FPÖ participation in government (in coalition with the ÖVP). In fact, Haider publicly distanced himself from German chauvinism (*Deutschtümelei*) in 1995, and the party developed policy concepts on matters such as EU integration, immigration, pensions, family, and social policy (Luther 2006b: 21–2; 2008: 107; see also Heinisch 2010: 11–12). 'Hard' topics (e.g. anti-immigration, fight against corruption and crime) were supplemented by 'soft' topics. In 1999, the FPÖ made the 'children's check' the core of its election campaign (Müller 2000b: 194). The ÖVP and the FPÖ moved closer to each other. A study of members of the national parliament, carried out in 1997–8, revealed that in socio-economic and socio-cultural matters the ÖVP MPs were closer to those of the FPÖ than to those of the SPÖ (Müller and Jenny 2000: 143–51). As Haider continued to eliminate past and potential future rivals, thereby depriving the FPÖ of people with the executive and policy experience necessary for public office, his office-seeking strategies remained 'incomplete at best,' however (Heinisch 2010: 12).

6.3   The ÖVP-FPÖ coalition of 2000–2003 (cabinet Schüssel I)

6.3.1   History

On 4 February 2000 the ('new') FPÖ's exclusion from government participation at the national level came to an end. After coalition negotiations between SPÖ and ÖVP had failed, Federal President Thomas Klestil saw no alternative but to swear in the new 'black-blue' (ÖVP-FPÖ) government. The ÖVP, though having suffered the worst election result since 1945 (it received 415 votes less than the FPÖ), nominated the federal chancellor (Wolfgang Schüssel) for the first time in thirty years. In order to enable his party to enter the government, the most controversial FPÖ politician, Jörg Haider, did not join the cabinet and formally resigned as party chairman. Susanne Riess-Passer was elected new party chairwoman and took over the position of vice chancellor. Haider remained governor in the province of Carinthia and the de facto strong man of the party, however (Luther 2010: 83–5).

By request of the federal president, a preamble was inserted in the coalition pact in which the government declared its commitment to Austria's membership in the EU, its respect for democratic values and the rule of law, its will to fight against xenophobia, anti-Semitism, and racism as well as for the respect of human rights for anyone irrespective of his or her origin, religion, and ideology. In the face of national and international critics the ÖVP held the preamble to prove that its coalition partner had become a 'responsible government party' (Fallend 2001: 240–3).

The ÖVP and the FPÖ split the cabinet portfolios equally. Each party got six ministries; the two most influential positions, chancellorship and ministry of finance, were also divided between them. The FPÖ was assigned influential portfolios; in addition to the vice chancellery and finance it was responsible for social affairs, innovation, defence, and justice. The ÖVP hesitated to assign the ministry of the interior, responsible for immigration, to the FPÖ after the latter had exploited and roused xenophobic sentiments in many an election campaign. The FPÖ had big troubles in finding competent personnel. Within one year the party had to exchange half of its cabinet members (Fallend 2001: 243–5). Although both parties were equally strong with respect to the distribution of portfolios, it was clearly the more experienced ÖVP that dominated governmental policy making.

Furthermore, the FPÖ leadership was soon confronted with its unsatisfied rank and file and a loss of voters. Provincial elections and opinion polls showed that the ÖVP was able to stabilize or enlarge its support, while the FPÖ was weakened, sometimes dramatically. The neoliberal economic policy, the priority of a zero budget deficit by 2002, and the restrictive social policy stood in sharp contrast to the electoral promises of the party and alienated many working people (Heinisch 2003: 113–14; Luther 2010: 90). The claim to combat patronage and corruption was undermined by the fact that personnel decisions in the public service were not objectified, as was claimed, but in many cases 'red' (SPÖ-near) incumbents were simply replaced by 'blue' (FPÖ-near) or – more often – 'black' (ÖVP-near) ones (Luther 2010: 87). This, in turn, alienated 'progressive' FPÖ voters.

This all resulted in the breakdown of the first 'black-blue' coalition. In 2002, the FPÖ cabinet members, because of the costs of the summer floods, agreed to postpone for one year a reduction of taxes for people with low income, which according to the coalition agreement should have come into effect in 2003. Encouraged by former party chairman Haider, a majority of FPÖ delegates to the national party congress opposed the decision, arguing that it undermined the image of the party, which had always fought for the interests of the 'little man in the street.' The rebellion provoked the resignation of the party chairwoman (and vice chancellor), the minister of finance, and the chairman of the FPÖ's parliamentary group (Fallend 2003: 889–91; Luther 2003: 139–41; Müller 2004: 346–7). It demonstrated clearly that the FPÖ had not yet developed into a 'responsible government party.' Chancellor Schüssel used the rebellion as an opportunity to call for premature elections, in which the FPÖ experienced a huge defeat (see Table 6.1).

6.3.2   Positive effects

According to hypothesis 4 (see Chapter 1), it can be argued that the right-wing populist FPÖ, during its opposition years, had had a positive effect on the quality of democracy, in that it had given voice to groups that had not felt represented by the elites. As a matter of fact, in 1999, thirty-six per cent of the FPÖ voters were motivated by a wish to teach the coalition parties (SPÖ and ÖVP) a lesson (see Table 6.2). With government participation, the FPÖ now had the chance to represent these sections of society who felt excluded and to implement policies they preferred. Indeed, according to opinion polls, the share of people who believed that 'People like me have no influence on what the government does' declined from thirty-two per cent in 1996 to twenty-five per cent in 2001. Plasser and Ulram (2002: 104–5) claim that this decline was due above all to FPÖ supporters, who rated the responsiveness of the new government more positively.

As far as policy issues are concerned, it can be hypothesized (see also Chapter 1) that the FPÖ contributed to a deepening of the quality of democracy in that it focused on issues the elites had neglected (i.e. SPÖ and ÖVP). Immigration (or the 'foreigner question') was a prominent issue in FPÖ election campaigns and a primary motive for its voters (see Table 6.2). The party was successful in putting the issue on top of the political agenda, despite the fact that the majority of the voters had other priorities.[5] In 2002, the FPÖ campaign focused more on social issues and on Euroscepticism, less on immigration (Müller 2004: 349). The Euroscepticism theme, however, can also be regarded as an attempt to take up an issue reflecting widespread public attitudes. According to the Eurobarometer survey carried out in autumn 2002 (European Commission 2003: 32), only forty-six per cent of the Austrians viewed

[5] According to exit polls after the general elections in 2002, the issue of 'more restrictive immigration rules' was considered 'very important' by forty-eight per cent of the respondents. This seems high, but eleven other issues (education, jobs, pensions, and so forth) were ranked higher (SORA 2002: 23–4).

EU membership to be a 'good thing' (compared to fifty-five per cent in the then EU-15).

If one regards an increase of conflicts as 'positive' (and this can be argued for a political system like Austria, which often had been characterized as 'hyper-stable'), then it can be hypothesized that FPÖ participation in government deepened the quality of Austria's democracy. In fact, it resulted in a growing polarization between governing and opposition parties to the extent that party competition eventually assumed a bi-polar structure (Müller and Fallend 2004). Surely unwanted by the governing parties, it also revitalized civil society. Two weeks after the inauguration of the new government, some two hundred and fifty thousand people demonstrated in Vienna for an 'open Austria' and against intolerance and racism (Fallend 2001: 246).

The FPÖ also contributed to enhancing democratic accountability in that the influence of the neo-corporatist arena (the so-called social partnership), which the FPÖ denounced as 'ancillary government,' was reduced. Thereby, it can be argued that the FPÖ's government participation had a positive effect by transferring important issues and policies, in this case from an economic, extra-constitutional realm, to the political realm (see Chapter 1). However, the downgrading of social partnership had already started in the 1980s (with economic recession, rising unemployment, impending EU membership, and so forth), and it was also a major instrumental goal of the ÖVP, which feared that via social partnership the SPÖ-dominated trade unions and the Chamber of Labour might undermine the envisaged neoliberal economic reforms (Tálos 2006: 335–7).

Finally, it cannot be denied that the mere fact of the FPÖ entering government can also be seen as an increase in democratic accountability. It demonstrated that Austria does not have to be ruled forever by an SPÖ-ÖVP cartel, with negative collusion effects, but that democratic change is possible. However, the exclusion of the FPÖ from government had an additional arresting effect on the two major parties in that competition between them decreased after 1986 (Heinisch 2008: 69).

Another aspect of the now increased political dynamics, this time to the detriment of the FPÖ, could be observed in the 2002 general elections, when the party became victim of an 'unceremonious cannibalisation' (Bale 2003: 85) by its coalition partner. The 'sovereign' punished the party's disastrous performance, which had led to the breakdown of cabinet Schüssel I, so that about half of the FPÖ voters of 1999 turned to the ÖVP. This seemed to indicate, first, that not a strategy of exclusion, but 'a strategy of co-optation and castration by the bourgeois parties might well be the best way to fight right-wing populism' (Luther 2003: 150), and, second, in a more general sense, that Austrian democracy provided for efficient mechanisms to deal with the 'problem' of a radical party which fights remorselessly against the (other) elites and breaks all political taboos.

6.3.3   Negative effects

Potential negative effects on the quality of democracy, as a consequence of government participation of the FPÖ, were an international concern from the beginning. Immediately after its inauguration, the governments of the other fourteen EU member states (not the EU as such), in a historically unprecedented move, imposed diplomatic measures on the new government, referring to the violation of (diffuse) 'European values' (see Gehler 2003; Merlingen et al. 2001). The diplomatic measures, in Austria called 'sanctions,' proved counterproductive, however. They brought the governing parties even closer together, pointing to the fully democratic process of government formation (after all, Austria was no 'banana republic'). In addition, the sanctions had no legal basis in the EU treaties, were decided before the Austrian government took office (i.e. before it was even in a position to violate any norms), and without hearing the 'accused.' That no such sanctions had been imposed when Prime Minister Silvio Berlusconi of Italy had invited the post-fascist National Alliance (AN) and the right-wing populist Northern League (LN) into his government in 1994 seemed to suggest that double standards were applied between a large and a small EU member state (Falkner 2006: 89–91). Finally, it was argued that domestic reasons, rather than 'European values,' led to the sanctions. The leading proponents of the sanctions were the French president, Jacques Chirac, and the Belgian prime minister, Guy Verhofstadt, both engaged at home to maintain a *cordon sanitaire* against the right-wing populists (Merlingen et al. 2001: 69). In Austria, the sanctions roused national feelings against the 'foreign intervention.' In an opinion survey, carried out two months after the inauguration of the new government, forty-eight per cent of the respondents agreed with the statement that 'we should not let the EU dictate which government we have to elect'; forty-six per cent were of the opinion that 'the accusations of the EU against Austria are a blatant injustice' (IMAS 2000).

To examine the political situation in Austria (and to find an exit option), the EU-14 mandated three 'wise men.' They concluded that the new government was 'committed to the common European values' and that the FPÖ ministers had 'by and large worked according to the Government's commitments' (Report 2000: 108, 113). Specifically, the report stated that the

Austrian Government's respect in particular for the rights of minorities, refugees and immigrants is not inferior to that of the other European Union Member States. (...) In some areas, particularly concerning the rights of national minorities, Austrian standards can be considered to be higher than those applied in many other EU countries. (Report 2000: 108)

Of course, this evaluation took place at the beginning of the government term, focused on the legal state of affairs, and cannot be taken as final proof of how the FPÖ treated minorities, refugees, and immigrants.

As a matter of fact, the report also criticized the FPÖ and classified it as a 'right wing populist party with radical elements' which had 'exploited and enforced xenophobic sentiments in campaigns' and thereby 'created an atmosphere in which openly expressed remarks against foreigners became acceptable' (Report 2000: 110). Attempts of FPÖ politicians 'to silence or even to criminalize political opponents if they criticize the Austrian Government' were pointed out as one of the most problematic features of the party (Report 2000: 93). The last point referred to the fact that in 2000 former FPÖ chairman Haider had suggested prosecution under criminal law of members of parliament who do not 'defend their country' abroad. He had the opposition in mind, which had refused to join the governing parties in denouncing the 'sanctions.' The minister of justice, an FPÖ nominee, found the idea one 'to pursue' (Fallend 2001: 247). In spite of these criticisms, the EU-14 followed the recommendation of the 'wise men' and lifted the 'sanctions' on 12 September 2000.

Normally, one would think that an international organization committed to democratic standards (like the EU) should be able to restrict (negative) effects of populism on liberal democracy. The case of the sanctions of the EU-14 against the Austrian government shows that an international organization, even if committed to democratic standards, can also have a negative effect on democracy. Mouffe (2005a: 56–9, 65–8) criticized the sanctions, like the politics of exclusion of the FPÖ from government participation up to 2000, as expressions of a moralization of the political discourse. Right-wing populism was not fought politically, but condemned morally and demonized. Instead of trying to understand the reasons for the success of the FPÖ (and other right-wing populist parties), a frontier was drawn between 'us' – the 'good democrats' – and 'them' – the 'evil extreme right.' According to her, democracy is not so much endangered by right-wing populists as by a moral discourse that avoids the necessary political confrontation with them.

With respect to the treatment of national minorities, refugees, and immigrants, the positive evaluation of the 'wise men' has to be differentiated in the light of later developments. In Carinthia, the constitutional right of the Slovene minority to bilingual local signs was ignored by the former FPÖ and later BZÖ chairman, Governor Haider (see Section 6.5 below). Concerning immigration policy, the FPÖ was able to exert influence even if it was not responsible for this government portfolio. The ÖVP, which had been more favourable towards labour migration and family reunion in the past, now took over the more restrictive line of the FPÖ (Bale 2003: 76, 82). Not all proposals of the FPÖ were implemented (see e.g. Fallend 2002: 911), but immigration policy was increasingly connected with security arguments and became tougher (though in accordance with the global reaction against 9/11 and supported by public opinion). As hypothesized in the introductory chapter, the right-wing populist FPÖ used the notion of popular sovereignty ('the people do not want it') to ignore or limit minority rights.

Popular sovereignty and plebiscitary arguments were also used in the case of the 2002 people's initiative against the nuclear power plant of Temelín in the Czech Republic. Despite the fact that the Austrian representatives had agreed to close the energy chapter in the EU enlargement negotiations with the Czech Republic, Haider demanded that the nuclear power plant, which is close to the Austrian border, be closed. Otherwise, the FPÖ should veto the accession of the Czech Republic to the EU. To mobilize public support, a people's initiative was started (against the will of the FPÖ party leadership, it has to be admitted), which in January 2002 was signed by 914,973 people (15.5 per cent of the electorate). The ÖVP, which opposed the initiative of its coalition partner, tried to play down the turmoil in the coalition and declared its unfaltering support for EU enlargement (Fallend 2004b: 125–6). Obviously, the FPÖ, though now part of the government, had not forgotten the plebiscitary instruments it had used successfully during its opposition years. However, it failed because of the determined stance of its coalition partner. Thus, as hypothesized in Chapter 1, a plebiscitary transformation of politics was envisaged by the FPÖ, but it did not take place. As was to be expected, in the end the Nationalrat agreed nearly unanimously, with the exception of two FPÖ MPs, to admit the Czech Republic to the EU, although the combated nuclear power plant is still in operation.

The ÖVP and the FPÖ also enacted several controversial institutional reforms, which served above all to enhance the government's grip on, for example, the chief social insurance organization or the organization administering the state-owned shares in enterprises (Fallend 2002: 906–8). However, these reforms can hardly be judged as undermining the foundations of the democratic system. In general, government policies did 'not bear the mark of right-wing extremism or excessive populism' in the 2000–2 period (Heinisch 2003: 106). Luther (2003: 138) described the government's actions as 'not nearly as illiberal as some had predicted.' Nor can it be argued that the FPÖ significantly threatened the institutional guarantees which Robert Dahl postulated as necessary to ensure public contestation and political participation in a liberal democracy (see Chapter 1). On the other hand, the FPÖ's conviction to wage a cultural war (*Kulturkampf*) against foreigners, especially from Muslim countries, as well as against the political left, was clearly not 'tamed' by government participation (Heinisch 2003: 106–9; Luther 2003: 138; Minkenberg 2001: 16–18). In this confrontation, the FPÖ depicted itself as the only party 'really' standing up for the interests of 'the people.' In this respect, the FPÖ conformed to the expectation that populism would foster a moralization of politics, which made political compromises difficult to achieve (see Chapter 1).

6.4   The ÖVP-FPÖ/BZÖ coalition of 2003–2007 (cabinet Schüssel II)

6.4.1   History

As a consequence of its landslide victory in the 2002 general elections (see Table 6.1.), the ÖVP was the pivotal actor in the ensuing government formation. Numerically, it could form a majority government with any other party. A renewal of the ÖVP-FPÖ coalition seemed rather irrational, given that the FPÖ had been responsible for the breakdown of cabinet Schüssel I, had in fact imploded afterwards, and had been punished by the voters severely. However, although the ÖVP leadership could not be sure whether the new FPÖ chairman, Herbert Haupt, had full control over the party's rank and file (especially over the Carinthian faction under Haider), it decided to continue the 'black-blue' coalition. Coalescing with a weakened FPÖ promised greater spoils of office compared to a coalition with a much stronger SPÖ. In addition, the ÖVP leadership feared that a return of the FPÖ into opposition would free the party to resume its strategy of irresponsible outbidding, which would probably be the best way to allow it reassert itself (Luther 2003: 148). The public was not amused: Sixty-one per cent of the respondents in a survey considered the ÖVP decision 'irresponsible' (*Der Standard*, 5 March 2003).

The change in power relations between the ÖVP and the FPÖ necessitated a reshuffle in the ministerial composition of government. The FPÖ was reduced to three out of twelve ministries: justice, social security, and innovation. The new party leadership interpreted the electoral disaster as an order for the FPÖ to give up some of its 'radical' positions. In fact, in the coalition agreement, the FPÖ had capitulated on all issues that had been subject of the intra-party rebellion half a year ago (Luther 2010: 95). The ÖVP, which was four times stronger than its coalition partner at this time, clearly took over the leading role in governmental policy making. The FPÖ was more than once overrun by ÖVP initiatives and struggled to justify why it had entered government at all (Fallend 2004a: 942–5). This, of course, weakened the party chairman, who was replaced as vice chancellor after eight months and had to accept Haider's sister as managing party chairwoman at his side (nine months later she was elected formal party chairwoman).

Nonetheless, the FPÖ continued to lose public support. In each of the six provincial elections of 2003 and 2004, with the exception of Carinthia, it lost between 10.9 and 14.4 per cent of the votes, that is, between one-half and two-thirds of its former voters; in the elections to the European Parliament in 2004 even 17.1 per cent. Intra-party critics blamed the submissive politics of the party leadership vis-à-vis the ÖVP and the neglect of its former anti-EU stance as the main reasons for the defeat in the EP elections. The FPÖ's nationalist wing, whose candidate had led a successful campaign for preference votes and had ousted the official top candidate to capture the only remaining seat for the party in the European Parliament, called for a new start (Fallend 2005: 948).

As a consequence of the internal turmoil, the FPÖ split in April 2005. The government members as well as the majority of the MPs of the FPÖ left the party and formed the BZÖ (Fallend 2006: 1043–5). The mastermind behind the split was former party chairman Haider, who recommended the FPÖ leadership get rid of the 'destructive forces' in the party. After the great majority of the new BZÖ MPs had declared their support for the government and its programme, Chancellor Schüssel continued the coalition (now with the BZÖ) and returned to business as usual.

Unexpected to its operators, however, the BZÖ plane did not take off. In fact, the BZÖ failed to enter parliament in all three provincial elections held in 2005 (none were held in 2006). Only by resorting to aggressive vote-seeking strategies was it able to surpass the four per cent threshold in the 2006 national elections.[6] Because of the weakness of the BZÖ, Chancellor Schüssel could act as if he headed a single-party

[6] To get four per cent of the votes nationwide is one route to parliamentary representation. The alternative is to win a basic mandate in one of the forty-three regional electoral districts. In spite of Haider's high popularity in Carinthia, the BZÖ failed to win a basic mandate in one of the four electoral districts in the province.

government during the remainder of his cabinet's term. The FPÖ, on the other hand, which had returned to vote-seeking strategies right after the party split and had strongly emphasized the immigration issue, had no problems entering parliament in 2006 (Luther 2008: 110–11).

6.4.2   Positive effects

The FPÖ (in government until 2005) was not able to yield a strong influence on government policy during the cabinet Schüssel II, due to its decimation in the 2002 general elections. However, as expected (see Chapter 1), it tried to give voice to groups it thought were not represented appropriately by the ÖVP. A good example of this is the major pension reform of 2003. A government proposal containing significant cuts of future pensions for workers met strong resistance (notably by the trade unions and the opposition parties). As a consequence, even the FPÖ demanded that the pension systems of other, allegedly 'privileged' groups (e.g. civil servants, railway workers, farmers) be harmonized with the system for workers. FPÖ party chairman Haupt took up an idea first proposed by Haider and pleaded for a referendum on the issue. Four provincial party chairmen objected to a new, revised government draft. After a wave of strikes organized by the trade unions (with, according to their own estimation, up to one million participants), Haupt suggested that the federal president chair a 'roundtable,' assembling representatives of government, opposition, provincial governors, and social partners. Then Haider mobilized eight FPÖ members of the Nationalrat to block the reform unless several amendments were introduced. After intensive negotiations a less radical reform was passed. Chaos was complete when the FPÖ members of the upper house, the Bundesrat (again mobilized by Haider), disagreed both with the bill containing the pension reform and a resolution *not* to veto the bill. As a consequence, enactment was stalled for eight weeks. The ÖVP was fuming about its coalition partner (Fallend 2004a: 942–4; Luther 2010: 96). This episode might be viewed as an attempt by the FPÖ to win back some of its reputation as a fighter for the interests of the 'little man in the street.' However, it can be taken for granted that the limited revision of the government plans was above all due to the pressure exercised by the trade unions. The FPÖ's role was confined to slowing down the decision making process.

Because of their weak status in cabinet Schüssel II, the FPÖ, and later the BZÖ, were hardly in a position to represent excluded sections of society by implementing policies they preferred in this period. The continued restrictive immigration policy was as much a concern of the ÖVP (responsible for it) as of the FPÖ. Opposition parties accused both the FPÖ and the BZÖ of being nothing more than 'stirrup holders' (*Steigbügelhalter*) for the ÖVP (Fallend 2006: 1046). By siding with critics of government proposals it had originally agreed to, the FPÖ certainly added to the conflictive dimension of politics– its actions, however, primarily contributed to chaos.

6.4.3   Negative effects

Like in its opposition years and during cabinet Schüssel I, the FPÖ continued its restrictive line on immigration policy during cabinet Schüssel II (in accordance with the ÖVP, however). Occasionally, new provisions did not pass the Constitutional Court. In 2004, for example, the court repealed major parts of a new asylum law, in particular the barring of asylum seekers from bringing forward new arguments during appeal and the possibility of their expulsion before the end of the proceedings (Fallend 2005: 951).

In 2005 the BZÖ, under pressure to show a clearer profile to guarantee its survival in the next general elections, argued for a more restrictive asylum law. Finally, parliament (by the votes of the ÖVP, the BZÖ and almost all MPs of the SPÖ) sanctioned a new law that increased the time during which asylum seekers could be deported (from six to ten months) and allowed force feeding of asylum seekers who go on hunger strike as well as the deportation of traumatized people. At the suggestion of the BZÖ minister of justice, 'misguidance to the abuse of applications for asylum' was entered into the criminal code, a provision directed against lawyers and NGOs trying to help asylum seekers (Fallend 2006: 1049–50). In his campaign for the 2006 general elections, the BZÖ top candidate promised to expel three hundred thousand foreigners (i.e. about a third of them). According to his claims, this figure corresponded to the share of foreigners who were criminals, unwilling to integrate themselves into society, and abusing the right of asylum (Fallend 2007: 880).

Although the FPÖ and the BZÖ cannot be made directly responsible for it, trust in political institutions declined during their years in government. According to the European Values Study (EVS), trust in parliament fell from forty per cent in 1999 to twenty-eight per cent in 2008. Only sixteen per cent of the respondents trusted government in 2008; political parties ranked at the bottom of the list of institutions with only fourteen per cent. FPÖ sympathizers showed the lowest levels of trust; only twenty-three per cent of them trusted parliament, for instance. From 1999 to 2008 the share of those who were 'satisfied' or 'very satisfied' with the way 'democracy functions in Austria' decreased from seventy-three per cent to fifty per cent. The decrease was highest among people who considered themselves to be 'right' (from eighty-three per cent to forty-three per cent) and among FPÖ sympathizers (from sixty-three per cent to thirty-six per cent) (Friesl et al. 2009: 216–21).

Of course, one has to be careful when trying to read long-term trends out of opinion surveys, which may only measure current attitudes. In 2008 Austria was again governed by a rather unpopular SPÖ-ÖVP coalition characterized by permanent internal conflicts, so it seems no wonder that forty-three per cent of the people believed democracy to 'have difficulties in making decisions' and that 'there is too much quarrel and controversy' (Friesl et al. 2009: 222–3). It is also clear that the negative public attitudes towards institutions and democracy cannot be attributed to the behaviour of the FPÖ and the BZÖ alone. On the other hand, their behaviour has obviously not contributed to more positive attitudes.

6.5   FPÖ/BZÖ effects on sub-national democracy: The case of Carinthia

Haider and his FPÖ (since 2005 BZÖ) did not only influence the political discourse, policies, and quality of democracy at the national level, but also at the provincial level, notably in Carinthia. There, Haider successfully used the issue of immigration and the claims of the Slovene minority to bilingual local signs to win the relative majority for his party in the 1999 and 2004 general elections. As the provincial constitution prescribes that all major parties have a right to take part in government according to their strengths in parliament (the so-called *proporz* system), the FPÖ had to share power with the SPÖ and the ÖVP. However, from 1999 until his death in 2008, Haider occupied the influential position of governor. He had inflicted lasting damage on the hitherto dominating SPÖ and put himself in the centre of a political system 'characterized by an illiberal milieu, little transparency, and no substantive democratic control mechanisms' (Heinisch 2010: 8). Haider profited from the fact that the province lacks independent centres of power; interest groups, the media, and civil society posed little challenge to him. By involving himself in every aspect of policy making, he also reduced the autonomy of the civil service (ibid.: 16). Thus, as hypothesized in Chapter 1, he reduced the possibilities of public contestation in 'his' province.

Haider was successful in maintaining the FPÖ's (and the BZÖ's) grip on power in Carinthia by symbolic politics, co-optation of the other parties into complicity, divide-and-conquer strategies, bread and circuses, and superior image making and political branding (Heinisch 2010: 20–6). Only in Carinthia were the right-wing populists 'able to implement what we might call populist governance' (ibid.: 27). By directly subsidizing people of low income and providing for cheaper oil and free kindergarten, Haider, in a truly populist manner, implemented his 'Carinthian model' for people feeling excluded. In this sense, his influence on Carinthian politics and policies can be seen positively.

On the other hand, Haider's rule also had negative effects on the quality of Carinthian democracy in that he used the notion of popular sovereignty to contravene the checks and balances and separation of powers of liberal democracy and in that he used the notion of majority rule to circumvent minority rights (see Chapter 1). The most striking example in this respect concerns the issue of bilingual (German and Slovenian) local signs in the ethnically mixed districts of Carinthia. In 2001, the Constitutional Court ruled that the federal law which regulated the setting up of bilingual local signs violated Article 7 of the Treaty of Vienna of 1955, in which the rights of the Slovene and Croatian minorities in Austria are guaranteed. The court stipulated that bilingual local signs had to be put up in all districts where Slovenes make up at least ten per cent of the population (the law said twenty-five per cent). As this would have increased the number of bilingual local signs from seventy to 394, Haider refused to implement the ruling. He accused the court of having made a 'political' decision that ignored the will of the majority of the Carinthian population and threatened to 'correct' it by initiating a consultative referendum. In fact, some constitutional lawyers acknowledged that the court might have exceeded its authority and that parliament was actually responsible for settling the matter. However, they left no doubt that the Carinthian state authorities were obliged to implement the ruling. The SPÖ and Greens saw in Haider's actions a serious danger for the constitutional state and called upon Chancellor Schüssel to bring the Carinthian governor to reason (Fallend 2003: 896). The fact that the FPÖ (and later the BZÖ) was a coalition partner, however, prevented the ÖVP and its chancellor from enforcing the ruling.

Over the years, several 'consensus conferences' to deal with the issue were organized by the federal chancellery. In 2005, Haider called off a compromise, which would have included the setting up of 158 additional signs, an 'opening clause' for further signs, and subsidies for cultural activities of the Slovenian minority (Fallend 2006: 1050–1). In 2006, he organized a consultative referendum in eighteen south Carinthian municipalities to back up his position and replaced bilingual signs with monolingual (German) signs supplemented by small Slovenian signs (Fallend 2007: 889–90). In vain, the opposition parties, constitutional lawyers, and media pointed to the fact that the conflict questioned the authority of the Constitutional Court and put a shame on Austria in the world at a time when national boundaries in Europe were about to disappear.

Only in 2011 did the federal chancellery, the Carinthian provincial governor, and three Slovenian organizations, after extensive negotiations, reach a compromise. The lower chamber of parliament, the Nationalrat, almost unanimously (against the votes of only three MPs of the Green Party) passed a new law on ethnic groups. By a constitutional provision the Nationalrat determined that bilingual signs had to be set up in 164 localities. Although the baseline for this was a minority share of 17.5 per cent of the population (not ten per cent, as the Constitutional Court had ruled) and although one of the three Slovenian organizations later demanded further improvements, the solution was generally welcomed as a major step forward (*Die Presse*, 6 July 2011).

Conclusions

Austria is a consolidated democracy, and the two right-wing populist parties, the FPÖ and the BZÖ, participated in coalition governments – both times at the side of a much more experienced coalition partner; the second time also in numeric terms in a clearly subordinated role. Thus, the effects of right-wing populism on the quality of democracy were not expected to be very significant, neither in a positive nor in a negative direction (see hypothesis 3).

To begin with the positive effects, the FPÖ (and later the BZÖ) certainly influenced the political agenda with respect to two issues where broad segments of the population have rather negative attitudes, European integration and immigration. However, the direct effect of the two parties on government policies, even in these two fields, remained limited. The ÖVP as the dominant governing party was strongly committed to European integration (in spite of the 'sanctions' against the new government in 2000), and immigration was handled by the Ministry of the Interior, directed by the ÖVP (which did not prevent a restrictive policy, however). The fact that the FPÖ and the BZÖ were able to participate in government can be regarded positively, from a non-normative perspective, as it showed that after years of 'grand coalitions,' political change was possible. To what extent the increased conflictive dimension of politics, which also led to a high polarization between government and opposition, should be viewed positively, is a matter of controversy.

Government participation of the two right-wing populist parties also had negative effects on the quality of democracy. The rights of minorities were either ignored or reduced during the ÖVP-FPÖ/BZÖ coalitions; not only those of the ethnic minority of the Slovenes in the province of Carinthia, but also those of immigrants, especially of asylum seekers. Institutions which should guarantee these rights, in particular the

Constitutional Court, were harshly attacked and their regulations, with reference to the principle of majority rule, ignored. The fact that Jörg Haider dominated the political scene in Carinthia and was very popular allowed him to get away with his provocations of the court. Although these remained exceptional cases, the democratic principles of separation of powers and rule of law were damaged. Therefore, one may argue that the case of Austria confirms hypothesis 5, which claims that populism in government will have moderate negative effects on the quality of democracy. At the same time, the FPÖ and the BZÖ contributed to a political climate in which culture wars were fought and compromises exacerbated. This, however, did not start with government participation, but characterized Austrian politics already during the FPÖ's opposition years.

To sum up, the analysis of the case of Austria shows that (right-wing) populism in government had both positive and negative effects on the quality of democracy. Whether the effects were stronger in government than in opposition (as hypothesis 1 suggests) is difficult to say. On the one hand, once in government, the FPÖ and the BZÖ had greater possibilities to influence policies and to change the institutional structure of the political system. On the other hand, they could not do everything they probably wanted as they were only junior coalition partners in a parliamentary system. What is more, the major coalition partner was not only more experienced in governing, but in the second phase of government participation (during cabinet Schüssel II) also much stronger. As a consequence, by government participation the (right-wing) populists in Austria were not only accepted in the 'club,' but certainly 'tamed' at the same time. That they also demonstrated their inability to govern might satisfy critics who had feared the end of democracy when the FPÖ entered government in the year 2000.

7 Populism and democracy in Venezuela under Hugo Chávez

Kenneth M. Roberts

Introduction

The rise of Hugo Chávez to power at the end of the 1990s not only marked a watershed in Venezuelan politics, but also transformed the scholarly debate about the revival of populism in Latin America's neoliberal era. In the 1980s, populism was widely presumed to have run its course, a victim of the debt crisis and austerity measures that undermined state-led models of industrialization to which populism was historically attached (Dornbusch and Edwards 1991). As new leaders with populist tendencies emerged in the 1990s, however, scholars debated whether and how populism could be reconciled with market liberalization (see Roberts 1995 and Weyland 1996 and 2001 for an overview of these conceptual debates). The meteoric rise of Chávez transcended these debates by demonstrating conclusively that more traditional, statist forms of populism were not consigned to the dust bins of history; they were, instead, making a vigorous comeback in a post-liberalization order marked by social dislocation and a crisis of established representative institutions.

Indeed, Chávez was arguably the most quintessential populist figure Latin America had seen since Juan Perón, the legendary Argentine leader who was virtually synonymous with populism in the region. However populism was defined, Chávez fit, as he seemingly embodied whatever core and ancillary properties were attached to the concept. In accordance with the conceptualization of populism in this volume, the ideology and discourse of *Chavismo* morally constructed an antagonistic duality between a virtuous 'people' (*el pueblo*) and an incorrigibly venal and corrupt elite (the oligarchy or, more colourfully, the 'rancid oligarchy' in the parlance of *Chavismo*). Although both sides of this duality were sociologically heterogeneous, each was ideologically constructed in relatively homogeneous and undifferentiated terms in the political arena, with *el pueblo* unified by the leadership of Chávez, and the oligarchy defined by its adversarial status.

136

The rise of *Chavismo* transformed the debate over Latin American populism in three fundamental (and inter-related) ways. First, it largely eclipsed the 1990s debate over the compatibility of populism with neo-liberalism. The election of Chávez, from the outset a strident opponent of 'savage neoliberalism,' was the first in a series of unprecedented electoral victories by populist and leftist leaders in the region. By 2011, eleven countries representing two-thirds of the regional population were governed by left-of-centre presidents. Most of these leaders were more cautious than Chávez in challenging neoliberal orthodoxy; none of them, after all, had the luxury of Venezuela's windfall oil rents and the political latitude this bounty provided. Nevertheless, the 'Left turn' clearly reflected an erosion of the technocratic consensus for market liberalization that had prevailed in Latin America since the late 1980s, and it placed the search for alternatives to neoliberalism front and centre on the region's political agenda (Levitsky and Roberts 2011; Weyland et al. 2010). Following the rise of Chávez, then, the issue was no longer whether populism could co-exist with neoliberalism, but rather whether it could construct meaningful and viable alternatives to it.

Second, this search for alternative models of development re-politicized social and economic inequalities in Venezuela and other Latin American countries. In the aftermath to the 1980s debt crisis, the demands of economic stabilization and the weakening of historic labour movements had marginalized political actors committed to redistributive policies. Chávez's brand of populism, however, was explicit in promoting the social and economic inclusion of subaltern groups by invigorating the state's developmental, social welfare, and redistributive roles. In contrast to other populist figures in the 1990s, like Alberto Fujimori in Peru, Chávez did not merely pose an outsider challenge to the political establishment; he confronted much (though not all) of the business community with his redistributive policies and his vigorous reassertion of state control over the economy. Therefore, while *el pueblo*, for Chávez, was not defined strictly in class terms – indeed, it notably excluded much of Venezuela's organized labour movement, which remained tied to traditional parties like Democratic Action (AD) – it nevertheless had a pronounced popular and lower-class bias.

Third, and most important for the themes of this volume, *Chavismo* expressed in unusually stark terms the varied tensions between populism and liberal democracy in Latin America. Similar to populist predecessors like Fujimori, Chávez is notorious for concentrating power in the executive branch, undermining institutional checks and balances, and marginalizing opposition forces from governing institutions. Indeed, Chávez has repeatedly mobilized popular majorities in a plebiscitarian manner to bypass established representative institutions and refound the constitutional order. In contrast to leaders like Fujimori, however, who made little effort to create new channels for popular participation in the political process, Chávez has set out to construct a more radical or 'protagonistic' form of democracy based on plebiscitarian expressions of popular sovereignty and grassroots participation in community organizations and self-governing structures. For Chávez, then, popular inclusion does not rest solely on the formation of new electoral alternatives or the delivery of social benefits to marginalized sectors of the population. It includes, as well, the construction of multiple channels for popular protagonism in the design and implementation of public services.

Clearly, efforts to construct radical democracy from below in Venezuela clashed with the reality of highly concentrated executive authority. Indeed, the rhythms and institutional expressions of popular mobilization were heavily conditioned by Chávez, whose shifting preferences and strategic priorities led to very high levels of improvisation and organizational fluidity at the base of his movement. Grassroots expressions of *Chavismo* were often launched with great fanfare, only to be displaced by new initiatives down the road, leaving multiple and overlapping communal organizations that operated on the margins of a weakly institutionalized official party (itself in a state of constant flux). But despite this lack of institutionalization – or, quite possibly, because of it – popular protagonism in Chávez's self-proclaimed 'Bolivarian Revolution' was authentic, and it provided a textbook illustration of the ways in which populism's inclusionary dynamic can expand opportunities for democratic participation at the same time that its majoritarianian logic restricts institutional spaces for effective democratic contestation. The Venezuelan case, therefore, is highly instructive for understanding the tensions between the participatory and competitive dimensions of democracy, as discussed by Mudde and Rovira Kaltwasser in the introduction to this volume (see also Dahl 1971). These tensions – which ultimately reflect differences between democracy understood as popular sovereignty and democracy conceived as institutionalized pluralism – are the central focus of the analysis that follows.

7.1   The crisis of Venezuelan democracy and the rise of *Chavismo*

The contradictory relationship between *Chavismo* and democracy can only be understood if the populist phenomenon is analyzed in the context in which it was spawned – namely, a profound crisis of Venezuela's democratic regime, a collapse of the party system that undergirded it, and a popular backlash against several aborted and ineffectual attempts to liberalize an economy based on state-controlled oil rents. Whereas most Latin American countries experienced democratic transitions in the 1980s, Venezuela's democratic regime had been in place since 1958, and until the early 1990s it was widely regarded as one of the most stable and consolidated democracies in the region (Peeler 1992). The progressive unravelling of this regime after 1989 is one of Latin America's great political enigmas, and it heavily conditioned the character of Venezuela's anti-system, leftist variant of populism under Chávez.

This experience makes it difficult to categorize the Venezuelan case. Venezuela is clearly an example of populism in power, so the potential exists for more profound effects on democracy than in a country where populism is merely an opposition force (see hypotheses 1 and 2 in the introduction). Likewise, this is not a case of populism arising under a new, unconsolidated democracy (hypothesis 3), as the democratic regime was long standing and seemingly consolidated through the late 1980s. By the early 1990s, however, the regime was in crisis, and patterns of decay were clearly at work. Consequently, although it would probably be misleading to characterize the regime as unconsolidated in the 1990s (hypothesis 7), the deepening crisis made Venezuelan democracy more susceptible to the effects of populism than hypothesis 6 would predict for a case with a fully consolidated democratic regime. Indeed, the rise of *Chavismo* caused Venezuela's post-1958 democratic regime to be swept aside and replaced by a new regime that was more 'popular,' but also more illiberal.

In contrast to countries like Chile, Brazil, and Uruguay, where established centre left parties in the 2000s elected presidents in contexts of increasingly consolidated democratic regimes and competitive party systems that narrowed their room for manoeuvre, Venezuela's turn to the left occurred under a populist outsider who capitalized on the crisis of representative institutions to mobilize opposition to the political establishment. As eloquently stated by Panizza (2005: 9), populism 'is the language of politics when there can be no politics as usual: a mode of identification characteristic of times of unsettlement and de-alignment, involving the radical redrawing of social borders along lines other than those that had previously structured society.' Not surprising, then, Venezuela's populist alternative was committed, from the outset, to a refounding of the constitutional order and a reconstruction of democratic institutions – options that simply did not exist for leftist parties where democratic regimes and broader party systems were not in crisis.

Likewise, the leftist character of Venezuela's populist alternative reflected the failure of the country's crumbling party system to offer viable programmatic alternatives to market liberalization (Morgan 2007), despite widespread opposition to neoliberal reforms and their marginal success at alleviating a deepening economic crisis. Indeed, market reforms were erratically implemented in a bait-and-switch fashion by elected leaders who had campaigned against them – a pattern of crisis management tailor made for a populist movement that outflanked and attacked the political establishment from the left.

Like all populist movements, however, *Chavismo* was eclectic and rather ill-defined ideologically, blending strong currents of Venezuelan and more regional 'Bolivarian' nationalism with Marxist influences that became more pronounced over the course of Chávez's government. The origins of the movement are found in a small clandestine group known as the Bolivarian Revolutionary Movement 200 (MBR 200), formed by Chávez and other junior officers within the Venezuelan armed forces in 1983 as a deepening debt-fuelled economic crisis dashed the illusions of permanent prosperity created by the oil boom of the 1970s. The MBR 200 embraced the symbols of Simon Bolívar and other nineteenth-century nationalist figures while adopting a critical stance towards the country's increasingly corrupt two-party system and the socio-economic inequalities tolerated under democracy. The military conspirators developed contacts with several small radical left parties and hardened their opposition to the regime as Venezuelan democracy entered into crisis in the late 1980s.

In particular, Chávez and his allies were deeply disillusioned when the military was called on to repress a massive outbreak of urban riots known as the *Caracazo*, which followed the adoption of austerity measures and neoliberal reforms by President Carlos Andrés Pérez of the traditionally centre left AD, shortly after he took office in February 1999 (Hawkins 2010a: 16–17; López Maya 2003: 74–8). These market reforms, implemented in collaboration with the IMF, were a classic case of bait-and-switch liberalization (see Stokes 2001). Pérez had been president during the free-spending oil boom in the 1970s, and his election campaign promised a return to prosperity and was replete with criticisms of neo-liberalism and international financial institutions. As such, the election campaign gave little indication that Pérez and his party were about to embark on a radical change of direction.

Sensing a growing delegitimation of the political establishment – Pérez's public approval rating had fallen to a dismal six per cent by 1992 (Romero 1997: 15) – Chávez and the MBR 200 organized a military coup in February 1992. The coup attempt failed, landing Chávez and his co-conspirators in prison, but not before the charismatic young officer was given an opportunity to address the public on television. Chávez assumed responsibility for the coup and conceded defeat, but he promised to continue the struggle for political and economic change, converting himself into a symbol of steadfast opposition to the status quo.

The political institutions that upheld that status quo, meanwhile, were gradually breaking down. Although Pérez survived a second military uprising in November 1992, he was impeached on corruption charges, found guilty by the Supreme Court, and removed from office by the congress in May 1993. National elections later that year provided graphic evidence of alienation from the political process, as well as an erosion of the traditional two-party system, which had allowed AD or its conservative rival COPEI to win every presidential election in Venezuela's post-1958 democratic regime. Rates of electoral abstention increased sharply (Hellinger 2003: 45; Maingón and Patruyo 1996: 101), while party identification plummeted, with the percentage of Venezuelans who claimed to be members or supporters of a party falling from 48.7 per cent in 1973 to 32.4 per cent in 1990 and a mere 22.8 per cent in 1994 (Molina Vega and Pérez Baralt 1996: 224). By the mid 1990s, an astonishing ninety-one per cent of Venezuelans expressed a lack of confidence in political parties (Luengo D. and Ponce Z. 1996: 70), while only thirty per cent expressed satisfaction with the performance of the country's democratic regime (Latinobarómetro 1998: 6).

This dissatisfaction was rooted, in part, in the characteristics of the party system and its two dominant parties. AD and COPEI were hierarchical and disciplined party organizations with a track record of collusion that had allowed them to monopolize the political arena. While dominating labour unions, business associations, and other organized groups within civil society (Coppedge 1994), they possessed relatively weak ties among the growing urban poor and informal sectors of society. Furthermore, despite their origins on the political left and right, respectively, AD and COPEI largely ceased to offer programmatic alternatives to the electorate, especially after AD shifted towards the right with Pérez's embrace of neoliberal reforms in 1989. Although these reforms were staunchly resisted within AD (Corrales 2002), most of the party leadership continued to support market liberalization in the 1990s, creating vacant political space to the left of centre that would eventually be filled by new contenders (Morgan 2007).

Clearly, however, dissatisfaction was also attributable to the abysmal performance record of the dominant parties in managing Venezuela's oil-based economy. The spending binge, structural distortions, and rampant inefficiencies associated with the mid 1970s oil boom quickly degenerated into a debt crisis when oil prices declined, leading to two decades of chronic economic hardship. By the late 1990s, GDP per capita had declined by twenty per cent, returning to levels last seen in the 1960s (Crisp 2000: 175).

The political effects of this economic decline were magnified by two critical factors conducive to the rise of a populist challenger, especially one with a leftist orientation. First, Venezuelans overwhelmingly perceived their country as wealthy because of its oil resources; as such, they blamed the political establishment and its corruption and mismanagement of the economy for any hardships they endured. Surveys found, for example, that ninety-four per cent of Venezuelans agreed with the statement that 'If Venezuela were honestly administered and corruption eliminated, there would be enough money for all and more' (Romero 1997: 21).

Second, economic hardships were disproportionately borne by the middle and lower classes, allowing new leftist alternatives to politicize the country's gaping inequalities. While per capita income shrank by twenty per cent, the real industrial wage and the real minimum wage plunged more than sixty per cent between 1980 and the mid 1990s (International Labour Organisation 1998: 43). Indeed, the two-thirds decline in the purchasing power of the minimum wage left it below the level of the early 1950s (Evans 1998: 12). Open unemployment increased from 6.6 per cent to 15.4 per cent of the urban work force between 1980 and 1999 (Economic Commission for Latin America and the Caribbean 2000: 744), while underemployment swelled the ranks of the informal sector. Consequently, poverty rates more than doubled, reaching two-thirds of the population by the mid 1990s, while social inequalities became more pronounced. The income share of the bottom forty per cent of the population fell from 19.1 per cent in 1981 to 14.7 per cent in 1997, while that of the top ten per cent increased from 21.8 to 32.8 per cent (Economic Commission for Latin America and the Caribbean 1999: 63). Indeed, all but the wealthiest quintile lost income shares during this two-decade-long economic slide. The socio-economic terrain was thus highly amenable to the mobilization of excluded and underprivileged groups by leftist alternatives that promised to support redistributive policies (see Ellner and Hellinger 2003).

Such alternatives emerged in the 1990s as AD and COPEI lost their capacity to integrate Venezuelan citizens into the democratic order, steadily eroding their historic dominance of the electoral arena. A leftist party known as Radical Cause (La Causa R) captured the mayorship of Caracas in 1992, then made a serious bid for the presidency in a close four-way race in the national elections of 1993, winning twenty-two per cent of the vote (compared to 23.6 per cent for AD and 22.7 per cent for COPEI). The election was won by aging former president Rafael Caldera, who

Table 7.1. *Presidential election results in Venezuela, 1993–2006*

Party/Coalition	1993	1998	2000	2006
AD	23.6	–	–	–
COPEI	22.7	–	–	–
Convergencia	30.5	–	–	–
Causa R	22.0	.11	37.5	–
MVR	–	56.2	60.3	62.8
Opposition coalitions*	–	40.0	–	36.9
Others	1.3	3.7	2.2	.3

* Multi-party opposition to Chávez coalesced behind the candidacy of Henrique Salas Römer of Proyecto Venezuela in 1998, Fernando Arias Cárdenas of Causa R in 2000, and Manuel Rosales of Un Nuevo Tiempo in 2006.

Source: Political Database of the Americas, Georgetown University, at: http://pdba.georgetown.edu.

formed an independent label known as Convergencia (Convergence) after breaking with COPEI, condemning Venezuela's neoliberal reforms, and tacitly legitimizing the coup attempt against Pérez (see Table 7.1). In office, however, after an initial experiment with macro-economic hetero-doxy, Caldera reluctantly shifted towards neoliberal policies in response to a deepening economic crisis and declining oil export revenues. With leaders of AD and the centre left Movement for Socialism (MAS) collaborating with this new policy shift, the stage was set for the rise of a populist outsider who could channel discontent with both the political establishment and the process of market liberalization (however incomplete the latter may have been).

Hugo Chávez proved to be that leader. Following a presidential pardon from Caldera in 1994, Chávez left prison and travelled across the country to broaden the base of his movement. Although the MBR 200 initially advocated electoral abstention, claiming that a national constituent assembly should be chosen to overhaul regime institutions, it changed its mind in 1997 and created a new electoral front known as the Fifth Republic Movement (MVR, for Movimiento Quinta República) to compete in the 1998 national elections (López Maya 2003: 81–3). Meanwhile, the two traditional parties sank deeper into crisis: Having lost the presidency for the first time in 1993, both AD and COPEI eventually withdrew their candidates for the presidency in 1998, opting instead to support other independent figures in a desperate bid to block

Table 7.2. *Legislative election results in Venezuela, 1998–2010*

Party/Coalition	1998	2000	2005*	2010
AD	30.0	20.0	–	–
COPEI	13.5	3.6	–	–
Causa R	2.9	1.8	–	–
Convergencia	1.9	.6	–	–
MVR/PSUV	22.2	55.8	69.5	57.5
Other Pro-Chávez**	8.2	4.2	30.5	1.2
MUD***	–	–	–	38.3
Others	21.3	14.0	–	1.2

Note: Percentage of seats in Chamber of Deputies/National Assembly.
   * Most of the parties in opposition to Chávez boycotted the 2005 legis-
    lative elections.
  ** Includes the Movimiento al Socialismo (MAS), Patria Para Todos
    (PPT), Podemos, and other small pro-Chávez groups.
*** In 2010, AD, COPEI, and a number of newer opposition groups coa-
    lesced in the Mesa de la Unidad Democrática (MUD), which cap-
    tured sixty-four seats in the 167-seat national assembly.
Source: Political Database of the Americas, Georgetown University,
at: http://pdba.georgetown.edu, and *Consejo Nacional Electoral* (CNE),
Gobierno de Venezuela, at: http://www.cne.gov.ve/estadisticas.

Chávez's ascendance. Chávez, nevertheless, swept to a landside victory with 56.2 per cent of the vote, and proceeded with his plan to disman-tle the constitutional framework of the democratic regime that had gov-erned Venezuela since 1958.

7.2.   Populist ideology and discourse under Chávez

Chávez's appeal, and the discourse that secured it, are vintage populism in the dualistic terms in which Laclau (2005a) has defined it. Certainly, *Chavismo* fits the minimalist ideological conception of populism outlined by Mudde and Rovira Kaltwasser in the introduction, while combining this 'thin-centred ideology' with heavier doses of nationalism, socialism, and a charismatic style of political mobilization. As stressed by Hawkins, Chávez interprets politics in highly moralistic and Manichean terms as a 'cosmic struggle' between forces of good and evil (2010a: 55). Indeed, Zúquete characterizes *Chavismo* as a form of 'missionary politics' in which a charismatic figure 'leads a chosen people gathered into a moral community struggling against all-powerful and conspiratorial enemies, and engaged in a mission toward redemption and salvation' (2008: 92).

Although this dualistic political ideology was highly consistent, the com-position of its poles – that is, the identity of friends and enemies, or *el pueblo* and the oligarchy – evolved over time. Initially, Chávez defined the enemy primarily in terms of the political establishment against which he had launched his ill-fated coup attempt in 1992. In particular, he condemned the leaders of AD and COPEI as a corrupt, entrenched, and self-serving political elite that made a farce of representative democracy. Chávez went so far as to claim that Venezuela was 'advancing toward a more authoritarian and repressive state … of a fascist dictatorial type' (Blanco Muñoz 1998: 368).

After coming to power and relegating traditional parties to the side-lines, however, Chávez became increasingly vocal in challenging other elements within Venezuela's power elite, including corporate-controlled media outlets that were vocal opponents of his rule. And while Chávez had always been critical of U.S. imperialism and its ties to elite interests in Venezuelan society, he intensified his critique in response to Washington's thinly veiled support for the military coup that briefly removed him from office in April 2002. Thereafter, alleged U.S. conspiracies played heavily into the *Chavista* discourse about foreign and domestic enemies who sought to derail his Bolivarian Revolution.

From the outset, Chávez framed his challenge to the establishment in revolutionary terms, in accordance with his cosmic and redemp-tive conception of political struggle. Initially, however, he eschewed a Marxist or class-based definition of this political dualism, in part because Venezuela's AD-controlled labour movement lacked a proletarian or revo-lutionary consciousness. The central antagonism in the *Chavista* duality was not between labour and capital, but rather between the dominated and the dominant, or the exploited and the exploiters. Middle classes, for Chávez, were firmly located in the more popular, exploited category. In his words, 'The middle class today is becoming an exploited class. Here there are two poles: a minority of exploiters and a great majority of exploited. If that is class struggle, then there is an explosive element today in Venezuela' (Blanco Muñoz 1998: 397). Although Chávez did not lump all sectors of capital together in the category of exploiters, he left little doubt that monopoly sectors bound to the interests of global capitalism were part of the rapacious power elite that preyed on the com-mon people.

This dualistic conception of political struggle was not initially framed in terms of socialist objectives. In the early stages of *Chavismo*, it was nation-alism – not socialism or Marxism – that provided the primary source of ideological inspiration. Chávez repeatedly invoked the symbolism of Bolívar and other nineteenth-century national heroes, mythically linking the redemptive character of his populist movement to historic struggles for national independence and regional integration (Zúquete 2008: 107–9). Virtually by definition, then, political adversaries were framed as anti-patriotic forces, typically with ties to the interests of imperial power.

Under this ideological construction, *Chavismo* could define itself in opposition to international capital and globalized neoliberalism, without rejecting capitalism or capitalists per se. Indeed, Chávez came to power advocating a 'humanistic' mixed economy that borrowed from both capitalist and socialist development models, with a market freed from monopoly control and a developmentalist state committed to nurturing national producers, both public and private (see Blanco Muñoz 1998: 611–14). This nuanced stance allowed him to garner early support from 'elite outliers' within the business community who sought access to a resource-rich petro-state (Gates 2010). Although Chávez believed the state should promote small- and medium-sized private producers, he rejected the privatization of social services and the national oil company, arguing that strategic sectors of the economy should remain in public hands.

Early *Chavista* discourse, then, did not promise to replace neoliberalism with a futuristic socialist alternative. Instead, it harkened back to the 'third way' logic, between capitalism and socialism, of historic populist figures like Perón, with their commitments to inward-oriented, state-led capitalist development. Indeed, it bore a politically awkward and unacknowledged resemblance to the oil-fuelled rentier statism of Venezuela's AD-COPEI duopoly prior to the turn towards neoliberalism at the end of the 1980s. The more radical discourse related to the construction of 'socialism for the 21st century' only emerged later, in the period after 2004 (see Hawkins 2010a: 83), when the Chávez government steadied itself politically and economically after a series of regime-threatening confrontations in the early 2000s.[1] It isn't clear whether Chávez was radicalized by these confrontations or whether – having survived and defeated the opposition at every step of the way – he simply felt secure enough to reveal his true preferences. What is clear is that the economic content of Chávez's ideological discourse shifted after 2004, and that public policies moved towards the left as well, with a growing number of nationalizations, an expansion of social programmes or *misiones*, and the creation of communal self-governing structures parallel to the representative institutions of municipal governments.

---

[1] The confrontations in the early 2000s included a business backlash against the beginnings of land reform and other statist measures, mass rallies and protests by opposition groups, the 2002 military coup, a devastating two-month management and labour strike at the national oil industry, and a presidential recall referendum in 2004.

If the radical character of Chávez's economic project only crystallized over time, the radical character of his political project was more evident from the very outset of his movement. Indeed, it could be seen in the constant invocation of revolutionary symbols and objectives, the military rebellion with which *Chavismo* made its public debut, and the insistent demand to refound the constitutional order along participatory (and not simply representative) democratic principles. It is to these issues, and their implications for the relationship between populism and democracy, that I now turn.

7.3 Democracy, inclusion, and popular participation under Chávez

To understand the implications of Chávez's left populism for democracy in Venezuela, and how it differed from more conservative variants of populism like *Fujimorismo*, it is vital to recognize that political redemption in the ideology of *Chavismo* did not rest solely in sweeping aside the partisan-based political establishment and electing a new leader who embodied the aspirations of *el pueblo*. Neither was it simply a matter of providing new social or economic programmes to respond to their claims for material improvements.

For Chávez, the political inclusion of neglected, excluded, and exploited sectors of society – that is, the construction of popular sovereignty – required their active participation in a new, more 'protagonistic' form of democracy that was conceived as an alternative to the liberal or representative democracy of the post-1958 regime. This vision of protagonistic democracy spawned novel forms of popular mobilization and grassroots organization that facilitated the inclusion of new societal actors in the political process, albeit at considerable cost to the quality of democratic contestation.

For Chávez, popular participation was not simply a normative or ideological commitment that differentiated his mode of democratic governance from what came before it. It was also, more instrumentally, a political resource that provided greater leverage to overcome the constraints of existing regime institutions. In short, popular participation helped Chávez refound the constitutional order, sideline the political establishment, and deliver social and economic benefits to a broad range of potential supporters. Participation, then, was both an end and a means for *Chavismo* – an integral component of democracy conceived as popular sovereignty, as well as a mechanism for constructing new forms of popular power.

Under Venezuela's post-1958 democratic regime, popular participation occurred primarily through electoral mobilization – which, as described earlier, declined sharply by the 1990s – and semi-corporatist forms of interest group representation, which linked relatively privileged and well-organized business and labour associations to the dominant parties and a wide array of state consultative and policy-making boards (see Crisp 2000). The relative closure of these formal institutional channels to community-based groups that were not tied to traditional parties, especially among the urban poor, contributed to increased levels of social protest in the 1990s (López Maya 2005). Simply put, while the existing democratic regime formally enfranchised the Venezuelan citizenry, it left large swaths of the population on the margins of the political system, disillusioned with the available options for partisan and electoral representation, and largely devoid of opportunities for meaningful participation in the policy-making process.

Chavismo adopted a two-pronged strategy to overcome this de facto exclusion. First, it relied heavily on plebiscitary measures to mobilize a new popular majority behind an agenda for radical institutional change, effectively giving citizens a direct voice in the refounding of the constitutional order. A central plank in Chávez's 1998 election campaign had been a promise to convene a constituent assembly to redesign Venezuela's democratic institutions, and the new president moved quickly to uphold this pledge after taking office. In his inaugural address on 2 February 1999, Chávez issued his first decree, which ordered a consultative popular referendum on whether a constituent assembly should be convened. Although only 37.8 per cent of eligible voters participated in the April referendum, Chávez obtained a strong mandate to proceed with his plans, with 86.4 per cent of voters supporting the election of a constituent assembly (see Table 7.3). These elections were held in July 1999 under a plurality electoral formula that allowed Chávez's supporters to claim 121 of the 131 seats in the assembly.[2] In a rebuke to the political establishment, and a symbol of the desire to incorporate new voices in the political arena, public office holders were not allowed to stand as candidates for the constituent assembly.

This convocation of a constituent assembly to 'refound' the republic was a classic exercise in popular sovereignty, as it largely bypassed and eventually dissolved the inherited constitutional rules and procedures. Venezuela's 1961 constitution contained no provision for electing a new constituent assembly; when asked to rule on the matter shortly before Chávez took office, the Supreme Court declined to state whether a constitutional amendment would be necessary to elect such an assembly,

---

[2] This information is from http://www.constitutionnet.org/en/country/venezuela (accessed 22 July 2010).

Table 7.3. *Popular referendums and presidential recall election in Venezuela, 1999–2009*

Vote	Convoke Constituent Assembly (1999)	Approve New Constitution (1999)	Presidential Recall (2004)	Approve Constitutional Reforms (2007)	Approve Constitutional Amendment (2009)
Yes*	86.4	71.4	41.7	49.3	54.9
No	13.6	28.6	58.3	50.7	45.1

* In all of these referendums, with the exception of the presidential recall, the 'Yes' vote represented the pro-Chávez position.
Source: Political Database of the Americas, Georgetown University, at: http://pdba. georgetown.edu.

although it recognized the legality of holding a popular referendum to gauge public opinion on the matter.[3] The opposition-controlled congress bitterly opposed the election of a constituent assembly, knowing that such an assembly would assume its legislative powers. Nevertheless, Chávez imposed his will, armed by his plebiscitary mandate and seventy per cent approval ratings in public opinion surveys. Upon convening, the new constituent assembly claimed 'supra-constitutional power,' a claim subsequently upheld by the Supreme Court, and moved quickly to dissolve both houses of the national congress as well as state legislative assemblies, effectively eliminating institutional checks on executive power that were located in other elected bodies. By December 1999, a new constitution had been drafted and approved in yet another popular referendum by a crushing majority of 71.4 per cent of voters, and a committee was formed out of the constituent assembly to exercise legislative powers in place of the disbanded national congress.

The new constitution made no mention of political parties, instead emphasizing the direct, participatory, and protagonistic role of citizens and civil society in the democratic process (see Álvarez 2003: 151–5). While strengthening the powers of the presidency, the constitution also recognized the role of referendums in the exercise of popular sovereignty, including recall elections that would allow citizens to remove public officials and judges after the midpoint of their terms in office. Ironically, the opposition to Chávez employed this mechanism in an attempt to remove him from office in 2004, but after a lengthy and contentious petition drive to gather the signatures needed to convoke the referendum, Chávez

[3] Ibid.

defeated the recall bid with a comfortable 58.3 per cent majority vote in the referendum. He fared less well in a December 2007 referendum on a package of constitutional reforms that, among other measures, would have eliminated term limits on the presidency. For the first time, Chávez was defeated in a referendum by a narrow margin of 50.7 per cent to 49.3 per cent of the vote. Although he accepted this defeat and acknowledged shortcomings in his administration that undermined its popular support, Chávez quickly regrouped and implemented some of the reform measures by presidential decree. A new referendum on a streamlined constitutional amendment eliminating term limits on the presidency and other elected offices was then held in 2009, and this time the amendment was ratified with 54.9 per cent of the vote (see Table 7.3).

The *Chavista* conception of protagonistic democracy, however, was not limited to referendums and plebiscitary measures that allowed for the direct expression of mass sentiments on major issues of constitutional order. Even more fundamentally, perhaps, it nurtured community-based forms of popular participation in local governance, the provision of social services, and productive activities. Indeed, the Bolivarian Constitution of 1999 proclaimed that 'assemblies of citizens' could make binding decisions, even overriding those of elected local, regional, or national governments (Álvarez 2003: 154). Although this proved difficult to implement in practice, the Chávez government did experiment with an evolving mix of grassroots organizations dedicated to a variety of social, economic, and political purposes. Some of these were informed by the innovative experiences of Causa R governments at the local level, as a faction of the leftist party had broken off and joined the coalition led by Chávez's MVR.

Although Chávez was initially averse to creating a mass party organization, he began to organize grassroots 'Bolivarian committees' after his release from prison in 1994. These were coordinated at the municipal level and vertically linked to regional and national organs of his movement, as well as local and regional assemblies. After 1997, when the MBR 200 shifted its stance from electoral abstention to electoral participation, grassroots organizational efforts became closely tied to the tasks of electoral mobilization in the 1998 presidential campaign, along with the sequence of popular referendums associated with the constitutional overhaul. Many civic groups with links to *Chavismo* were also actively engaged in the debates over constitutional reform, ultimately developing 624 proposals for consideration by the constituent assembly, over half of which were incorporated in some form in the final draft of the constitution (García-Guadilla 2003: 186). Nevertheless, upon taking office, Chávez initially relied heavily on military personnel rather than civic groups to coordinate public works projects and the delivery of social services (Norden 2003: 104–6).

After completing his constitutional overhaul, however, and winning new national elections in 2000, Chávez shifted his attention increasingly to social and economic reform, progressively radicalizing his 'Bolivarian Revolution' and, in the process, intensifying elite opposition. This dynamic provided a new stimulus to grassroots organization and popular mobilization, in part to help carry out social and economic reforms, and in part to provide a counterweight to the de facto power of elite groups in the business community and mass media (see Roberts 2006). Initially, the centrepiece of community-based popular organization were the so-called Bolivarian circles, which formed in low-income districts beginning in 2001 and ultimately collaborated with the government in a broad range of education, health care, nutrition, and other social programmes. These Bolivarian circles played an important role in the popular protests that helped reverse the April 2002 business-backed military coup, which briefly removed Chávez from office. By 2003 the government claimed, probably with some exaggeration, to have registered 2.2 million members in two hundred thousand local circles (Hawkins 2010a: 177).

After this initial burst of energy, the Bolivarian circles became less active and were largely displaced by a plethora of more specialized community-based organizations, including dozens of community water councils, local planning councils in each municipality, and over six thousand urban land committees with an estimated membership at 1.6 million to assess land claims and deliver titles (Hawkins 2010b: 43). Many of the social 'missions' of the Chávez government – programmes related to health, education, nutrition, and other social needs – also had a strong participatory character, with local committees formed to assess community needs and administer government assistance, which amounted to as much as 3.5 per cent of GDP by the middle of the decade. Hawkins (2010b: 36–43) estimates that some sixty-five hundred local health committees with close to three million participants were formed as part of the Barrio Adentro health care mission, whose benefits reached nearly half the adult population, according to public opinion surveys. The subsidized food mission known as Mercal reached an even higher percentage of the adult population, with 71.6 per cent of survey respondents claiming to have used its services, while over two million students participated in new educational missions at the primary, secondary, and university levels. As part of its strategy to build 'socialism for the 21st century,' the government also encouraged the formation of over sixty thousand local cooperatives to engage in productive activities and the service sector of the economy (Goldfrank 2011).

Finally, starting in 2005, the government made a major push to promote the formation of participatory Communal Councils (CC), which function parallel to and independent of elected municipal governments. The CCs make planning decisions through local assemblies of citizens, form sub-committees to oversee the implementation of programmes in different areas, and obtain funding directly from the central government for local infrastructure, housing, and development projects. By 2008 some eighteen thousand CCs had been formed (Handlin and Collier 2011), and surveys indicated that 35.5 per cent of the adult population had participated in their activities. As Hawkins (2010b: 42) states, this level of participation far surpasses that of the highly touted participatory budgeting initiatives launched by the Workers' Party (PT) in Brazil, which typically engage '2 to 8 per cent of the population in municipalities with the programme' and reach 'as high as 10 per cent only in the most successful areas.' With independent authority to plan public works and secure government funding, the CCs clearly go beyond a mere consultative role in the process of community development.

Given their dependence on state initiative and resources, CCs (and other community-based organizations) were often criticized by the opposition for being clientelistic and partisan instruments of *Chavista* control. Although more rigorous scholarly research has found little evidence of overt clientelistic manipulation of government programmes at the level of individual recipients, there is evidence to suggest that political loyalties influence the allocation of resources at the district level, and certainly there is a pro-Chávez partisan bias in the profile of programme participants (Hawkins 2010a: ch. 7). Nevertheless, public opinion surveys suggested that state-sponsored community organizations provided channels of participation for citizens whether or not they supported Chávez, even if his partisans were more likely to take advantage of participatory opportunities. Thirty-nine per cent of Chávez supporters, for example, reported that they participated monthly in meetings of CCs or other community-based associations – but so did twenty-eight per cent of the supporters of other parties and twenty-one per cent of non-partisans. These figures all dwarf those recorded in Chile, Brazil, and Uruguay, where more institutionalized leftist parties governed, but provided weaker stimulus for participation from below (see Handlin and Collier 2011). Furthermore, survey evidence indicates that 'Bolivarian associations are mobilizing new Venezuelans, particularly sectors of the population, such as women and the poor, that have traditionally been excluded from politics' (Hawkins 2010b: 54).

Undoubtedly, the CCs and other grassroots forms of popular organization were plagued by a number of problems. The constantly evolving maze of communal groups suggested that they remained highly dependent on state (and particularly executive) priorities, initiatives, and resources, and they were undoubtedly poorly institutionalized and thus prone to deactivation (as seen with the Bolivarian circles). Their status relative to elected municipal governments remained an ongoing source of political contention, and in a context of state-allocated oil rents, there is an ever-present danger of being transformed into mere vehicles for clientelistic political manipulation. Nevertheless, state-sponsored community associations under Chávez clearly offered mechanisms for social and political inclusion and grassroots participation that exceeded those created by other leftist governments in Latin America and far exceeded what had existed previously in Venezuela. This activation at the grassroots level, moreover, carried over into more explicitly partisan affairs. As Handlin and Collier (2011) show, Venezuelan citizens were four times as likely to attend meetings of Chávez's political party than all other parties combined, and nearly three times as likely to participate in campaign activities of Chávez's party or to identify with his party.

To summarize, on the basic Dahlian dimension of democratic participation or inclusion, Chávez's brand of leftist populism clearly led to significant advances. Chávez attracted sectors of Venezuelan society that felt alienated or excluded from the existing democratic regime, directed appeals specifically to subaltern groups within a broader conception of 'the people,' mobilized a new popular majority through electoral and plebiscitary means to refound the constitutional order, and opened new channels for grassroots participation in the political process. What remains to be seen, then, is what this new expression of popular sovereignty, with its heavy reliance on charismatic authority, implied for the other core dimension of democracy – that of contestation.

7.4   The Chávez regime and democratic contestation

As Rovira Kaltwasser and Mudde suggest in Chapter 1, the construction of new forms of popular sovereignty by populist movements may well enhance democratic inclusiveness and participation at the expense of democratic contestation. These tradeoffs are not inevitable, however. Popular majorities can be built without violating the rights of political minorities or undermining political pluralism, while plebiscitary and participatory mechanisms can be developed to supplement rather than displace or circumvent representative institutions.

Nevertheless, in the Venezuelan case tensions and tradeoffs between the two primary dimensions of democracy have clearly been present (see Coppedge 2008). These tradeoffs can be seen in two principal areas.

First, *Chavismo* used plebiscitary measures to concentrate power in the executive branch, in particular in the hands of a charismatic leader, in the process weakening the institutional checks and balances associated with liberal democracy. Second, this erosion of institutional checks and balances has undermined the protection of civil and political liberties for opposition groups and thus weakened democratic contestation. Although Venezuela remains politically competitive and pluralistic – *Chavismo* has not created a single-party regime and suppressed all political opposition the way another populist-turned-Marxist did in Cuba fifty years ago – it is today probably closer to Levitsky and Way's (2002) model of 'competitive authoritarianism' than it is to liberal democracy.

Clearly, power is highly concentrated, both within *Chavismo* as a political movement and within the broader political regime. Within *Chavismo*, Chávez's charismatic authority is essentially unchecked by rival political leaders or institutionalized mechanisms of accountability. Secondary leaders have come and gone, and sometimes returned, at a dizzying pace, but none have been allowed to consolidate a personal base of power to rival that of Chávez. Chávez has the power to make or break the political careers of subordinates, and this dependency accentuates the autocratic tendencies within his leadership. Furthermore, Chávez, like Perón, initially took only half-hearted measures to institutionalize his movement as a party organization, and when he did finally adopt a more ambitious party-building strategy after 2006, with the formation of the United Socialist Party of Venezuela (PSUV), it remained very much an instrument of his personal authority.

There is, of course, nothing very novel about political parties serving as instruments of personal authority in Latin America, or in Venezuela for that matter. What is more problematic for democratic contestation is the extent to which political authority in the larger regime is also highly concentrated in the presidency, and the ways in which this concentration has steadily eroded the horizontal checks and balances provided by other regime institutions. As previously mentioned, Chávez used his plebiscitary power to first bypass, and then dissolve, the opposition-controlled legislature in the process of rewriting the constitution, and he crafted new electoral rules that ensured his movement an overwhelming majority in the constituent assembly.

The new constitution strengthened executive powers in a number of significant ways: The presidential term was lengthened and re-election was allowed, and the president was given the power to dissolve congress, control military promotions, and convoke popular referendums or constituent assemblies. The refounding of the constitutional order also allowed for new elections in 2000, giving Chávez's MVR an opportunity to capture a majority of seats (see Table 7.2), which it then used to grant Chávez expanded decree powers. These decree powers were instrumental in the turn towards more statist and nationalistic economic policies in the early 2000s. Additionally, the constituent assembly dissolved provincial legislatures and declared a judicial emergency, leading to the dismissal of some 200 judges. A judicial reform bill passed in 2004 allowed the government to appoint twelve new Supreme Court justices, helping *Chavismo* to consolidate its control over the judiciary as well.

Largely relegated to the margins of formal regime institutions, opposition forces turned increasingly to extra-institutional measures to contest Chávez's rule. A series of civic protests in early 2002 culminated in the short-lived military coup in April of that year. When the coup was reversed, the opposition tried a new tactic: a damaging two-month strike in the national oil company in late 2002 and early 2003, which Chávez finally broke by firing some eighteen thousand managers and staff and placing trusted allies in charge of the company. The oil strike triggered a severe recession in 2003, but as oil prices started a steady climb and the economy began to recover, the government used its newly enhanced control over the oil windfall to redirect revenues to the missions and other social programmes (Corrales and Penfold 2010). Chávez's public approval ratings increased sharply following a decline in the early 2000s, and he was able to comfortably defeat the opposition's attempt at a presidential recall in the referendum of 2004.

An increasingly demoralized opposition 'barely contested' sub-national elections in October 2004 (Corrales and Penfold 2007), allowing Chávez supporters to capture twenty-one out of twenty-three state governments and more than ninety per cent of municipalities. The following year, the opposition made a last-minute decision to boycott national legislative elections entirely, in part as a response to concerns that the government could trace voter identities through the automated voting system.[4] This boycott allowed the MVR and other parties sympathetic to Chávez to capture all the seats in the national assembly. By 2005, then, *Chavismo* effectively controlled the national executive, legislative, and judicial branches of government, as well as other regime institutions like the National Electoral Council (CNE).

---

[4] For example, the names of Venezuelan citizens who signed the petition for a recall election against Chávez in 2004 were subsequently revealed by electoral officials and published on the Internet, in blatant violation of the norm of voter anonymity. In response to opposition concerns, Venezuelan electoral authorities reached an agreement with the Organization of American States to withdraw controversial digital fingerprint scanners prior to the 2005 legislative elections, but this did not induce the leading opposition parties to participate in the electoral process.

Clearly, the closing of institutional space for opposition forces was not unrelated to their own political weakness and ineffectiveness. AD and COPEI retreated into political insignificance after 1998, and fragmented opposition forces repeatedly failed to coalesce behind a new party organization or political movement capable of challenging *Chavismo* in the electoral arena. Lacking confidence in their ability to compete against a charismatic leader on an unlevel playing field, many opposition groups abandoned institutional spaces and opted for quasi-insurrectionary forms of resistance to try to force Chávez from power, such as the 2002 coup and the national oil strike. These tactics, however, created political instability and economic hardships that made it difficult for the opposition to win over undecided citizens, and the coup, in particular, cast doubt on the democratic credentials of the opposition itself. Indeed, it played into the hands of a populist figure who framed political struggle in highly confrontational and conspiratorial terms.

The institutional marginalization of opposition forces was also attributable, however, to Chávez's manipulation of popular sovereignty – mobilized through plebiscitary means – to evade or override institutional checks and balances and then alter the rules of the game in ways that tilted the playing field. Likewise, it reflected the concentration of resources in the hands of the state, as Chávez had control over special funds for social programmes independent of central bank oversight, and the CNE was lax in enforcing restrictions on the use of state resources, public office, and television advertising in electoral campaigns (Corrales and Penfold 2007 and 2010). The Chávez government was clearly in a position to use state contracts, revenues, licensing powers, regulatory authority, and legal sanctions (for example, on corruption charges) to reward loyalists and exclude or punish opponents in a wide range of economic and social activities.

Indeed, concerns mounted over time that these forms of financial and legal leverage were being used to hamstring the political opposition (Human Rights Watch 2008). Tensions were especially acute with the mass media, as the country's leading private television channels and newspapers were strident opponents of Chávez, and in some cases they had openly sympathized with civic protests against the regime and the 2002 military coup. Chávez sought to 'democratize' the media by expanding public television and radio outlets and supporting community-based radio programming, but he also clamped down on opposition media – for example, by denying the renewal of a broadcasting license for one major television station and filing charges against the director of another for defamation and disseminating false information. Similar charges were used to imprison an opposition former state governor in 2010 (Human

Rights Watch 2010). As Venezuela moved towards national legislative elections in September 2010, at a time of deepening economic crisis and social unrest, Chávez decreed the formation of a new public office with potentially wide-ranging censorship powers.

Despite these measures to weaken or intimidate the opposition and tilt the political playing field, it is important to recognize that voting procedures under Chávez have generally remained free from fraud. As such, *Chavismo* can still be challenged in the electoral arena, as the 2010 legislative elections clearly demonstrated. After abstaining from legislative elections in 2005, opposition forces opted to form a new coalition to contest *Chavismo* in 2010, confident that they could garner newfound support in a context of soaring crime rates, a severe recession triggered by the global financial crisis, and spot shortages of basic goods in the marketplace. Although Chávez's PSUV narrowly defeated the opposition coalition and captured a majority of seats, it fell short of fifty per cent of the vote for the first time in competitive elections, and even gerrymandered electoral districts did not provide the official party with the two-thirds majority of legislative seats required to pass certain types of organic laws or award Chávez executive decree powers. Therefore, as Chávez prepares to run for yet another re-election in 2012, he will be forced to compete in a political environment with meaningful institutional checks and balances for the first time since he came to office.

Where, then, does this leave the balance sheet for assessing the quality of democracy under Chávez? Assessments that prioritize one of Dahl's dimensions over the other can easily come to radically different conclusions, either lauding democratic advances under Chávez (Wilpert 2006) or decrying the descent into authoritarianism (Brewer-Carías 2010). Looking at the two dimensions together, however, suggests that the record is a mixed one, and that the regime has a hybrid character that combines elements of democracy and authoritarianism (see Corrales and Penfold 2010). In terms of democratic inclusion and participation, the Chávez regime made substantial gains in comparison to the crisis-ridden and discredited democracy of the 1990s. Indeed, at the height of its popularity in the mid 2000s, the Chávez regime fared strikingly well in comparison to other Latin American democracies. In regionwide public opinion surveys conducted in 2005, for example, Venezuelan citizens were the least likely in all of Latin America to say that politics was too complicated to understand, the second most likely (after Uruguayans) to express satisfaction with the performance of their democratic regime, and the most likely to characterize their regime as democratic (Latinobarómetro 2005). Clearly, *Chavismo* made popular sovereignty meaningful for a large number of Venezuelans. At the same time, however, it concentrated power, undermined checks and balances, and made opposition rights increasingly tenuous. Nevertheless, Chávez did not completely suppress opposition forces; he left open channels for electoral contestation that the opposition has recently shown it can exploit, even if the playing field is tilted to the president's advantage. Only time will tell whether Chávez keeps this space open, and whether the opposition can continue to make gains within it.

Conclusion

The Venezuelan case lends support to many of the propositions about populism outlined in the introduction to this volume. *Chavismo* demonstrates how populism's moralizing discourse can polarize society into antagonistic camps, and how its thin-centred ideology can complement and undergird both nationalist and socialist ideological influences. It also demonstrates that populism in power can have profound effects on democratic institutions and practices, even under relatively longstanding democratic regimes. Although fully consolidated democracies provide institutional safeguards against populist manipulation, regimes in a state of advanced decay may prove surprisingly susceptible to change wrought by populist mobilization. Indeed, opposition to an entrenched but discredited regime was the primary rallying cry for populist mobilization in Venezuela.

Such mobilization is not inherently anti-institutional, much less anti-democratic. In a context of acute political crisis, populist figures may assault established representative institutions as regime and party system outsiders. If given access to state power, however, they may well rebuild new and more powerful regime institutions, along with grassroots channels for popular participation, even if they are loathe to create intermediary institutions that might restrain their freedom to manoeuvre. And while these new regimes may consolidate, their relationship to democracy is likely to be highly contradictory, with gains in inclusion offset by limited contestation and opposition rights. Chávez, for example, prioritized new and more inclusive expressions of popular sovereignty while undermining the checks and balances required for effective democratic contestation or institutionalized pluralism.

Chávez's challenge to liberal democracy in Venezuela had deep roots in the crisis of the post-1958 democratic regime and the opportunities this provided for anti-system and anti-establishment populist mobilization. The collectivist ideologies of nationalism and socialism that were attached to populism in Venezuela were neither necessary nor sufficient for the vitality of such a challenge; as the chapter on Peru by Levitsky and Loxton shows, populist ideology attached to a pro-market agenda may be just as threatening to democracy as that attached to more collectivist goals. The inclusionary and participatory character of *Chavismo*, however, was more clearly rooted in its socialist aspirations to enhance the welfare of lower-class groups by strengthening their voice in the political process. Although 'the people,' for Chávez, potentially included anybody outside the disdained political establishment, the poor occupied a privileged space in the populist camp. Consequently, *Chavismo* in power not only polarized Venezuelan society politically – driving a wedge between supporters and opponents of Chávez and his regime – but also socio-economically, given the class distinctions that underlay the political cleavage.

Placed in a larger, comparative perspective, the Venezuelan case clearly continues the long tradition of political tension between populism and democracy in Latin America (de la Torre 2010). More specifically, it sheds new light on the dual participatory and contestatory dimensions of democracy that do not always co-exist in harmony with one another. Redemptive to some, and threatening to others, populism is likely to remain an integral part of the regional political landscape so long as institutions are weak and citizens are excluded from meaningful participation.

8 Populism and competitive authoritarianism: the case of Fujimori's Peru

Steven Levitsky and James Loxton

Introduction

Populism is a remarkably recurrent phenomenon in Latin America. For nearly a century, whenever competitive elections have been permitted in the region, populist strategies of political mobilization have been widespread. Given this persistence, the question of populism's relationship to democracy is a crucial one. Is populism a threat to democracy, a corrective to democracy, or, as the editors of this volume contend, both?

This chapter raises questions about the 'double-edged' nature of populism, arguing that in Latin America, the notion that populism is a corrective to democracy works better in theory than in practice. The 'populism as corrective' hypothesis rests on an abstract definition of democracy as the 'combination of popular sovereignty and majority rule' (Chapter 1), in which liberal rights are not a defining feature. In practice, however, democracy without liberalism is always ephemeral. In the absence of liberal rights, those empowered by majority rule in round one all too frequently use the state to block or distort the formation of alternative majorities in subsequent rounds. Thus, although populism has typically been inclusionary in Latin America, it has rarely been democratizing in the sense of institutionalizing majority rule. Rather, successful populism frequently leads to competitive authoritarianism.

We illustrate the argument through an examination of the case of Peru under Alberto Fujimori (1990–2000). As a populist outsider, Fujimori won the presidency by successfully mobilizing marginalized sectors of Peruvian society against the political elite. In power, Fujimori's anti-political establishment discourse led to severe executive-legislative conflict and, in 1992, an *autogolpe* (presidential coup) that closed the congress, dissolved the constitution, and purged the judiciary. The *autogolpe* was backed by a solid popular majority, which allowed Fujimori to impose a new constitution and win re-election in 1995. However, the destruction of institutional checks and balances allowed Fujimori to massively abuse state institutions and skew the political playing field against opponents. Successful populism thus facilitated a plebiscitarian assault on liberal democratic institutions, which pushed Peru into competitive authoritarianism.

8.1   Populism, democracy, and competitive authoritarianism

Populists mobilize subaltern mass constituencies, in a personalistic manner, against the entire political and/or economic establishment (Di Tella 1965; Roberts 1995; Weyland 1996, 2001). Central to populism, then, is an anti-elite appeal, made by a politician who credibly presents himself or herself as an outsider. A central claim of this volume is that populism can be both friend and foe of democracy: populism's inclusionary tendencies often serve as a corrective to existing democratic regimes, but at the same time, its illiberal and hegemonic tendencies can pose a threat to those regimes. Although we share this view of populism as fundamentally double-edged, we offer a slightly different take.

In Latin America, populism tends to be inclusionary but is rarely democratizing. It is inclusionary in that it involves the mobilization of marginalized groups against the established elite. Successful populists at least partially displace the existing elite and open up the political establishment to new actors. They may appoint representatives of marginalized groups to positions in the state, create new channels of access, and/or use public authority to advance policies that benefit, materially and symbolically, previously excluded groups. In the 1930s and 1940s, many Latin American populists extended formal rights, including suffrage and basic labour rights, which had long been denied to important sectors of the population (Collier and Collier 1991). Contemporary populists have introduced constitutional reforms to enhance citizen participation, extended new rights to indigenous people and other marginal groups, and brought members of these groups into positions of authority.

Yet populism is not necessarily democratic. Populist majorities guarantee only a snapshot of democracy – a democratic moment rather than a democratic regime. For majority rule to be meaningful, popular majorities must be generated over multiple rounds. Democracy – or specifically, a democratic *regime* – can only be said to exist where existing majorities can be easily reconfigured and new majorities can freely emerge. In practice, this has always required the Dahlian (1971) set of liberal rights. In the absence of such rights, a government generated by a popular majority at T=0 may use state power to limit others' ability to construct alternative majorities at T=1 or T=2. In our view, then, what Rovira Kaltwasser and Mudde describe as the 'internal contradiction of liberal democracy,' that is, the tension between the democratic promise of majority rule and the reality of constitutional protection of minority rights,' makes sense in theory, but breaks down in practice. Liberal rights may limit the scope of majority rule, but without them, majority rule is unlikely to persist.

In Latin America, successful populism has frequently pushed fragile democracies into competitive authoritarianism. Competitive authoritarianism may be defined as a civilian regime in which democratic institutions exist and are viewed as the primary means of gaining power, but in which incumbent abuse of state institutions skews the playing field to such a degree that the opposition's ability to compete is seriously compromised (Levitsky and Way 2010). In such regimes, competition is real but unfair: although opposition parties play, and occasionally even win, the democratic game, they compete on a highly uneven playing field. Government critics are often harassed or arrested, access to resources and the media is skewed, and incumbents politicize state institutions – including the courts, tax authorities, security forces, and electoral authorities – and use them as weapons against the opposition. To quote Castañeda (1995: 131), competitive authoritarianism is like a 'soccer match where the goalposts [are] of different heights and breadths and where one team include[s] 11 players plus the umpire and the other a mere six or seven players.'

Successful populism tends to lead to competitive authoritarianism for several reasons. First, many populists are political outsiders who have little experience with, or interest in, the institutions of representative democracy. Most career politicians spend years working within parties, legislatures, courts, and local governments, during which they acquire skills – such as negotiation, compromise, and coalition building – that help those institutions work. And because working within the institutions of representative democracy is their livelihood, most professional politicians are committed to those institutions. Populists, by contrast, are often amateur politicians who emerge from outside the established party system.[1] Without experience in the day-to-day politics of legislative, judicial, or other democratic institutions, outsiders often lack the skills – or patience – to pursue their political objectives through those institutions. And many of them lack a serious commitment to the institutions themselves. Indeed, every Latin American president who has closed congress since 1990 –Fujimori, Hugo Chávez, Rafael Correa, and Jorge Serrano – has been an outsider.

---

[1] For example, Alberto Fujimori (Peru), Jorge Serrano (Guatemala), Hugo Chávez (Venezuela), Lucio Gutiérrez (Ecuador), and Rafael Correa (Ecuador) had never held elected office before winning the presidency.

Second, successful populists earn a mandate to bury the political establishment. The core message of populist campaigns is that the established political elite is exclusionary, corrupt, and unrepresentative, and that existing regime institutions are therefore not really democratic. Fujimori, Chávez, and Correa all claimed that their countries were not democracies but 'partyarchies' (i.e. a system of 'rule by the parties' rather than by 'the people'), and all of them campaigned on a pledge to destroy the old elite in the name of 'true' or 'authentic' democracy. Where such appeals succeed, populists win a mandate to sweep away the political elite and 'refound' the political order. The problem is that in contemporary Latin America, the system against which populists campaign is usually a democracy: thus, the 'corrupt' or 'unrepresentative' institutions that they promise to sweep away are political parties, legislatures, and judiciaries.

Finally, populists' incentive to assault representative institutions is often reinforced by the fact that the political elite that they mobilized against and defeated in elections continues to control these institutions. Lacking strong parties, populists often fail to translate their electoral success into a legislative majority. And as outsiders, they generally have had little influence over the appointment of Supreme Court justices, electoral authorities, and other state officials. Indeed, most of these positions are held by established party appointees. Of course, populist presidents could respond by negotiating and sharing power with the established parties (as did Lula, for example, a non-populist leftist in Brazil). Having been elected on an anti-establishment appeal, however, such a move would constitute a betrayal of their mandate, which could be politically costly. Thus, populists have a strong incentive to assault representative democratic institutions: to circumvent or close the congress, pack or dissolve the Supreme Court, or rewrite the constitution.

For these reasons, the election of a populist to the presidency often triggers an institutional crisis in which a newly elected outsider with a mandate to sweep away corrupt and unrepresentative institutions is pitted against an established political elite who views those institutions as a last bastion of defence. In some cases, populists lose these showdowns and are removed from office – as in the cases of Jorge Serrano in Guatemala in 1993 and Lucio Gutiérrez in Ecuador in 2005. More frequently, however, the president wins, for several reasons. First, because populists win office in a context of widespread societal disaffection with the status quo, public opinion generally favours the president – often overwhelmingly.[2]

---

[2] Chávez and Correa, for example, both enjoyed very high public approval ratings when they launched their assault on existing constitutional arrangements, and Fujimori's public approval soared to eighty per cent following his 1992 coup.

At the same time, the 'traditional' parties that lead the opposition tend to be discredited and lacking in public support. Moreover, the opposition tends to suffer from organizational weakness. Populist victories almost invariably occur in the context of inchoate or collapsing party systems. The electoral success of an outsider often accelerates the deterioration of established parties by serving as a signal to other politicians to avoid association with 'traditional parties' (Levitsky and Cameron 2003). As the established parties decompose, the opposition as a whole fragments, and with it the capacity to act collectively and mobilize against governmental abuses.

When populist presidents prevail in such institutional showdowns, the result is usually a skewed playing field. Presidents may be able to close Congress and elect a new one with a pro-government majority; pack the judiciary, the electoral authorities, and other key state institutions with their supporters; rewrite the electoral laws to weaken opposition parties; and impose a new constitution that strengthens the executive branch and extends the president's term in office. In the absence of institutional checks and balances or strong opposition parties, little prevents presidents from violating other democratic norms and procedures, including basic civil liberties, in an effort to weaken or pre-empt future opposition. All of this is a recipe for competitive authoritarianism. In the sections that follow, we show how populism contributed to greater inclusion *and* a slide into competitive authoritarianism in Fujimori's Peru.

8.2   'A president like you:' populism and Fujimori's rise to power, 1990–1992

The presidency of Alberto Fujimori has been described as 'a prototypical case of neopopulist leadership' (Weyland 2006: 13; also Roberts 1995). Fujimori was a classic political outsider. Described by *The Economist* as 'the man from nowhere' (in Conaghan 2005: 16), Fujimori was a little known mathematics professor and university rector – of Japanese descent – who had never held elected office or belonged to a political party. His victory in the 1990 presidential election has been described as the 'biggest electoral surprise in the political history of [Peru]' (Panfichi 1997: 226–7). Unable to secure a nomination from a major party, Fujimori created his own party, Change 90, to run for senate in 1990 (Roberts 1995: 95). He reportedly tossed his hat into the presidential race only as a means to gain publicity for his senate bid (Schmidt 1996: 330–1). Six weeks before the election, Fujimori stood at less than one per cent in the polls (ibid.: 321); indeed, the erstwhile frontrunner, novelist Mario Vargas Llosa (1994: 434), claims to have never given 'a single thought to him' until ten days before the election.

Fujimori's rise from obscurity to the presidency was rooted in a triple crisis. First, Peru suffered a spectacular economic collapse in the late 1980s, marked by a deep recession and hyperinflation. Second, the mounting insurgency of the Maoist Shining Path brought the Peruvian state to the brink of collapse. In 1989 and 1990 alone, police recorded nearly six thousand insurgent attacks and seven thousand deaths due to political violence (Tanaka 1998: 108). By decade's end, the guerrillas controlled a quarter of Peru's municipalities and had penetrated the shantytowns surrounding Lima, raising the spectre of a Shining Path victory (see Burt 2007; Mauceri 1996). A third, and related, problem was a crisis of political representation. In 1990, the four-party system that had existed in the 1980s was on the verge of collapse (Cameron 1994; Tanaka 1998). The two largest parties, Popular Action (AP) and the American Revolutionary Popular Alliance (APRA), had governed during the 1980s and were widely held responsible for the country's economic and security crises. The United Left (IU), which might have taken advantage of the major parties' failure, suffered a schism in 1989 and never recovered. The conservative Popular Christian Party (PPC) was an elitist, Lima-centredorganization with little support among the urban poor or in the interior (Cameron 1994: 19). The crisis of representation was exacerbated by the growth of the urban informal sector, which encompassed roughly half of Lima's economically active population in 1990.[3] Informalization eroded the established parties' already tenuous linkages to society, weakened class-based organizations, and inhibited collective action among the poor (Grompone 1991; Roberts 1998).

In this context of triple crisis, public disaffection with the established parties soared. A 1990 survey found that only ten per cent of respondents identified with one of the four major parties, down from forty-three per cent in 1986, whereas eighty per cent identified themselves as independents (Kenney 2004: 47). Another survey found that only seventeen per cent of respondents in Lima expressed any confidence in the country's political parties (Tanaka 1998: 226). Indeed, hostility towards all politicians soared, especially among the poor. According to Aldo Panfichi (1997: 230), a survey carried out in ten low-income districts in Lima found

almost unanimous negative views toward politicians. Ninety-four per cent of those interviewed said they were in agreement that 'the people are always deceived by

---

[3] On the growth of the informal sector and its impact, see Cameron (1994), Grompone (1991), and Roberts (1995, 1998). For a dissenting view, see Kenney (2004: 48–59).

politicians.' The same percentage said that 'politicians always end up arranging things among themselves,' and 89 per cent agreed that 'the politicians and the wealthy are always in collusion.'

The crisis also eroded public confidence in Peru's democratic system more generally. A 1990 survey in Lima found that fifty-nine per cent of respondents believed that the country was 'only a little democratic' or 'not at all democratic' (Mauceri 2006: 252). In another survey, carried out in low-income neighbourhoods in Lima, only forty-four per cent of respondents believed that Peru had a democratic system (Roberts 1995: 98).

The triple crisis provided fertile ground for political candidates who could present themselves as 'outsiders' (Roberts 1995). A radio personality, Ricardo Belmont, won the 1989 Lima mayoral election as an outsider, and as the 1990 presidential race approached, celebrated novelist (and political neophyte) Mario Vargas Llosa emerged as the early frontrunner. However, Vargas Llosa's free-market platform and open call for economic shock measures limited his appeal among the poor (Conaghan 2000: 264). Moreover, his decision to align himself with two established conservative parties, AP and PPC, undermined his 'independent' or 'outsider' status in the eyes of many voters (Cameron 1994: 123–4). It was ultimately Fujimori, not Vargas Llosa, who tapped most successfully into the public disaffection with the political elite.

Fujimori's presidential campaign was populist in several senses. First, it mobilized groups and individuals who felt excluded under the existing political system. Lacking a party or strong ties to the establishment, Fujimori had little alternative but to build a coalition of outsiders. Thus, he mobilized constituencies that operated at the margins of politics, particularly evangelical Christians and the informal sector (Daeschner 1993: 170–4; Murakami 2007: 207–8; Roberts 1995: 99–100). These constituencies 'shared a sense of alienation from a political system that had historically accorded special favors to a privileged few' (Schmidt 1996: 328). In line with this strategy, Fujimori named as his two vice-presidential running mates Máximo San Román, the president of Peru's most important small business association, and Carlos García, an influential Baptist minister. He also appointed an evangelical Christian as general secretary of his party, Change 90 (C90), and awarded fifty of the party's 240 congressional candidacies to evangelical Christians (Conaghan 2005: 17). Several other C90 candidates 'spoke Quechua and worked in the informal economy' (Daeschner 1993: 261). By contrast, the legislative candidate list presented by Vargas Llosa's Democratic Front (FREDEMO) coalition 'read like a who's who of the Peruvian political establishment' (Cameron

1997: 43).[4] Fujimori's campaign explicitly targeted the informal sector. His platform included promises to legalize street vendors and create a new bank to provide credit to the informal sector (Roberts 1995: 100). During the second-round debate, he declared:

> Those Peruvians who work in the streets ... are a labor force that we must respect. They have chosen the path of honesty and work instead of vagrancy and crime. For that reason, we will recognize their associations and ... integrate them into a legal and formal framework, as is their aspiration. (In Intercampus 1990: 67)

These alliances were critical to Fujimori's initial success. Badly outfinanced by FREDEMO and other major parties,[5] Change 90 had no choice but to adopt a grassroots campaign based on word of mouth rather than mass media (Daeschner 1993: 171–2; Murakami 2007: 208). Informals and evangelicals served as the campaign's 'muscle' and 'arms and legs' (Daeschner 1993: 174; also Degregori and Meléndez 2007: 26–7). Evangelical pastors distributed Fujimori campaign materials while conducting door-to-door missionary work; truck drivers provided transportation between Lima and rural areas; and businesspeople campaigned for Fujimori among the urban poor (Daeschner 1993: 171–4; Murakami 2007: 208).

Second, Fujimori successfully presented himself as an outsider and a 'man of the people.' Surveys showed that Fujimori's 'newness' and lack of partisan ties were his greatest electoral assets, while Vargas Llosa was hurt by his perceived ties to established parties (Cameron 1994: 140).[6] Yet Fujimori's outsider status went beyond partisanship. As a (non-white) child of working-class Japanese immigrants, Fujimori could credibly present himself as a Peruvian everyman who stood outside (and ultimately, in opposition to) the entire social, economic, and political elite (Panfichi 1997). The fact that he was a child of poor immigrants who had worked their way out of poverty resonated with Lima's poor, since many had migrated from the countryside to the city in search of a better life (Daeschner 1993: 144–5; Panfichi 1997: 228–30).

Fujimori's campaign made effective use of his non-elite background. Adopting the slogan 'A President Like You,' Fujimori mixed freely with the poor in rural villages, urban slums, and public marketplaces. He drove

---

[4] FREDEMO included Vargas Llosa's Liberty Movement, the PPC, AP, and the smaller Solidarity and Democracy (SODE).
[5] According to Schmidt (1996: 321), Vargas Llosa's advertising spending exceeded Fujimori's by a twenty to one margin.
[6] Alma Guillermoprieto (1995: 81) reports an exchange in which a street vendor is asked by a left-wing politician why she intends to vote for Fujimori, and she responds: 'Because he hasn't done anything yet.'

a tractor, dubbed the 'Fuji-mobile,' in order to illustrate his connectedness to the rural poor (Murakami 2007: 207–8). As Conaghan (2005: 17) put it, 'Fujimori was at ease in his role as "man of the people" – riding a bicycle, wearing a poncho, speaking his folksy and ungrammatical Spanish.' By contrast, Vargas Llosa 'arrived at events in an armor-plated Volvo, surrounded by bodyguards, and appeared to suffer through the long programs of speeches and folklore,' all of which made him look 'like an envoy from the upper class.'

Fujimori's ability to present himself as a 'man of the people' was reinforced by his ethnic and family background (Degregori and Grompone 1991). As a Japanese Peruvian, Fujimori belonged to a small ethnic minority. However, given widespread disaffection with Peru's predominantly white political elite, Fujimori's ethnic background proved to be 'an asset rather than an obstacle,' as his 'facial features, migratory experience, and modest origins were more reminiscent of Peru's *mestizo* and indigenous majority than those of the Europeanized Vargas Llosa' (Roberts 1995: 95). For many Peruvians, Fujimori's ethnic origins 'meant, above all, that he was not white, and was therefore one of them' (Guillermoprieto 1995: 78). Deftly taking advantage of this status, Fujimori embraced the nickname 'El Chino,' often referring to himself as such during campaign events (ibid.: 82). The racial background of Fujimori's vice-presidential candidates, Máximo San Román (a dark-skinned *mestizo*) and Carlos García (who was of partially African ancestry), further differentiated him from the political elite. As San Román put it: 'We were the ticket most representative of Peru: the *Chino*, the *Cholo*, and the *Negro*' (in Daeschner 1993: 122).

Fujimori's outsider status helped catapult him into a second-round runoff against Vargas Llosa. Fujimori's populist strategy deepened in the second round. Vargas Llosa was backed by virtually the entire Peruvian elite, including the business community, the Catholic Church, the bulk of the media, and most of the cultural and intellectual elite. This enabled Fujimori to run as a David against the Goliath of Peru's discredited political establishment – a strategy facilitated by racist and xenophobic attacks against Fujimori carried out by some of Vargas Llosa's supporters (Guillermoprieto 1995: 82; Vargas Llosa 1993: 472–3, 476).[7] Fujimori's discourse grew increasingly Manichean in the second round, dividing society into 'the pure people' and 'the corrupt elite.' He defined the election as a 'confrontation between the white elite … and the nonwhite common people' (de la Torre 2000: 124), positioning himself as the representative of Peruvian *cholos* (brown-skinned poor), in opposition to the

---

[7] It should be noted that Vargas Llosa himself publicly rejected these racist attacks.

blanquitos (whites), the *ricos* (the rich), and the *pitucos* (wealthy whites) (Carrión 1996: 286–7; Degregori and Grompone 1991: 96–7). Fujimori claimed to represent the 'real Peru, *cholo* Peru' (in Intercampus 1990: 22), declaring at one campaign rally: 'We may be *chinitos* and *cholitos*, but we are the real people' (in Daeschner 1993: 241). If Vargas Llosa won, Fujimori declared, Peru would be governed by 'whites,' but if he were elected, the government would be made up of a '*chinito* and four *cholitos*' (in Carrión 1996: 287). Fujimori relentlessly portrayed Vargas Llosa as out of touch with the common people and scarcely even Peruvian. In the second round debate, he attacked Vargas Llosa for having taught at foreign rather than Peruvian universities and at one point declared: 'You think we Peruvians are monkeys' (in Daeschner 1993: 252).[8]

Fujimori's strategy was effective. Vargas Llosa was unable to shake the image of being a 'white, privileged member of the Peruvian social elite with little understanding of the problems facing *las clases populares*' (Conaghan 2000: 264). Fujimori won the runoff election overwhelmingly, with 62.5 per cent of the vote. Whereas Vargas Llosa's vote was drawn primarily from the better-off strata of society, Fujimori won overwhelmingly among the poor (Cameron 1994: 127, 143).

8.3   Populism in power: political conflict and democratic breakdown, 1990–1992

The character of Fujimori's populist appeal changed somewhat after he assumed the presidency in 1990. Facing deep economic and security crises, Fujimori turned programmatically to the right, borrowing much of Vargas Llosa's platform and several of his top advisors (Conaghan 2000: 256; Murakami 2007: 228–33). Indeed, '[t]he most notable characteristic of Fujimori's first cabinet was that it included no one who had voted for him in the April elections' (Kenney 2004: 126). Fujimori's shift to the right permitted a rapprochement with Peru's economic and technocratic elite. By 1992, he had forged a 'a tacit alliance' with the '*de facto* powers of Peruvian society – the military, leading elements of the business community, major media outlets, and transnationalized technocrats linked to international financial institutions' (Conaghan 2000: 257). This new alliance undermined Fujimori's original coalition of outsiders. Although marginal groups were well represented in Change 90's legislative bloc, Fujimori kept the party at a distance, ignoring its legislators, sacking its

---

[8] The reference to monkeys was based on a FREDEMO television spot that featured a monkey dressed as a civil servant defecating on a desk, apparently in order to illustrate the need for state reform (Daeschner 1993: 108–9).

evangelical general secretary, and closing down its main headquarters (Planas 2000: 347–51). Emblematic of the rupture was the fact that Fujimori's two vice presidents, evangelical leader Carlos García and small business leader Máximo San Román, became two of his most trenchant public critics.

Notwithstanding these changes, however, Fujimori remained unmistakably populist after assuming the presidency. Although he dropped the class-based elements of his anti-elite discourse, he stepped up his attacks on the *political* elite: 'no longer "the people" versus "the oligarchy," it became instead "the people" – represented by their elected president – versus the "political class"' (Roberts 1995: 98). Indeed, soon after taking office, Fujimori launched a 'systematic attack on Peru's political elites and the establishment institutions they controlled – namely, the political parties, Congress, and the judiciary' (Ibid.: 97). He publicly attacked legislators as 'unproductive charlatans' and judges as 'jackals' (in Conaghan 2005: 30), and he decried politicians' 'irresponsible, sterile, antihistoric, and antipatriotic behavior, which favors the interests of small groups and party leaders over the interests of Peru' (in Gorman 1997: 325).

Using the presidency as a bully pulpit, Fujimori attacked 'the party system as a whole' (Conaghan 2000: 265), claiming that the established parties were corrupt and unrepresentative – and that they were actively blocking his efforts to carry out the public will and resolve Peru's economic and security crises. Indeed, he began to argue that Peru was not really a democracy, or rule by the people, but rather a 'partyarchy,' or rule by the parties (Roberts 1995: 98; Kenney 2004: 220). In a speech to business leaders, Fujimori asked:

Are we really a democracy? And the democracy (...) is it a government of the people, by the people, and for the people or a government of the majority? I find it difficult to say yes. We are a government that in truth has always been governed by powerful minorities. (In Conaghan 2005: 30)

Fujimori's populist strategy contributed to a regime crisis. Change 90 controlled only thirty-two of 180 seats in the chamber of deputies and fourteen of sixty-two seats in the senate. The vast majority of legislative seats remained in the hands of the established parties.[9] Moreover, the judiciary, a key player in Fujimori's counterinsurgency programme and in evolving constitutional battles between the executive and the congress, was in the hands of judges appointed by APRA and other established

---

[9] In the chamber of deputies, APRA controlled fifty-three seats, AP held twenty-six seats, the PPC held twenty-five seats, and the IU held sixteen seats (Kenney 2004: 91).

parties (Conaghan 2005: 32; Kenney 2004: 196–7). Rather than negotiate with the established parties, however, Fujimori continued to attack
them, entering into a 'chicken game' with both the congress and the
judiciary (Tanaka 1998: 212–13). Fujimori increasingly circumvented
Congress via executive decrees (Kenney 2004: 172–7). Calling Fujimori
'The Emperor,' congressional leaders moved to limit his presidential powers and threatened to impeach him (ibid.: 177–91). As one government
official put it, the conflict reached a point 'where either the Congress
would kill the president, or the president would kill the Congress' (in
Cameron 1997: 56).

In April 1992, Fujimori – backed by the military – carried out a presidential coup (*autogolpe*), closing the congress, dissolving the constitution,
and purging the judiciary and other state institutions. Most major media
outlets were occupied by the armed forces, several leading journalists
and members of congress were arrested, and ex-president Alan García
was forced into exile (Cotler 1994: 209–10). Fujimori defended the coup
as a step towards what he called a 'true' (in Daeschner 1993: 289) and
'*sui generis*' democracy (in Conaghan 2005: 7). He claimed that the pre-
existing regime was not a democracy but a 'dictatorship of *partidocracia*,'
or a 'government supposedly of the people but in reality by the parties
and for the parties' (in Kenney 2004: 220). Thus, Fujimori asserted that
the coup was 'not a rupture of democracy but rather a rupture of the
chain of corruption' (in Cameron 1997: 63). As he later explained: 'I had
two remaining options: to defend a minority of the population or the vast
majority. Obviously I chose the majority' (in Daeschner 1993: 294).

Populism was a central cause of the 1992 coup. First, as a political
outsider, Fujimori lacked partisan allies in other branches of government
(Kenney 2004: 91, 196–7). Thus, in addition to assuming office in the
worst possible circumstances, including hyperinflation and a raging insurgency, Fujimori faced the challenge of divided government. Scholars have
argued that opportunities existed for Fujimori to forge the legislative alliances necessary to govern democratically (Cameron 1997 54–5; Cotler
1994: 206–8; McClintock 1996: 64), much as Presidents Cardoso and
Lula da Silva would later do in Brazil.[10] Many of Fujimori's programmatic
initiatives in 1990–2 enjoyed legislative support, particularly on the right
(Kenney 2004: 129, 136) and within APRA (Daeschner 1993: 276–7).
However, this legislative support was not automatic, but rather 'subject
to renegotiation' (Conaghan 2000: 257). In other words, the construction

---

[10] Indeed, Vargas Llosa (1994: 470–1, 475) even claims to have offered to drop out of the
second round of the 1990 election and forge a coalition government under Fujimori's
leadership. For more pessimistic accounts about the prospects for forging a legislative
coalition, see Kenney (1996) and Murakami (2007: 272–80).

of a legislative majority would have required consultation, negotiation, and power sharing. Yet as a political amateur, Fujimori lacked experience with legislative coalition building, and indeed, he showed little interest in such arrangements (McClintock 1996: 64–6). Rather, he viewed the congress as 'worse than a nuisance' (Cameron 1997: 49). According to one of Fujimori's aides, he simply 'couldn't stand the idea of inviting the President of the Senate to lunch in the Presidential Palace every time he wanted to pass a law' (in McClintock 1996: 65).[11]

In part, Fujimori's lack of interest in legislative coalition building was rooted in a different conceptualization of democracy. Fujimori viewed democracy in terms of results that benefitted the majority, even if that meant circumventing liberal democratic procedure. Thus, his attitude 'was that of responding to the expectations of the people with specific results, worrying more about the efficiency of the procedures used to obtain these concrete achievements than their democratic or anti-democratic character' (Murakami 2007: 274). Often described as 'the politics of anti-politics' (Degregori 2000; Panfichi 1997), this plebiscitarian, result-oriented approach to democracy had little room for what he called '*palabrería*,' or the 'excessive, useless talk' of the political parties and political elite (in Conaghan 2005: 4). As Fujimori put it:

> Democracy now should not include the participation of political parties. The people have learned a lot. They have said: Enough of this kind of democracy. We want a democracy that is more efficient, that resolves our problems. Democracy is the will of the people – good administration, honesty, results. (In Conaghan 2005: 3)

Efficient problem solving on behalf of the people required a free hand in decision making, rather than having to seek out 'understandings, consensuses or broad agreements' (Murakami 2007: 224).

Whatever his view of democracy, it is clear that a populist strategy worked to Fujimori's political advantage. Fujimori had won the presidency with an anti-elite discourse. Taking advantage of broad public disaffection with the political elite, he effectively sought and won a popular mandate to sweep away that elite. Now, as president, Fujimori confronted a congress dominated by the established political parties he had vilified, and defeated, in the 1990 campaign. Although Fujimori could have negotiated alliances with those parties, such alliances would have betrayed his popular mandate. Given widespread public hostility towards

---

[11] As Cameron (1997: 50) writes: 'Having built his career by attacking major institutions in Peruvian society – political parties and politicians, the bureaucracy, the courts, even the Catholic Church – Fujimori's *autogolpe* was consistent with his anti-political style.'

the congress, the judiciary, and the established parties,[12] a plebiscitarian attack on these institutions was more likely to mobilize public support than were efforts to negotiate with them (Cameron 1997: 50). Indeed, public opinion data suggest that conflict with the political elite worked to Fujimori's advantage: public confidence in the congress, the judiciary, and political parties declined further in 1991 and 1992, while support for Fujimori increased (Kenney 2004: 234–5; Tanaka 1998: 225–6). Thus, a populist strategy not only won Fujimori the presidency but also proved essential to his political success in office.

Perhaps the clearest evidence that successful populism contributed to the 1992 *autogolpe* was the public reaction to it. Peruvians overwhelmingly *supported* the coup. Post-coup surveys found more than eighty per cent supported the dissolution of the congress and ninety per cent supported the reorganization of the judiciary (Conaghan 2005: 33; Kenney 2004: 228). Likewise, Fujimori's approval rating soared from fifty-three per cent to eighty-one per cent (Carrión 2006: 129). Thus, while the president 'was greeted enthusiastically by crowds' as he walked through the streets of Lima in the aftermath of the coup (Cameron 1997: 50), '[v]eteran politicians were mortified by the jeers that greeted them in Lima's cafes and restaurants' (Conaghan 2005: 45). Indeed, most Peruvians not only endorsed the closure of the congress but accepted Fujimori's interpretation of the events as a 'popular uprising' rather than a coup (in ibid.: 33). According to an April 1992 poll in Lima, fifty-one per cent of respondents characterized the coup as 'democratic,' while only thirty-three per cent viewed it as 'dictatorial' (Kenney 2004: 231).

Opposition parties' efforts to mobilize resistance to the coup failed (Cameron 1997: 62–4). Already discredited, the established opposition parties weakened and fragmented after the coup (Tanaka 1998: 229–30). As the success of Fujimori's plebiscitarian strategy became clear, politicians began to abandon the established parties en masse, reinventing themselves as 'independents' (Planas 2000: 42, 370–4). Consequently, the opposition that led the defence of democracy after 1992 was fragmented, disorganized, and lacked even a minimal capacity to mobilize resistance to the new regime (Levitsky and Cameron 2003).

In sum, Fujimori's decision to carry out an *autogolpe*, and his ability to get away with it, were rooted in his populist rise to power. Fujimori was elected in opposition to the entire political elite, effectively earning

---

[12] Polls in late 1990 found public approval of President Fujimori to be nearly triple that of the congress (Kenney 2004: 235). In an early 1991 survey, only nineteen per cent of respondents expressed confidence in the legislature, sixteen per cent expressed confidence in the judiciary, and thirteen per cent expressed confidence in political parties (ibid.: 234).

a mandate to bury that elite. Negotiating an alliance with the elite after coming to power would have constituted a betrayal of his mandate. Moreover, given widespread public disaffection with the old elite, a plebiscitarian strategy clearly worked to Fujimori's political advantage. Thus, the logic of populist mobilization led to a severe institutional crisis and, ultimately, the breakdown of Peruvian democracy.

8.4   The rise of competitive authoritarianism, 1992–2000

The regime that emerged after the April 1992 *autogolpe* was competitive authoritarian (Levitsky and Way 2010). Initial plans to govern in a dictatorial manner were abandoned due to international pressure, which forced the government to restore an electoral regime (Ferrero 1993: 34–7; McClintock and Vallas 2003: 136–8).[13] Elections for a constituent assembly (CCD) were held in late 1992, followed by a referendum on the constitution in 1993 and presidential elections in 1995. In addition to writing a new constitution, the CCD would serve as an interim congress until legislative elections were held in 1995.

Although these steps satisfied the international community by restoring the outward appearance of democracy, the regime that emerged after 1992 was not democratic. For one, Fujimori took advantage of the seven-month 'institutional vacuum' (Conaghan 2005: 43) to reconfigure state power in ways that facilitated authoritarian rule. In the absence of checks and balances, the government issued hundreds of decrees 'recasting government institutions and their operating procedures' in ways that 'concentrated more powers and control in the executive branch' (ibid.: 41). The decrees legalized the purge of the judiciary and other public agencies that occurred after the coup, dramatically elevated the status of the National Intelligence Service (SIN), and created a new presidential 'superministry' that enhanced the executive's ability to distribute patronage (ibid.: 41–3). In addition, millions of dollars in public money were siphoned into slush funds in the SIN to be used for Fujimori's re-election campaigns and other political purposes (ibid.: 41).

Moreover, between 1992 and 1995, Fujimori used his broad public support to consolidate authoritarian rule through plebiscitary means. Fujimori's public approval rating remained steadily above sixty per cent throughout the 1992–5 period (Carrión 2006: 128–9), which enabled him to win successive electoral majorities. Fujimori's C90/New Majority coalition won an outright majority of seats in the new constituent

---

[13] On the initial plans for dictatorial rule developed by the military in the late 1980s, see Cotler (1994: 208); Cameron (1997: 51, 57); and Rospigliosi (2000: 74–86, 106).

assembly, which allowed him to dominate the new body and unilaterally impose a new constitution expanding executive authority and permitting presidential re-election (Conaghan 2005: 56–9). In 1995, Fujimori was overwhelmingly re-elected, capturing sixty-four per cent of the vote (defeating former UN secretary-general Javier Pérez de Cuéllar, a prominent member of the old elite) and an outright majority in the congress. These popular majorities allowed Fujimori to describe the post-1992 regime as a 'truly representative democracy' (in Kenney 2004: 220).

Yet if Fujimori enjoyed clear majority support between 1992 and 1995, he used those temporary majorities to skew the playing field in ways that would distort or prevent the emergence of alternative majorities in the future. In the absence of institutional checks and balances, Fujimori and his intelligence advisor, Vladimiro Montesinos, were 'able to monopolize a level of power unheard of in Peru in decades' (Degregori 2003: 220). Montesinos used this power to construct a vast illicit network that systematically corrupted state institutions and deployed them against opponents (Conaghan 2005; Rospigliosi 2000). Montesinos used the SIN to spy on opposition and media figures (Bowen and Holligan 2003: 290–1; Rospigliosi 2000: 157–8, 202), and as videotapes later documented, he bribed and blackmailed hundreds of public officials, legislators, judges, military commanders, media owners, journalists, and opposition politicians.[14]

Fujimori and Montesinos used the SIN's shadow state to skew the political playing field in several ways. First, they established a firm grip on the judiciary. Not only did the government engage in a massive court-packing scheme in the aftermath of the 1992 coup,[15] but a 'staggering' number of judges, including several Supreme Court justices, received bribes or favours from the SIN in the post-1992 period (Conaghan 2005: 167). The politicized courts served as a 'shield for friends of the regime and a weapon against its enemies' (Durand 2003: 459). Judicial and tax authorities became 'instruments of persecution' (ibid.: 463), targeting opposition politicians, businesspeople, journalists, and media owners, forcing some of them into exile (Avendaño 2001; Durand 2003: 459–61).[16] The National Elections Board (JNE) was also packed, and as

---

[14] At least sixteen hundred people, including four Supreme Court justices, a majority of the National Elections Board, two attorneys general, and dozens of legislators, were videotaped accepting bribes or favours from Montesinos (Cameron 2006; Conaghan 2005; Rospigliosi 2000).

[15] Eighty per cent of sitting justices, including thirteen Supreme Court justices, were sacked (Pease García 2003: 286–90, 300–1; Rospigliosi 2000: 103–4; Youngers 2000: 26–32).

[16] For example, after the Channel 2 television network ran a series of critical news stories in 1997, the government revoked the citizenship of its owner Baruch Ivcher, a naturalized Peruvian citizen, and forced him into exile on tax charges (Conaghan 2005: 141–53).

a result, complaints of electoral abuse were routinely buried (Conaghan 2005: 92–3, 168).

The Fujimori government also skewed access to resources and the media. At least $146 million was transferred illicitly from various state agencies into Fujimori's campaign coffers between 1992 and 2000 (Conaghan 2005: 164). Moreover, the SIN organized and financed Fujimori's electoral campaigns, and the army was mobilized to campaign for him (Bowen and Holligan 2003: 344–72; Rospigliosi 2000: 202). The government controlled much of the private media through manipulation of debt and judicial favours, strategic use of state advertising, and massive bribery (Ames et al. 2001: 229, 232; Bowen and Holligan 2003: 340–4, 361–2). By the late 1990s, four of Peru's five private television networks were receiving monthly payments from the SIN; likewise, more than a dozen tabloid newspapers received up to $2 million a month to publish articles faxed from the SIN (Bowen and Holligan 2003: 361–2; Fowks 2000: 68–72).

The authoritarian nature of the regime became particularly manifest during Fujimori's second term. Fujimori faced two major challenges after 1995. First, his public support began to erode, slipping below fifty per cent for the first time since 1991 (Carrión 2006: 130). Second, his own constitution barred him from seeking a third term in 2000. Unwilling to give up power, yet lacking a viable successor, the government adopted a strategy of 're-election at any cost' (Cotler 2000: 53). In 1996, Fujimori's majority in congress passed the Law of Authentic Interpretation, which declared that because Fujimori's first term began under the old constitution, it did not count under the new one, therefore leaving him free to seek another re-election in 2000 (Conaghan 2005: 121–2). The law was 'considered absurd by most constitutional experts' (McClintock and Vallas 2003: 144). However, when the constitutional tribunal voted to declare the law 'inapplicable,' the government ignored the ruling and, shortly thereafter, the congress impeached the three members of the court who had voted for it (Conaghan 2005: 126–30). Opposition groups launched a petition drive to call a referendum on the re-election issue. Despite broad public support for the referendum (Carrión 2006: 143), this, too, was derailed through institutional manipulation.[17] Finally, the government packed the National Elections Board in order to ensure that Fujimori's candidacy would not be disqualified (Avendaño 2001: 131–3).

---

[17] In 1996, the congress passed a law requiring that referenda be approved by forty per cent of the congress, which 'ensured that no referendum could pass without the support of the government' (Conaghan 2005: 124). The referendum project ultimately died in the congress.

The 2000 election was unfair. Opposition parties 'faced a steeply tilted playing field – indeed, a virtual cliff' (McClintock 2006a: 255). Candidates from the opposition were spied on and their campaigns were disrupted by SIN-orchestrated mob attacks and power outages (Youngers 2000: 63–4). Media coverage was biased, and the SIN-controlled media launched a 'dirty war' against opposition candidates, accusing them of everything from terrorism to homosexuality.[18] On election night, the government appeared to manipulate the results in order to avoid a run-off against Alejandro Toledo.[19] External and domestic pressure forced Fujimori to accept a second-round vote (McClintock and Vallas 2003: 150), but an opposition boycott – in the face of the government's refusal to level the playing field – allowed Fujimori to run uncontested in the runoff. Although the regime imploded soon thereafter,[20] Fujimori succeeded in securing an illegal third term.

In sum, although Fujimori's popular majorities enabled him to declare his government 'truly democratic,' they also facilitated a slide into competitive authoritarianism. The 1992 coup and electoral victories in 1992 and 1995 effectively eliminated institutional checks on Fujimori's power, which enabled him to skew the political playing field against opponents. In effect, temporary majorities were used to inhibit the emergence of future alternative majorities. A majority of Peruvians eventually came to oppose Fujimori's increasingly authoritarian behaviour in the late 1990s; by then, however, that majority lacked the institutional mechanisms to stop him.

8.5   How inclusionary was *Fujimorismo*?

The case of Fujimori's Peru clearly illustrates the potential of populism to weaken the contestation dimension of democracy. But how inclusionary was *Fujimorismo*? Borrowing from Filc (2010), this section evaluates *Fujimorismo*'s inclusionary effects along three dimensions: material, political, and symbolic.

---

[18] Studies found that Fujimori received more than twice as much coverage as all other candidates combined (Boas 2005: 36; García Calderón 2001: 52). Television networks generally ignored opposition candidates and often refused to run their ads (Ames et al. 2001: 78). On the media 'dirty war,' see Bowen and Holligan (2003: 377–8), Degregori (2000: 151–68) and Fowks (2000: 69–70).

[19] Credible 'quick counts' showed Fujimori ahead of Toledo but short of the fifty per cent needed to avoid a runoff (Ames et al. 2001: 139). When Fujimori's official vote share began to rise later in the evening, OAS representative Eduardo Stein declared that he had 'no idea where these results [were] coming from,' and that 'something sinister [was] going on' (in Bowen and Holligan 2003: 384).

[20] In November 2000, a leaked videotape showing Montesinos bribing an opposition legislator triggered a regime crisis, forcing Fujimori to call new elections and eventually abandon the presidency (and the country). See Cameron (2006).

In terms of material inclusion, that is, an improvement in the 'material conditions of subordinate groups' (Filc 2010: 13), *Fujimorismo* brought relatively little change. Fujimori had campaigned in opposition to neo-liberal 'shock' policies in 1990, but he reversed course upon taking office and 'administered what is considered one of the most drastic economic restructuring programs in Latin America' (Carrión 2006: 135). The economic reforms succeeded in ending hyperinflation and restoring growth, thereby earning broad public support (Weyland 1998: 556), and the government used revenue from privatizations to increase public spending, mainly in the form of expanded public works and large-scale state clientelism (Roberts 1995; Schady 2000). However, *Fujimorismo* did little to redistribute wealth, create jobs, or create enduring social welfare policies. Indeed, with respect to employment and average income, 'Peruvians were no better off in 2000 than in 1990' (Carrión 2006: 126).

In terms of political inclusion, which Filc (2010: 14) defines as providing marginalized groups with 'access to political power,' Fujimori's record was mixed. In his initial presidential bid, Fujimori clearly mobilized previously marginal groups, most notably evangelical Christians and the informal sector. As a political outsider without a real party or ties to the establishment, Fujimori needed allies in order to mount a presidential campaign, and the groups available for mobilization were those that remained at the margins of the political system. Thus, Fujimori built a coalition of outsiders, and his victory in 1990 brought these outsiders unprecedented access to power. For example, *Fujimorismo* dramatically increased the presence of evangelical Christians in public office: in 1990, evangelicals won the second vice presidency, fourteen seats in the chamber of deputies and four seats in the senate (López Rodríguez 2008: 134).

Once he was securely in power, however, Fujimori's need for outsider allies diminished. Consequently, *Fujimorismo* grew less inclusionary after 1992. The number of 'technocrats, specialists and businessmen' in Fujimori's cabinet increased over time (Murakami 2007: 251), and whereas Fujimori's first party, Change 90, had recruited numerous politicians from marginal groups, his second party, New Majority (created in 1992), was an 'exclusive club' composed mainly of technocrats drawn from the Lima elite (Conaghan 2005: 52–3; Degregori and Meléndez 2007: 49–61). At the same time, Fujimori's alliance with evangelicals and informal business associations broke down. As early as 1990, the president purged Change 90 of many of its evangelical leaders, and a number of evangelical deputies resigned from the party (Degregori and Meléndez 2007: 37–42; Kenney 2004: 172). By 2000, the number of *Fujimorista* evangelicals in the congress had dwindled to one (López Rodríguez 2008: 135).

Fujimori's most significant and enduring move towards political inclusion came in the area of women in politics. Prior to 1990, women were 'almost invisible in the Peruvian political system' (Schmidt 2006: 150). No women were appointed to cabinet positions between 1980 and 1987, and relatively few were elected to the congress. The rise of *Fujimorismo* triggered a 'feminization of Peruvian politics' (ibid.: 173). As part as of Fujimori's coalition of outsiders, numerous women gained increased access to positions of power after 1990. In 1990, for example, women represented 9.4 per cent of Change 90 deputies and 14.3 per cent of its senators, compared to 5.4 and 4.5 per cent, respectively, for all other parties (ibid.: 154). Women were also appointed to a variety of key positions in the Fujimori government, including attorney general, minister of the presidency, minister of industry, and ambassador to the Organization of American States (ibid.: 153–5).

Unlike other marginal groups, women continued to make political gains throughout the Fujimori period. Three women served as president of congress between 1995 and 2000 and, when Fujimori took office for his illegal third term in 2000, all four members of the congressional leadership were women – unprecedented for Latin America (Blondet 2002: 51–2). The Fujimori government also created a Ministry for the Promotion of Women and Human Development in 1996, and in 1997 it pushed through a gender quotas law that required that women make up at least twenty-five per cent of each party's legislative candidate list (ibid.: 49–51). As a result, women's overall representation in the congress increased from six per cent in 1990 to twenty-two per cent in 2000 (Schmidt 2006: 154, 167). Although it is likely that women would have made political gains in the 1990s regardless of who was in power (Blondet 2002), the rise of Fujimori clearly accelerated this process (Schmidt 2006). The legacy of this advance was evident in the number of women holding high-level government positions in the post-Fujimori era.[21] Thus, the 'feminization of Peruvian politics' appears to be an enduring legacy of *Fujimorismo*.

Finally, Fujimori's most significant and lasting impact was almost certainly in the area of symbolic inclusion, which Filc (2010: 14) defines as a process in which 'the excluded group becomes part of the common "we."' *Fujimorismo* clearly opened up Peru's political class to historically marginalized groups. The visibility and stature of evangelical,

[21] These included prime minister (Beatriz Merino), finance minister (Mercedes Araoz), interior minister (Pilar Mazzetti), president of congress (Mercedes Cabanillas), and mayor of Lima (Susana Villarán). Others, including Lourdes Flores and Fujimori's daughter, Keiko, emerged as leading contenders for the presidency.

female, and *mestizo* politicians increased markedly under Fujimori. As one *Fujimorista* congressman put it:

The members of the ... opposition are the ones who have always held power. With Fujimori, people like me are in Congress. The opposition would never have allowed me into their ranks because I'm not like them. I'm not white. I'm not from Lima. And I don't have money.[22]

This symbolic inclusion appears to have had a lasting impact on the face of Peruvian politics. Whereas nearly all of the top politicians in Peru were white men drawn from a narrow socio-economic elite prior to 1990, this ceased to be the case after Fujimori. Indeed, the first president elected after Fujimori's fall from power, Alejandro Toledo, was of indigenous descent, and several of the leading contenders for the presidency in the 2000s were non-white (Ollanta Humala), female (Lourdes Flores), or both (Keiko Fujimori).

Overall, then, *Fujimorismo*'s record in terms of political inclusion was mixed. Although Fujimori mobilized the poor electorally, and although his initial victory clearly opened up politics to previously marginal groups, he did little 'to construct institutionalized partisan or corporatist channels' of access for marginalized groups (Roberts 1995: 100). Like many populists, Fujimori was not an institution builder and thus left behind few new mechanisms of popular participation.

Perhaps the clearest manifestation of the limited impact of Fujimori's inclusionary politics was the rise of Ollanta Humala, another populist who nearly captured the presidency in 2006 by appealing to the poor with a promise to bury the political elite in the name of 'authentic' democracy (McClintock 2006b). Humala subsequently won the presidency in 2011, albeit with a less populist appeal. This continued 'demand' for populist candidates suggests that *Fujimorismo* brought little permanent change in the area of political and socio-economic inclusion.

Conclusion

The Peruvian case confirms Mudde and Rovira Kaltwasser's hypothesis that populism in power weakens unconsolidated democracies. Populism in contemporary Latin America is almost always inclusionary, but rarely democratizing. Thus, in line with the editors' introductory propositions, Alberto Fujimori mobilized and gave voice to excluded groups, and his rise to power helped to revitalize public opinion. However, *Fujimorismo* also exhibited many of the negative effects of populism highlighted in

---

[22] Congressional deputy Erland Rodas, interviewed by Liz Mineo, 4 May 1999.

the introduction, including a 'plebiscitary transformation of politics' in which popular majorities are used to undermine checks and balances, minority rights, and other key elements of liberal democracy. More generally, this chapter has argued that in fragile democracies, the ascent to power of populists frequently triggers institutional crisis and, in many cases, a slide into competitive authoritarianism. Although we have focused on the case of Fujimori's Peru, the elective affinity between populism and competitive authoritarianism can be seen in other cases as well, including Argentina under Juan Perón, Venezuela under Hugo Chávez, Ecuador under Lucio Gutiérrez and Rafael Correa, and Bolivia under Evo Morales.

The evidence from Latin America thus suggests that populism is more of a threat than a corrective to democracy. To function as a corrective, Latin American populism would have to emerge in the context of strong liberal democratic institutions. In general, however, populists fare poorly in countries where liberal democratic institutions are strong (e.g. Chile, Costa Rica, Uruguay). Paradoxically, then, democracies strong enough to potentially benefit from populism's corrective effects are unlikely to experience populism, whereas the democracies that experience populism are unlikely to survive it.

9 Populism, democracy, and nationalism in Slovakia

Kevin Deegan-Krause

Introduction

Can populism and democracy co-exist? At first glance the case of Slovakia answers 'no!' Slovakia's democratic institutions suffered during governments commonly regarded as populist and recovered during the governments regarded as anti-populist. This conventional wisdom is not wrong, but it is too simple. A closer look at the case of Slovakia suggests a more subtle relationship between populism, democratic consolidation, and nationalism, which sheds light on all three concepts. The relationships among these three phenomena came into sharpest relief during two governments headed by Vladimír Mečiar during the mid 1990s, but for a full understanding of how populism affected democracy during this period, it is useful to also analyze the governments that came before, between, and since.

The comparisons suggest that the damage to Slovakia's democracy had less to do with the ideological aspects of populism – the discourse of a 'pure people' against a 'corrupt elite' – than with the related (but not identical) ideology of nationalism – in this case one ethnically defined people against another – and with the rejection of institutional limits, which is often related to populism, but is not at the core of the definition used in this volume. To the extent that populism did cause damage to democracy during the mid 1990s, the comparison also suggests – at least in the case of Slovakia – that age and institutionalization of a democracy diminish the negative impacts of populism and related phenomena, and that in the right circumstances the anti-corruption and anti-elite aspects of populism may not produce much damage; in fact, they may even prove beneficial. The case of Slovakia thereby points to the possibility of employing a non-normative understanding of populism and helps to define more clearly the areas in which populism might be expected to support or undermine democracy.

9.1 Measuring populism in Mečiar's Slovakia, 1992–1998

Although Slovakia has often found itself overlooked on the world stage, it has not lacked for scholarly attention. A number of full-length scholarly books and numerous articles detail the political developments of the country using categories that correspond closely to those defined in the first chapter of this volume (Deegan-Krause 2006; Haughton 2005; Henderson 2002; Leff 1997; Williams 2000). The task, then, is not to re-tell the oft-told story of Slovakia's political development, but rather to offer a brief recitation and then to translate the conclusions of those works and other research into specific indicators of populism. Building upon the definition used in this volume, populists will, in particular, (1) downplay differences *within* the category of 'the people'; (2) downplay differences *within* the category 'the elite'; (3) emphasize the moral distinctions *between* 'the people' and 'the elite.'

Following the regime changes in Poland, Hungary, and the Democratic Republic of Germany, Czechoslovakia's Communist Party relinquished its leading role in December 1989, after weeks of street demonstrations throughout the country. It ceded power to civic movements, Civic Forum (OF) in the Czech lands and Public Against Violence (VPN) in Slovakia, which were led by dissidents and experts, as well as some leaders from the 1968 Prague Spring era of reform. In the elections called for June 1990, the OF won a near majority in the Czech lands, with the rest of the votes split between former communists, Christian democrats, and Moravian regionalists, while VPN won about one-third of the Slovak vote, with the remainder split between communists, Christian democrats, and the separatist Slovak National Party (SNS). The civic movements and Christian democrats from both republics worked together to undertake political and economic reforms, but the tripartite structure of parliament proved limiting, as did the fragmentation of both civic movements in 1991. In the election of 1992, Czech votes gave a significant plurality to the Civic Democratic Party (ODS), a free market offspring of OF, while in Slovakia a large plurality of voters opted for the Movement for a Democratic Slovakia (HZDS), an offshoot of VPN that emphasized the need for strengthening Slovakia's place within the Czech and Slovak federation. ODS leader Vaclav Klaus and HZDS leader Vladimír Mečiar quickly negotiated an agreement to sever formal bonds between the two republics on 1 January 1993.

Only one seat short of a parliamentary majority after the 1992 election, Mečiar at first led a one-party HZDS government with support from the SNS, but defections from HZDS in spring 1993 required him to bring SNS into a formal coalition. Further defections from HZDS in spring 1994 put the coalition into the minority and a vote of no confidence brought into power a coalition of Christian democrats, former communists, and the defectors from HZDS. This coalition called new elections in fall 1994, but failed to gain a majority, and Mečiar (again with a significant plurality, though not a near majority) returned to government in coalition with the SNS and the Association of Workers of Slovakia (ZRS), a new left-wing splinter of the former communist party. This coalition governed with Mečiar as prime minister from fall 1994 until the fall 1998 elections, at which time it was again replaced by a government coalition of Christian democrats, former communists, defectors from Mečiar's party, and representatives of Slovakia's Hungarian minority. Elements of that coalition, under Prime Minister Mikuláš Dzurinda, governed from 1998 until 2006, but by that time Mečiar's party had dwindled so significantly that it played only a minor role as a junior coalition partner in the government of Robert Fico and his Direction-Social Democracy (Smer-SD) party. Fico governed from 2006 until 2010 when his coalition lost to a coalition much like Dzurinda's, under the leadership of Iveta Radičová.

Mečiar's governments during the 1990s are the most noteworthy for those interested in the impact of populism because the parties in power were also those that most strongly exhibited the characteristics of populism. Just how much, and in what way, is a question for the sections included later in this chapter, but two distinct summary measures – an analysis of party appeals during each parliamentary term shown in Figure 9.1, and an expert survey of the overall degree of populism during the same time periods shown in Figure 9.2[1] – point to high levels of populist appeals employed by Mečiar's party during the 1990s, and above average levels for its coalition partners SNS and ZRS during the same period.

For both measures the weighted level of populism was higher in the 1992 and 1994 Mečiar governments than for any other Slovak government before or since (though Fico's 2006–10 government comes closer than the others). Even Mečiar himself accepted the term during a 1991 interview, though he gave it a strongly positive connotation:

[Zmena reporter] They say that you are a populist.... Is the current identification of 'populist' with 'Mečiar' correct?

[Mečiar] What is said about populism here is not exactly right. As far as I know, this political direction was always viewed positively. It is not about something pejorative. It is and will be a relationship to the people. (Odbor 1996: 27)

It remains to seen, however, exactly *how* Mečiar's party and governments exhibited their populism. The following sub-sections therefore examine

---

[1] Figure 9.1 presents indicators for a broad range of populism-related appeals – including measures related to the discourse and organizational forms commonly associated with populism – for each party during each parliamentary term between 1992 and 2006. Figure 9.2 aggregates those figures into an average for each government (weighted by relative party size) along with the results of an expert survey that asked scholars of Slovakia's politics to provide their own definition of populism and rate each party during each parliamentary term according to that definition. The results prove nearly identical.

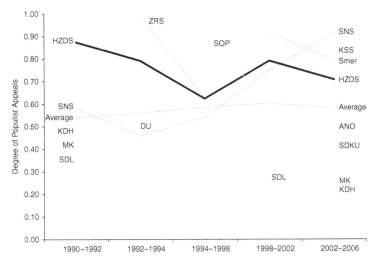

Figure 9.1. Use of populist appeals in Slovakia by Party, 1992–2008.
Source: Deegan-Krause and Haughton (2009).

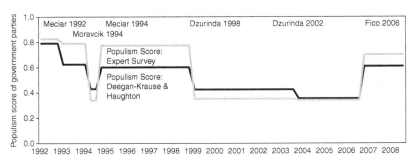

Figure 9.2. Indicators of populism in Slovakia by government, 1992–2008.

Note: Weighted average of government parties.

Sources: Deegan-Krause and Haughton (2008, 2009).

the performance of this government (and others as well, for the sake of comparison) on the specific indicators discussed previously.

9.1.1   *Downplaying differences within the category of 'the people'*

It is almost wholly correct to say that during the 1990s Vladimir Mečiar and his HZDS aimed their political messages directly at a segment of the population it defined as large and homogenous and referred to as 'the people.' Mečiar frequently noted that his party pursued its policies 'solely and exclusively in the interest of the people' (*Slovenská republika*, 15 June 1995) and stressed that 'every member of HZDS must realize that he serves the people' (*Slovenská republika*, 2 December 1996). Yet focusing on Mečiar's relationship toward 'the people' can miss the main underlying dynamic: After 1992, statements by Mečiar and his party about 'the people' referred almost exclusively to 'the *Slovak* people,' a population they defined in ethnic terms.

The specification of 'the people' in terms of a specific ethnic sub-group seems initially to violate the very definition of populism, which depends on homogeneity, but in this case, the 'Slovak people' is large enough to stand in plausibly for the people as a whole. Indeed such 'surrogate' categories for 'the people' are often more useful in populist efforts than 'the people' in generic terms, because the surrogate may also implicitly point to who stands outside of 'the people' (non-believers, capitalists, non-Slovaks). In the case of Slovakia, those who fall outside the definition of 'the Slovak people' can be distinguished from others not only by ethnicity, but by the intervention of 'external forces' on the behalf of non-Slovaks (whereas 'the Slovak people' lacked similar protectors). In the case of ethnic Hungarians, this meant intervention from Hungary; in the case of Roma, this meant intervention by the European Union and international human rights groups.

While in the early months of his public life Mečiar appealed to a wide spectrum of voters as 'one of their own,' an effective, no-nonsense leader who cared about their concerns (Učen 1999), over time he began to narrow his emphasis. As early as 1991, Mečiar acknowledged his use of the national principle as a way of building national unity and diminishing internal differences:

In the current complicated socio-political situation there must exist unity of the government and the people. On what principle should I have, as premier of the Slovak Republic, achieved this unification? I could not distribute social resources because none were available. I also could not leave the people without any alternative. The character of the nation, the character of the republic is always a unifying element, and I therefore returned to it. I always attempted to reach agreement with a wide political spectrum. The unification of this spectrum was in the interest of Slovakia, as well as in the interest of the party or movement. (Odbor 1996: 26)

The ambiguity here between 'the nation' and 'the republic' soon gave way to an almost exclusive emphasis on the *national* dimension, one that appears in the opening line of the new Slovak constitution, drafted in 1992 under Mečiar's leadership: 'We the Slovak nation' (Csergő and Deegan-Krause 2003).

Having shifted from 'the people' to 'the *Slovak* people,' Mečiar intensified his efforts to downplay internal distinctions within the category, appealing across major divides both to communists and to Catholics, to workers and to business owners. Particularly telling is Mečiar's attempt to downplay differences between rich Slovaks and poor ones by explaining his government's insider privatization efforts as an effort to keep firms in *domestic* hands:

Our path was one of creating a domestic entrepreneurial stratum, an attempt to make sure that capital remained home, and so that people, owners of capital, could then by means of the market, advanced technology and investment could enter into other international methods of cooperation. (*Slovensko do toho!*, 6 May 1998)

In defining even wealthy entrepreneurs as 'one of us,' as long as they were domestic, Mečiar offered a consistent vision of a unified people and then sought to enhance that unity by emphasizing the people's plight in the face of a unified 'elite' supported by those outside Slovakia's borders.

9.1.2   *Downplaying differences within the category of 'the elite'*

Defining 'the elite' posed a bigger problem for Mečiar than defining 'the people.' How can a popular prime minister and head of the country's largest party himself avoid the 'elite' label and still apply the elite label to others? The task was relatively easy during Mečiar's periods out of power in 1991–2 and 1994, but those periods were relatively brief. Mečiar's more notable success lay in his ability to sustain the image of an underdog fighting against a unified elite even while he exercised the full power of the state.

The first challenge was to portray his opposition as internally unified. Ironically, Mečiar's own centralization of power actually made this easier by giving his opponents common cause and inspiring previously unlikely forms of cooperation across ideological and ethnic divides; particularly exemplified by the coalition of HZDS defectors, Christian democrats, communists and Hungarians that removed Mečiar from the premiership in 1994 and replaced him in power in 1998. HZDS repeatedly re-emphasized the 'strange bedfellows' motif and characterized the entire opposition as simply 'anti-Mečiar' and 'anti-HZDS' (*Slovensko do toho!*, 18 June 1998), and not without reason (at least while Mečiar remained in power).

The more difficult challenge for Mečiar was to characterize his opposition – parties which together could not muster an electoral majority and lacked access to mass media and privatization-related clientelism – as *elite*. The answer in this case, involved the identification of the opposition parties with external powers. By linking domestic political opponents with larger and more powerful international actors, Mečiar could minimize his own elite status as head of government and claim that the true power – the true elite – was elsewhere.

9.1.3   Emphasize the moral distinctions between 'the people' and 'the elite'

The very principles that Mečiar and his party used to establish the homogeneity of 'the people' and the homogeneity of 'the elite' helped him to draw sharper lines between the groups. Since Mečiar's party emphasized that its opponents, the true 'elites,' had gained their power over Slovakia's societies through their ties to foreign powers – Czechoslovakia, Hungary, foreign investors, the European Union, and the United States – it was easy to identify those elites as disloyal. Mečiar, and especially his allies, thus could – and frequently did – characterize Slovakia's political competition as a *fundamental* conflict about the future of Slovakia fought between the Slovak people and the *anti*-Slovak elite (Deegan-Krause 2006: 219–21).

With such a fundamental distinction, it is hard to imagine that the antagonists would not characterize each other in moral terms. Mečiar himself sought at times to present a neutral face, and at the 1998 national assembly of his party, he announced that 'we do not seek enemies – they are only people with other opinions' (*Slovensko do toho!*, 6 May 1998). But at a party meeting two weeks later, Mečiar's own interior minister, Gustav Krajči, argued that 'at present Slovakia is grappling with a difficult test of vital importance. Will it succeed in its fierce struggle for survival or succumb and become forever the vassal of foreign interests' (*Slovensko do toho!*, 21 May 1998), and HZDS officials repeatedly voiced even sharper criticisms during the election campaign. While Mečiar and his allies did not hesitate to point out policy differences with the opposition, their real emphasis remained corruption, less in the financial sense – the opposition had not been in power long enough to engage in significant personal enrichment – than in the sense of moral decay. According to HZDS deputy Dušan Slobodník, chairman of parliament's foreign affairs committee, the opposition's activities could be characterized as a form of spiritual theft:

We have our own historical memory and will not let ourselves be deprived of it by advocates of Czechoslovakism and the idea of Great Hungary, by cosmopolitans who would like to rob Slovakia of its Christian and national gist. (*Slovensko do toho!*, 22 July 1997)

And according to HZDS parliamentary deputy Roman Hofbauer, opposition efforts stemmed from base motives of dishonesty and malice:

> Our citizens are justified in their asking why we have established our own state, if we do not protect it with a quiet determination as others do. They ask how it is possible that laws are being breached in Slovakia by the dissemination of irredentist ideas, disinformation, and lies about Slovakia, and why nothing is done to defend our truth! They ask what are the Slovak diplomats, both abroad and at home, good for if they do not act quickly and decisively on behalf of our nation and our state. They ask how it is possible that anyone can come to Slovakia at any time and spew his anti-Slovak hate, anti-Slovak lies, and anti-Slovak racism as much as he likes in the name of a fictitious cosmopolitanism and Pan-Europeanism. (*Slovenská republika*, May 1996)

The discourse used by Mečiar and his party thus closely resembles the behaviour that can be expected of a populist, but with a specific national flavour. So strong, in fact, was the emphasis on an ethnically defined Slovak people in conflict with rival ethnic groups and de-ethnicized cosmopolitans, that its uniquely populist elements are fairly obscure. The key difference lay not in Mečiar's moral tone or his assertion of the homogeneity of protagonists and antagonists, elements that many variants of nationalism and populism share, but in the identification of opponents as elite, rather than equal or inferior. Mečiar demonstrated a remarkable capacity to label his national opponents as privileged even when they were languishing in opposition, and to transform international sympathy for his opponents into a potential source of domestic oppression. The populist elements that Mečiar introduced into his party's nationalism thus allowed him to transcend ordinary nationalist appeals and magnify the severity of the potential threat. By the same token, the element of *international* threat that he introduced into his party's populism allowed him to identify himself with 'the people' even at the height of his domestic political power.

In light of this close inter-connection between Mečiar's nationalism and his populism, many analysts of Slovakia – including this author – have avoided the ambiguity and pejorative connotations of populism[2] and emphasized Mečiar's nationalism, but the framework chapter's precise and neutral definition makes the choice largely unnecessary. Mečiar's political behaviour followed both nationalist and populist patterns, with populism most prominent in the first year of HZDS, before the 1992

---

[2] My own 2006 book on the question of Mečiar uses the word *populism* only twice, both times as quoting others (and sceptically so). Haughton (2005) uses *populist/ism* three times, twice in quotations and only once in minor point by the author himself. Henderson (2002) uses the word only twice, Leff (1997) only three times, and Nedelsky (2009) only four times in minor roles.

election, and afterwards settling into its mutually dependent relationship with nationalism.

The framework chapter and other scholarship on the 'thin-centred' nature of populism make it clear that this kind of relationship is not unexpected and that populism's narrow range allows it to attach easily to other ideologies. The example of Slovakia helps to make it clear why such attachment is not only possible, but sometimes necessary. As an ideology of moral opposition to those in power, populism is ill-suited for *wielding* power. When populists find themselves in office, they must either find a new rationale for their political necessity ('keeping the old elites from returning' will only work for so long) or find a compelling explanation for why elected office does not shape the country's destiny. As an essentially *political* ideology, populism in office must therefore have a partner ideology that points outside the purely political realm towards other factors such as economics or ethnicity that prevent those in office from actually taking power into their own hands and becoming 'the elite.' Only by pointing outside the domestic political realm can populists continue to occupy political positions without losing their anti-elite appeal.

Mečiar, for his part, was adept at both the discourse of the populist underdog and of the defender of the nation, and he used each to shore up weaknesses in the other. Slovakia experienced a nationalist populism not in the sense of all-encompassing indictment against Mečiar commonly used by scholars during the 1990s (see for example Carpenter 1997), but in the very specific sense of an ideological appeal to re-take power now held by elites outside the boundaries of one's own ethnic group. This clears the way for the deeper question asked in this volume: To the extent that populism played a role in Slovakia's politics, how did it affect the development of democracy?

9.2   Assessing populism's impact in Mečiar's Slovakia, 1992–1998

The framework chapter's six positive and six negative aspects of populism can be conveniently sub-divided into five general categories of behaviours. Three of these relate to the nature of populist political competition. According to these hypotheses, populists may (a) seek a new basis for political competition, related to its distinctive (if thin-centred) ideology (Positive #4 and #5; Negative #3); (b) mobilize and represent excluded groups (Positive #1, #2, and #3); and (c) introduce a higher degree of intensity in political competition (Positive #6; Negative #4). It also poses hypotheses about the populist relationship to political institutions. While rejecting its definitional aspect, Mudde and Rovira Kaltwasser posit 'a logical connection to certain types of mobilization (e.g. charismatic leadership, direct communication leader to masses, suspicion of strong party organizations).' Accordingly, populists (d) may advocate for popular sovereignty and employ plebiscitarian mechanisms at the expense of institutional restraints (Negative #1 and #5). Finally, the framework chapter's list of harms speculates about another potential impact of populism, which goes beyond its definitional rejection of the political elite in favour of the people, to include rejection of the preferences of 'minorities,' which may or may not be identical with the minority constituted by the elite. Populists, according to this final potential indicator, (e) may use the notion and practice of majority rule to circumvent and ignore minority rights (Negative #2).

To understand the role of populism as harm or corrective in Slovakia (and thereby perhaps to understand its underlying dynamics), it is useful to consider whether Mečiar's populism produced any of the specified positive or negative behaviours, and whether these in turn had the predicted effects beneficial or harmful to Slovakia's democracy.

9.2.1   A new basis for political competition

Mečiar's creation of HZDS was itself an effort to change the fundamental basis of Slovakia's political competition, and his success shaped Slovakia's subsequent political life (though it also subsequently locked HZDS into that basis of competition and diminished its subsequent populist potential). HZDS began its political life by explicitly sidestepping the ideological and personality conflicts between anti-communists and communist and focusing instead on efficiency and responsiveness to popular needs (Učen 1999). The party quickly supplemented this shift with a call for a stronger constitutional position of Slovakia within Czechoslovakia, in a way that raised the national question without endorsing either independence or the status quo (Leff 1997) and allowed Mečiar to label both former dissidents and former communists as 'Czechoslovak.'

The party's search ability to move on to *new* bases of competition declined significantly after Slovakia achieved independence, however, as the party invested its identity building into the 'pro-Slovak' pole of the national dimension. That pole allowed room for minor shifts – particularly its attempt to link previously disparate 'Czechoslovak,' 'Hungarian,' and 'European' attitudes under the 'anti-Slovak' or 'anti-national' label (Deegan-Krause 2004) – but the party made no subsequent efforts at a radical shift in the basis of competition after 1992, effectively ceding the territory to a series of new parties that tried to shift competition from national issues to other dimensions.

Mečiar's populist attempt to re-frame political issues along a national dimension had a profound effect on Slovakia's political competition and indirectly affected its democracy. He realized the potential of the national dimension for drawing support and then mobilized nationally oriented voters so effectively that national questions dominated elections through the early 2000s (and returned again in the early 2010s). For a decade all governing coalitions included parties of the socio-economic left, right, and centre and for two decades, Slovakia's governments alternated between the two ends of the national spectrum, with no instances of parties crossing the line separating the two groupings. This in itself produced neither threat nor corrective, but simply a change in the kind of coalition and the nature of the cleavage that dominated the country's political competition.

The more consequential effect for Slovakia's democracy can be seen in the other ideological characteristics of the coalitions. Whereas a divide between socio-economic left and right might have saddled Mečiar with coalition partners unwilling to undermine Slovakia's democracy, the national dimension presented him in 1994 with two weak and relatively small coalition partners, which cooperated with his nearly successful efforts to dismantle horizontal (and eventually vertical) accountability in Slovakia (Deegan-Krause 2006, 76–9; Haughton 2005). It is difficult, however, to attribute this outcome to populism itself. The populist impulse that may have led Mečiar in early 1991 to strike out along a new dimension did not foreordain the authoritarian coalition of late 1994. It is likely that the ability to select among multiple dimensions increased his ability to justify authoritarian measures, at least compared to his counterparts in the Czech Republic (Deegan-Krause 2006), but the ability to make that choice had as much to do with Slovakia's underlying demographic heterogeneity as with Mečiar's populist entrepreneurship.

9.2.2   *Mobilizing and representing excluded groups*

The 'inclusion effect' of populism is hard to assess in Slovakia. It seems relatively minor in impact, but is closely related to the dimensions of political competition. During the period of Mečiar's political emergence, Slovakia's voters went to the polls in extremely large numbers (nearly eighty-five per cent), with high levels of participation cutting across ethnic, religious, economic, age, and regional lines. Since the demographics of Mečiar's 1992 supporters almost perfectly matched the demographics of the voting population as a whole (FOCUS 1990–2000), he does not appear at that time to have mobilized any particular demographically defined group. In 1994 and 1998 the groups that tended to favour his party were the elderly and rural constituencies that were already slightly overrepresented in the electorate as a whole.

A stronger claim can be made that Mečiar and his party did represent otherwise unvoiced *attitudes* and unchampioned policy options. In 1990 those who sought independence could vote comfortably for the Slovak National Party (SNS), but there was at the time no major party that articulately supported an option 'between [the status quo] and independence,' a position that consistently corresponded to the preferences of a quarter of the Slovak population (FOCUS 1992–2000; Academy of Sciences of the Czech Republic 1992–1998). Mečiar filled this gap by calling for a loose confederation between Czechs and Slovaks. While he worked hard to achieve this middle course, he ultimately found it necessary to choose one of the two extremes and opted for independence. The eventual separation of the two republics was welcomed more strongly by supporters of SNS than by those of Mečiar's own party (FOCUS 1992–2000), and the outcome limited his party's impact on the representation of excluded opinions about Slovakia's status. Furthermore, with the resolution of the independence question, the efforts of HZDS to seek out new groups or new opinions came more or less to a close, limiting the inclusion-related benefits to Slovakia's democracy from HZDS.

9.2.3   *Introducing a higher degree of intensity into political competition*

Because Mečiar engaged in intense political competition from his first days in public life early in the post-communist period, it is difficult to judge the degree to which he contributed to the intensity overall. It is safe to say that Mečiar always generated strong feelings. At first, these were almost uniformly positive, but within two years they had become widely split between active supporters and active opponents. It is likely, though difficult to demonstrate statistically, that Mečiar's polarizing effect helps to explain rates of voter turnout in Slovakia, which were significantly higher than the regional average (Cześnik 2009). But to the extent that turnout rates were already high, and that many voters turned out in 1994 and 1998 because they feared Mečiar's return to power, it is difficult to see this as an unambiguous positive outcome of his populism.

The polarization linked to Mečiar's nationally charged populism *did* arguably have a negative effect on democratic decision making in terms of consensus building, but for reasons quite different than those hypothesized in the framework chapter. In Slovakia's unicameral parliamentary democracy, the problem of gridlock did not emerge, and as the following sections indicate, the bigger problem related to the *ease* of decision making by whichever side of the polarized political field held a majority. This consequence, however, related far more closely to questions of institutional manipulation than to those of electoral competition discussed here.

In contrast to Mečiar's relatively harmless and increasingly infrequent use of populist electoral appeals, his attacks on Slovakia's institutional framework had a direct negative impact on Slovakia's democracy, and the severity of that problem increased over time. It is less clear, however, that this institutional manipulation can be attributed to populism.

9.2.4   *Advocating popular sovereignty and plebiscitarian mechanisms*

Mečiar and his HZDS nearly reversed Slovakia's democratic transition and consolidation. Numerous studies of Slovakia demonstrate that Mečiar pursued the systematic elimination of institutional restraints, particularly after his return to the premiership in late 1994 (Deegan-Krause 2006; Haughton 2005; Henderson 2002). He systematically marginalized the role of the opposition within parliament and oversight bodies, placed limits on the presidency, and undermined the independence of the police, prosecutors, and courts. In the public realm the explanations for these institutional encroachments followed the plebiscitarian pattern of a leader who 'embodies the "will of the people"' and whose decisions should not be 'bogged down in multiple layers of institutions (occupied by the political class) that are likely to misconstrue, ignore or delay effective representation' (Barr 2009: 40).

Long before Mečiar's party newspaper published the striking headline 'National Interests into the Hands of the Strongest Man' (*Nový deň*, 18 May 2001), party statements frequently emphasized sentiments like those of a group of HZDS-appointed regional officials that 'The pressure exerted by [the president] and the opposition does not permit full concentration on work for the benefit of developing sovereign Slovakia' (*Slovensko do toho!*, 21 November 1995). Mečiar himself emphasized the need for decisive leadership without the 'sick element' of the constitutional court (Innes 2001: 266) and criticized the 'continuing attempts by certain opposition parties and movements, and also by the president of the Republic, to destroy the political system in Slovakia' (*Slovensko do toho!*, 21 December 1995).

A nearly identical pattern of focus on Mečiar's personal leadership, at the expense of intermediaries, also emerged within his own party. While HZDS initially possessed a fairly wide range of prominent personalities, each with their own bases of support, the party saw a steady exodus of top-level elites, some departing of their own will and some expelled by the party (Deegan-Krause 2006: 88–97). New personalities emerged to fill the gap, but they depended heavily on Mečiar's favour for their positions (and even so many eventually left the party). At lower levels, Mečiar established direct personal ties to party activists, even to the extent of remembering their birthdays and the names of their children (Krause 2000: 257). And more than any other leader in Slovakia at the time, he sought out opportunities to communicate directly with party supporters through weekly newsletters and monthly rallies. Mečiar thereby managed the unusual feat of constructing strong and capable party institutions while maintaining plebiscitary leadership's characteristic 'absence of group autonomy within the movement' (Rybař and Deegan-Krause 2009: 42).

9.2.5   Emphasizing majority rule

In a manner consistent with their rejection of institutional constraints, Mečiar and his party adopted an increasingly vehement insistence on the absolute right of the majority. This mode of argument applied both to arguments about the rights of political majorities and ethnic majorities. On political questions Mečiar's party rejected participation claims by opposition parties: In 1994, for example, Mečiar removed opposition representatives from numerous oversight bodies and parliamentary commissions and reacted to opposition complaints by responding 'The elections are over, get used to it' (*Sme* 1994). On ethnic questions, the party ascribed to the ethnic Slovak population the unique position of the 'state-forming' nation of Slovaks and explicitly rejected the possibility of minority rights in favour of 'individual rights,' which would function in practice as majority Slovak rule (Csergo and Deegan-Krause 2011).

The institutional arguments relating to plebiscitary and majority rule appear to offer a strong cautionary tale about the dangers posed by populism. However, it is important to remember that although these plebiscitary elements appear in a wide variety of definitions of populism (e.g. Roberts 2008; Weyland 2001), the definition of this volume suggests a closer look at the causal connections between these manifestations and the core definition involving mass-elite antagonism. In that sense, it is hard to draw a necessary connection between Mečiar's antagonism towards the domestic opposition and its international supporters with his systematic encroachments. Of course, a leader who faces a significant and disloyal opposition may adopt extreme measures, but it is far easier to find evidence of opposition disarray than of opposition plots, and the populist anti-elite rhetoric is better understood as rationale than as genuine reason. Evidence points to the resonance of this rationale, at least for a particular class of voters (Deegan-Krause 2006: 185–90), and its effectiveness provides the strongest argument for the negative institutional effects of populism per se (though it must share that responsibility with the nationalism with which it was intertwined).

The weakness of any genuine causal connection between Mečiar's national anti-elitism and his institutional encroachments is fairly apparent in light of the consequences of those encroachments. To centralize power in the hands of the prime minister, at the expense of all other potential institutional rivals, is certainly a risky move if there was actually any chance that the country would soon be run by a government of mercenary anti-Slovaks subservient to foreign interests (Gould and Krause 1998). It is also worth noting that when confronted with hostile *majorities*, Mečiar and his party found it appropriate to adopt *anti*-plebiscitarian positions. Before the split of Czechoslovakia, Mečiar sought equal standing for Slovakia, rather than a unitary state that would have favoured the majority population of Czechs, and his party likewise rejected a referendum on the future status of Slovakia, which might – depending on the phrasing of the question – have produced a preference for a common state. In 1997 Mečiar and his party similarly rejected the notion of direct popular election of the president (an election the party feared it might lose) as well the notion of a referendum to decide on the direct presidential election question. In June of that year the party's efforts to stop the change overstepped legal boundaries, as Mečiar's minister of the interior violated election protocols to print and distribute referendum ballots that simply omitted the presidential election question altogether (Deegan-Krause 2006: 52–7).

These changing stances suggest that Mečiar used plebiscitarian mechanisms in a purely instrumental manner, emphasizing them only when they served his political needs and rejecting them when they limited his power. Underneath Mečiar's intertwined populism and nationalism was a win-at-all-costs reluctance to accept basic political rules and a willingness to use any political discourse that would contribute to a victorious outcome. Populist discourse on the problems of institutional intermediation provided a publicly acceptable rationale for Mečiar's efforts at political control – much as his populist emphasis on the opposition's assistance from international elites allowed him to raise the stakes of his national appeals – but it does not appear to have provided the motivation. Populism and nationalism together supported the goals of Mečiar's more fundamental impulse (perhaps ideology, perhaps merely mentality): a soft authoritarianism that rejected any exertion of accountability over the party leader, whether by minority *or* by majority.

9.3   Evaluating populism's impact beyond mečiar

Case studies are invitations not only to think deeply about a single set of circumstances, but also to think about the kinds of questions that we should ask when we look at other cases. Leaving cross-border comparisons for the editors of this volume, it is nevertheless useful to go beyond the case of Mečiar to see if the country's other governments confirm populism's relatively mild and indirect negative impact on democracy. Particularly useful in this regard is a comparison between Mečiar's governments and the government of Robert Fico between 2006 and 2010. The comparison is an appealing one, not only because Fico's government included Mečiar's HZDS (as a very junior partner, much reduced in size from its earlier days) as well as SNS, but also because observers inside Slovakia and abroad freely applied the label 'populist' to Fico and his government (Krastev 2007; Lewis 2008). Many even accused Fico of following directly in Mečiar's early footsteps (Bútora et al. 2009).

Initial evidence suggests that at least in terms of Fico's use of populist discourse, the analogy is entirely appropriate. Figure 9.2 shows that the Fico government ranked only slightly below the Mečiar governments on a broad-based definition of populist appeals (Deegan-Krause and Haughton 2009) and in the perceptions of experts on Slovakia's politics using a variety of definitions (Deegan-Krause and Haughton 2008).[3] The definition from the framework chapter of this volume describes Fico more closely than it does Mečiar. Fico's government identified a 'people' that theoretically encompassed virtually the entire population and was defined by its lack of access to the spoils of political power, lumping together all past elites and judging them sharply for their lack of concern for ordinary citizens (arguing, for example, that Dzurinda's government was as corrupt as Mečiar's had been). Like Mečiar, Fico eventually narrowed his definition of 'the people' according to specific qualities; though, unlike Mečiar, Fico began with socio-economic criteria and only later moved in an ethnic Slovak direction.

Yet despite the similarities, Fico's populism did not coincide with a significant erosion of democracy. It is true that the Fico government interfered with the independence of the judiciary, imposed restrictions on the use of the Hungarian language, and exhibited significant corruption. But unlike Mečiar Fico did not pose a fundamental threat to Slovakia's basic democratic institutions. Polity and Freedom House scores are hardly perfect indicators, but they do provide an acceptable

---

[3] The scores reflect the average of populism scores during the period in question, weighted by parties' share of seats in government.

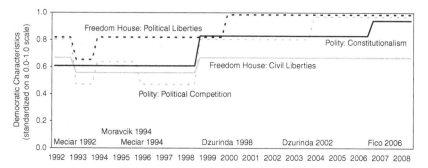

Figure 9.3. Indicators of democracy in Slovakia, 1992–2008.
Sources: Freedom House (2009), Polity (2009).

baseline for quantifying what we already know. Unlike the populism of the early 1990s, which went in tandem with a rise in various indicators of non-democracy, similar levels of populism under Fico produced no similar decline in democracy (see Figure 9.3).[4]

A broader look at all of Slovakia's governments during its independence suggests a similar pattern. Table 9.1 sorts Slovakia's post-communist governments on the axes used in the framework chapter for the whole volume. The table shows that Slovakia itself experienced the full array of combinations of populist governing status and democratic consolidation addressed by the volume as a whole, and appends to percentage point changes in an index of five quantitative indicators of democracy, two from Freedom House (political liberties and civil liberties) and three from Polity (democracy, constitutionalism, and political competition). The array shows in an approximate way that declines in Slovakia's scores happened exclusively during Mečiar's two governments, while all other governments saw increases.

In line with the hypotheses of the framework chapter, the table suggests that populism threatened Slovakia's democracy when populists were in government and when democracy was still unconsolidated. In the case of Slovakia, declines in the quality of democracy only occurred when *both* conditions were present.

Of course, given the limited number of cases, and especially the small number of governments with declining scores, it can be argued that Slovakia's declines were not caused in general terms by governing populists in an unconsolidated democracy, but rather by the specific efforts

---

[4] The 2009 Freedom House report did note problems, but not enough to change the country's scores from dual 1s (the best possible score).

Table 9.1. *Relationship by strength of populism and democracy in Slovakia with average percentage change in democracy-related scores during governmental term*

Populism Democracy	Government	Opposition
Consolidated	2006–2010 (Fico): +05	2010– (Radičová): No data 2002–2006 (Dzurinda II): +03
Unconsolidated	1994–1998 (Mečiar III): −03 1993–1994 (Mečiar II): −14	1998–2002 (Dzurinda I): +18 1994 (Moravčik): +06

Sources: Freedom House (2009), Polity (2009).

of Mečiar, who combined populism and nationalism in the service of specifically authoritarian goals, which other populists (including, perhaps, Fico) did not share. It may also be true that even if Fico's populism was as dangerous to democracy as Mečiar's, Slovakia had changed in the meantime in such a way as to render its democracy more resilient. The country that Fico undertook to govern in 2006 was different from the one Mečiar began to lead fourteen years earlier, particularly because of eight years of government by parties with extremely low levels of populist appeals.

The differences are clearer when one disentangles the various realms of democratic competition involved in populist appeals. At least five of these can be distinguished:

- *Majority-Minority Relations.* Populists build their appeals around the idea that political power has fallen into the hands of a distinct minority – often an economic or ethnic minority – whereas their opponents often raise the spectre of power in the hands of the irresponsible masses. As the previous discussion suggests, the key minority emphasized by Slovakia's populists was the 'foreign population,' particularly the Hungarian ethnic minority. Whereas 'Hungarians in government' offered Mečiar an easy scare tactic, Fico took office after eight years of Hungarian parties in important ministries. Although Dzurinda's coalition between Slovaks and Hungarians never lacked for internal struggles, it was reasonably successful in achieving its ends and Slovakia had not moved appreciably in the direction of Hungarian secession. Most Slovaks thus developed a sense that Hungarians did not threaten the fundamental project of Slovakia's independence.
- *Accountability.* Populists frequently seek to create a relationship between the people and their elected leader, whose power is shielded from the interference of other institutions with a less direct electoral

mandate, whereas the opponents of populists fear the excesses that might be committed as a result and prefer more indirect, institutional mechanisms. Mečiar significantly weakened the horizontal, institutional constraints on leadership, but the government that followed him, while far from perfect, made few institutional encroachments and actually created some rival institutional mechanisms (an ombudsman and a directly elected presidency) and accepted the European Union as a potential constant. When Fico took office in 2006 he could thus make stronger claims than Mečiar that 'real power' lay elsewhere, and at the same time could act on those claims without as great a risk of destabilizing the balance of power within the political system.

- *Party System Institutionalization.* Populists frequently cite the institutionalization of a party system as a restriction on the voice of the people, while the opponents of populism fear the instability that emerges from high volatility. Mečiar's party emerged as part of an enormous wave of party reconfigurations that followed the demise of the anti-communist umbrella movement VPN. Those waves kept coming in subsequent elections, but they were never quite as large, and although Slovakia's party system in 2006 could not be said to have fully stabilized, the election that brought Fico into government was also the first in Slovakia's short history in which no new parties gained election to parliament. While the tight centralization of Fico's government raised questions about the ebb and flow of his supporters if he should be forced from the political scene, the system by 2006 was better able to absorb the volatility.

- *Elite Circulation.* Populists warn the public against the rise of an elite class that controls political power and uses that control to siphon off public resources for partisan or personal gain. The opponents of populism, by contrast, fear that new elites will disrupt an effective system and may in turn use their newfound positions to feather their own nests. Mečiar's elevation to prime minister in 1994 marked the fifth change in that position in four years and he justified the fears of the anti-populists with a spectacularly obvious sell-off of state property to party supporters and donors. But Mečiar's removal in 1998 did not fully solve the problem and justified populist warnings about persistent corruption in the form of chronic (and profitable) irregularities in public contracts. Although Fico's 2002 campaign slogan, 'As They Stole under Mečiar, So They Steal under Dzurinda,' was technically incorrect (the scope and scale of corruption was smaller under Dzurinda than under Mečiar), Fico's emphasis on removing corrupt elites held at least the promise of improved governance. That

Fico's government did not fix the problem, especially in the area of entrenched corruption, relates more to the choices of the Fico government than to populism's *potential* corrective role in identifying and ameliorating corruption.

* *Intensity of Competition.* Populists point to the problem of voter apathy and disenchantment, whereas the opponents of populists raise fears about political competition that is too broad and too passionate. Mečiar inflamed new passions on top of those that remained from the political changes of 1989 and the split of Czechoslovakia, but passions began to dwindle during Mečiar's third term, and voter participation showed significant declines. Fico sought to gain office by bringing frustrated voters back into the electorate, and for a time the party even used the label 'The Third Way' as a way of attracting those disillusioned by the failures of the Mečiar and Dzurinda governments. These efforts did not counter the overall decline in turnout which did not end until 2010, and in that election the slight uptick in turnout may have been driven by opposition to Fico and *his* coalition's corruption.

In nearly every one of these categories Slovakia's conditions between 1992 and 2006 moved away from the populist norm (the extremes most feared by elites and other anti-populists) and towards relationships that were more institutionalized but (perhaps as a result) seemingly less responsive to the voices of ordinary citizens. Not only did the Fico government have more space to use populist manifestations without causing problems for Slovakia's democracy, in several areas the balance had actually shifted to the point that populism could serve as a *corrective*, particularly in the areas of corruption, policy responsiveness, and popular mobilization.

These five aspects suggest that the general ability of populism to threaten or correct democratic development depends heavily on the context in which those actions take place. By this understanding, populism does not have an inherently negative or positive impact on democracy, except to the extent that it moves a system towards the extreme. Whether a manifestation of populism helps or hinders democracy usually depends on the degree to which democracy is already securely in place.

The question of 'majority-minority relations' provides a useful example. As Mudde and Rovira Kaltwasser point out, the ambivalence of the relationship is directly related to the internal contradiction of liberal democracy, that is, the tension between the democratic promise of majority rule and the reality of constitutional protection of minority

Realm of contestation	Anti-populist extreme (What populists fear)	Populist extreme (What anti-populists fear)
Majority-minority relations	Tyranny of the minority	Tyranny of the majority
Accountability	Institutional but not electoral	Electoral but not institutional
Party system institutionalization	Stalemate or domination	Political instability
Elite circulation	Too little, yielding corruption	Too much, yielding inexperience
Intensity of competition	Apathy	Unrest

Impact of populism	Populist impulse	
	Populism as corrective	Populism as threat

Figure 9.4. Model of contextual influence on populism's potential for threat or correction.

rights. Since populism is clearly on the side of majority rule, the emergence of populist rule in an already majoritarian polity might threaten democracy itself. But, as the graphic in Figure 9.4 suggests, the majoritarian efforts of populists in a polity on the other end of the spectrum might actually help to redress the balance and protect democracy. Nor is majoritarianism the only aspect of democracy for which the impact of populism depends upon context.

Democracy depends on many balances of competing goods, many 'Goldilocks' variables' that cause problems if their values are too large *or* too small, and nearly all manifestations of populism affect at least one of these. Admittedly, excess in one direction may be less likely or less dangerous for some characteristics than for others, but even in seemingly obvious cases (such as 'full suffrage') there are limits to inclusion in age and comprehension beyond which democracies see dangers (and those limits were much greater and with much worry only a century ago when 'too much suffrage' was a genuine fear).

With the sole possible exception of Slovak-Czech relationships in Czechoslovakia, Mečiar moved the country away from the midpoint and towards the populist extreme. When Fico took power Slovakia had already pulled back from Mečiar-era extremes and lay closer to the opposite extreme. As a result, some of Fico's efforts actually pushed Slovakia *towards* the more democratic midpoint while others pushed beyond toward the populist extreme but from a much safer starting point.

Conclusion

With a better understanding of populism's dynamics and its interaction with context, we can finally begin to better understand the complex relationship between populism and democracy. The framework chapter's hypotheses about the impact of populism derive from two independent sets of conditions: the impact of populist participation in government and the degree of consolidation of democracy. The case of Slovakia is quite consistent with the framework chapter's hypotheses and offers some additional useful insights.

While there are probably few who doubt that government status affects the impact of populism, Figure 9.2 provides useful experimental evidence to compare the effect of populists in and out of government in Slovakia; particularly the comparison between the Mečiar governments and their immediate predecessors and successors. Since the parties' levels of public support and organization did not vary much across this period, shifts in the quality of democracy can be attributed in general to the actions of those *in government.*, and in particular to the specific actions taken by Mečiar's second and third governments (though this chapter suggests that Mečiar's ability to harm democracy had relatively little to do with the degree of his *populism.*)

The framework chapter's hypotheses regarding the relationship between populism and democratic consolidation are even more interesting, and evidence from Slovakia suggests that the variable is well chosen. Each of the five contextual conditions discussed in this chapter relate in some way to the consolidation of democracy. The contexts in which populism is most dangerous to democracy are those directly related to the creation of stable institutions, which counter the push of populism (depicted as left-to-right movement in Figure 9.4). This has two parallel effects: The first is to increase the need for populism as a corrective to overly restrictive institutions, and the second is to decrease the risks related to a populist correction. The further a country moves to the toward full institutionalization of democracy, the more populism it may need and the more it can actually afford without risking its democracy (though not without personal risk to those outside the category of 'the people'). The experience of Austria and other western European countries suggests that voters in overinstitutionalized contexts may opt for new parties to break political deadlock and inject new energy into the system, even though doing so sometimes means accepting the targeting of particular ethnic or social groups. The experience of Slovakia suggests that populism in underinstitutionalized (new) democracies may obey a different logic. The anti-elite appeals of populism did attract voters even in the weakly consolidated conditions of Slovakia in the early 1990s, intensifying Mečiar's primary appeal as the defender against dangers from *outsiders*, whether international, ethnic Hungarian, or disloyal Slovaks. But populism-fortified nationalism was not invincible, and Slovakia offers the encouraging message that citizens can become aware of populism's limits and that sometimes the voice of the people can recall government from the brink of populist-induced collapse.

10 Populism: corrective *and* threat to democracy

Cas Mudde and Cristóbal Rovira Kaltwasser

Introduction

Populism stands in tension with (liberal) democracy. In the opening chapter of this volume, we maintained that in order to understand this tension, it is necessary to move from theoretical discussions to empirical studies and demonstrate in concrete cases the ways in which populism can be a threat and/or a corrective for democracy. The chapters of this edited volume offer a rich basis for such analysis. Accordingly, in this concluding chapter, we provide a first analysis with the aim of assessing and rethinking the ambivalent relationship between populism and democracy. Particular emphasis will be given to identifying aspects that, on the one hand, might appear only in certain regional contexts, and on the other hand, might be present in diverse geographic and socio-political settings.

Without a doubt, both populism and democracy are today widespread in different parts of the world. This consequently begs the question whether the impact of populism on democracy is determined by the regional context or by generic factors. In other words, is populism related to specific factors that might be well more pressing in certain world regions than in others? At the same time, it can be argued that particular aspects of the relationship between populism and democracy go beyond regional particularities. For instance, populist forces always promote the repoliticization of certain topics, which either intentionally or unintentionally are not being addressed by the establishment.

In line with this cross-regional and intra-regional perspective, this concluding chapter draws upon the eight case studies of this edited volume and is structured in three sections. In the first section we turn our attention to the concepts and hypotheses developed in the theoretical framework, developed in Chapter 1, in order to assess their validity. Then, in the second section, we proceed from 'the empirics' to 'the theory;' that is, we present new insights on the basis of the eight case studies. Finally, in the last section, we propose lines of inquiry for further research on populism and democracy.

10.1   Assessing the concepts and hypotheses developed in the framework

The framework developed for this edited volume is based on Sartori's (1970) conceptual approach. We proposed minimal concepts of both populism and democracy, since this increases conceptual clarity, avoids conceptual stretching, and enables the cross-regional approach of this book. Indeed, Europe (both West and East) as well the Americas (both North and South) differ at many levels, which makes the comparison of the relationship between populism and democracy in these world regions a difficult task. In this sense, the use of minimal concepts has proven to be very valuable, because it has permitted us to 'travel' across different cases and even geographical areas.

As is well known, the downside of minimal definitions is that they do not provide enough analytical depth to distinguish relevant aspects of a common phenomenon (Keman 2009: 77). For instance, in this book it has been argued that quite dissimilar leaders, such as Vladimír Mečiar in Slovakia and Andrés Manuel López Obrador in Mexico, should be regarded as populist. Of course, both leaders are quite different in terms of their respective policy agendas and political aims, but they share an important commonality, which allows us to analyse them under the same conceptual umbrella. This means that the proposed minimal definition of populism must be seen as a starting point, based on which it is possible to (a) determine if particular cases might be considered as examples of populism or not; and (b) study to what extent, and in which aspects, particular cases of populism differ. Specifically, the proposed minimal definition of populism can be used for identifying two types of populism: exclusionary populism in Europe and inclusionary populism in Latin America (Mudde and Rovira Kaltwasser 2011).

In a similar vein, we consider Dahl's (1971) minimal definition of democracy as a crucial benchmark upon which a distinction between authoritarian and democratic regimes can be drawn. At the same time, this concept is useful for hypothesizing about the ambivalent relationship between populism and democracy. As we stated in the framework, populism can be seen as positive for democracy in terms of improving 'inclusiveness' and negative with regard to 'public contestation.' Do the case studies of the edited volume confirm or reject this thesis? Generally speaking, the evidence presented in this volume supports this argument. Both in Europe and the Americas populist actors seek to give voice and power to marginalized groups, but they also tend to combat the very existence of oppositional forces and transgress the rules of political competition (Rovira Kaltwasser 2012).

The way in which particular expressions of populism define 'the pure people' and 'the corrupt elite' determine the type and degree of inclusiveness that is promoted. In the words of Mouffe: 'What is problematic is not the reference to "the people." (...) The problem lies in the way in which this "people" is constructed' (2005a: 69). For example, in relatively affluent and egalitarian societies (such as the cases of Austria, Belgium, Canada, the Czech Republic, and Slovakia described in this edited volume) populist actors are prone to define 'the people' in ethnical terms, and in consequence, they reserve the notion of political participation to the native population. By contrast, in relatively poor societies (such as the cases of Mexico, Peru, and Venezuela) populist forces usually define the 'the people' as the socio-economic underdog, and therefore, they seek to promote the inclusion of vast groups which are objectively and subjectively excluded from society. Beyond this important difference, it is worth stressing a significant similarity that we find in all the chapters of the book: Populism's lack of respect of public contestation derives from its monist conception of society. Indeed, populism draws upon a Manichean distinction between the 'the pure people' and 'the corrupt elite,' which leaves little space for pluralism (de la Torre 2000; Hawkins 2009; Mudde 2004).

According to Dahl's minimal definition, real existing democracies differ on many levels. Hence, it is not surprising that scholars normally propose, either implicitly or explicitly, an expanded concept of democracy in order to differentiate between 'low quality' and 'high quality' democratic regimes. Against this backdrop, we were not only interested in studying the impact of populism on democracy as such, but also, and mainly, in the negative and positive effects that populism can have on the quality of democracy. This distinction is not trivial. There is an important difference between referring to a 'democracy *without* adjectives' and 'the quality of democracy.' While the former alludes primarily to majority rule and popular sovereignty, the latter indicate achievements or failures in relation to the model of *liberal* democracy.

Based on the case studies examined in this volume, a first general observation to be made is that populists usually mention and exploit a tension between two dimensions of the quality of democracy: They criticize the poor *results* of the democratic regime and, to solve this problem, they campaign for a modification of the democratic *procedures*. Put in another way, populists tend to claim that the rule of law and the 'checks and balances' anchored in the constitution not only limit the capacity of 'the people' to exercise their collective power, but also give rise to a growing discontent with the political system. This explains why populist actors normally favour, at least in theory, plebiscites and other forms of direct democracy.

The latter is conceived of as an appropriate method to give back power to the people and avoid the gap between the governors and the governed (Canovan 2005: 107). However, this does not mean that populism is at odds with democratic representation per se. It is more accurate to say that populism is against the alleged 'misuse' of the channels of democratic representation and to circumscribe the latter only to periodical elections. From this angle, populism can be seen as a sort of democratic extremism, in the sense that it is particularly suspicious of all kinds of unelected bodies, which are becoming increasingly powerful today (Vibert 2007).

It is not a coincidence that populist actors refer to and exploit a tension between these two dimensions (procedure and result) of the quality of democracy. By doing so, they appeal to the notion of popular sovereignty, arguing that 'the people' is the only authority that has the right to evaluate and legitimize the political system. This poses a real challenge to the theory of liberal democracy, which takes the existence of 'the people' for granted and, because of that, proceeds with the discussion of the legitimacy of the political regime. As Näsström (2007) has pointed out, liberal (as well as deliberative) democratic theory explains the process of people building by referring to the 'contingent forces of history,' that is, peoples are formed by accident, tradition, and, more often than not, wars. This means that 'the people' is conceived of as a *constituted power*, which normally is crystallized in a formal constitution that defines how political power should be exercised. By contrast, populist actors see 'the people' as an active entity, or what Kalvyas (2005) calls the *constituent power*, that is, the main actor of a democratic regime when it comes to (re)founding and updating the higher legal norms and rules that regulate the exercise of power.

In addition to this general observation, it is important to analyse whether populism does have a positive and/or a negative effect on the quality of democracy. To answer this question, we selected our cases on the basis of two criteria: (1) if the main populist actors are in opposition or in government, and (2) if the democratic regime is consolidated or unconsolidated. The first criterion indicates that the most relevant factor should be the actual power of the populist forces; that is to say, if populism is confined to the opposition, it has little room to manoeuvre and thus has a minor impact on the quality of democracy. The second criterion refers to the 'maturity' of the democratic regime and is based on the idea that when a democratic regime is consolidated, even governmental populism should have little impact on the quality of the democracy, since the latter is sufficiently robust to deal with the 'populist challenge.'

What do the eight case studies tell us about these two assumptions? The evidence of the book supports the first assumption. In fact, the four cases of 'populism in opposition' (Flemish Block/Interest in Belgium, Reform Party in Canada, 'Republicans' in the Czech Republic, and Andrés Manuel López Obrador in Mexico) all show that when populist actors are in opposition, they do not have great influence on the quality of the democratic regime. Nevertheless, this does not mean that populism in opposition should be considered irrelevant. This might be the case in the Czech Republic, where the Republicans flourished for a short period of time but did not challenge the established parties in a profound way. Yet in the other cases of 'populism in opposition' the situation seems quite different. By advancing certain topics that normally receive little attention in the public agenda and are considered improper by the establishment, populist forces challenge the mainstream parties and obligate them to adapt their programmes. For instance, Bruhn shows in her chapter on Mexico that López Obrador lost the presidential elections, but the winner (Felipe Calderón) was compelled to redefine the priorities of his government, and thus placed much more emphasis on the fight against poverty. In a similar vein, the cases of Belgium and Canada demonstrate that due to the emergence of a right-wing populist party, the mainstream right parties are prone to strengthen their conservative stance in order to avoid a loss of votes.

To sum up, populism in opposition can have a positive effect on the quality of democracy since it helps to give voice to groups that do not feel represented by the political establishment. Under these circumstances, the latter has to deal with issues raised by the populist forces. Interestingly, these issues are normally seen by most elites as disgusting and vulgar. Hence, and to paraphrase Arditi (2005: 90–1), populism acts like a drunken guest at a dinner party: While usually it does not respect the rules of public contestation, it spells out painful but real problems of the existing political order. From this point of view, populism per se cannot be considered as anti-democratic, but rather as an expression of the will of a neglected part of the people that might be at odds with certain procedures and results of liberal democracy.

With regards to the second assumption (the 'maturity' of the democratic regime), the evidence of the case studies reveals a mixed picture. While consolidated democracies are more resilient, and hence better suited than unconsolidated democracies to cope with the 'populist challenge,' they can also suffer a process of democratic erosion. As Roberts shows in his chapter on Venezuela, Hugo Chávez has built a new regime which has little respect for the 'checks and balances' that are inherent to the model of liberal democracy and, in turn, promotes a radical shift in terms of fostering political participation. But, as Roberts also indicates, the deterioration of the quality of Venezuelan democracy started *before*

Chávez came to power, and is closely related to the poor management of the country's oil economy by the established 'democratic' political actors, that is, AD and COPEI. In other words, if Roberts is right in indicating that contemporary Venezuela may well be closer to Levitsky and Way's (2002) model of 'competitive authoritarianism' than it is to liberal democracy, then it is relevant to stress that this process of democratic deconsolidation – or what O'Donnell (1992) has called the 'slow death of democracy' – started before Hugo Chávez came on the scene. This implies, in turn, that populism is not the only factor, and possibly not the most decisive, when it comes to explaining the erosion of the quality of democracy in current Venezuela.

This finding is very relevant, since the academic scholarship has tended to affirm that elite settlements – such as the one that Venezuela experienced in 1958 through the so-called Punto Fijo pact – have a positive impact on the consolidation of democracy (e.g. Higley and Burton 2006; Peeler 1992). In short, the case of Venezuela illustrates that a process of elite settlement might well lead to the formation of a political establishment, which in the long run is much more interested in preserving its own interests and wealth than in improving the quality of the democratic regime. In this sense, populist actors might be correct when they maintain that elite pact making is not only an anti-democratic form of interest representation, but can also have a negative impact on the quality of democracy.

However, the three other cases of consolidated democracies analysed in this edited volume confirm our thesis. Austria, Belgium, and Canada are countries in which the rise of right-wing populist parties has not provoked a process of democratic erosion. In all these cases the democratic 'checks and balances' are entrenched and, in consequence, populist actors have limited room of manoeuvre. While they have the capacity to put their concerns on the public agenda, they do not have the force to trigger a wide reform of the political system. Moreover, in all these countries several institutional protections can be enacted by the parliament and/or the constitutional court in order to 'defend democracy' from populist forces. Accordingly, the limited impact that populism has had on the quality of democracy in the cases of Austria, Belgium, and Canada derives not only from the relatively weak electoral performance of the respective populist parties, but also from the existence of a consolidated democracy that has several formal and informal mechanisms which seek to tame – or in extreme cases ban – the parties in question. As Capoccia (2005) has noted, while there must be legal limits to the 'tolerance for the intolerant,' it is also crucial to have inclusive strategies in the toolbox of democratic defence, that is, strategies that aim to socialize the populist forces into the rules of public contestation.

Finally, it is necessary to refer to the impact of 'populism in power' on unconsolidated democracies, the most threatening scenario. The two cases that we selected for this scenario leave us with a mixed picture. On the one hand, Mečiar in Slovakia can neither be portrayed as a 'pure democrat' nor as an 'authentic dictator.' Deegan-Krause's chapter shows that if the government of Mečiar did have any impact on the quality of democracy, it was rather positive and, in consequence, it contributed to the completion of Slovakia's democracy, that is, the movement from an unconsolidated to a consolidated democracy. In spite of this, the chapter also demonstrates that Mečiar was not only a populist, but also, and mainly, a nationalist who ethnicized Slovak politics and the Slovak state. On the other hand, as Levitsky and Loxton explain in their chapter on Peru, Fujimori represents a case in which the rise of a populist leader did lead to a process of democratic breakdown.

The answer might be, in part, provided by the difference in political system. In presidential systems, political outsiders can gain the presidency without having political support within the broader political system. This was the case with Fujimori, who was elected democratically, but had neither a majority in parliament nor any kind of party or grassroot organization supporting him (Tanaka 2005: 278). This situation provoked a deadlock, which Fujimori solved by undertaking a presidential coup (*autogolpe*). After closing the parliament in 1992, he formed a constituent assembly that drafted a new constitution and served as an interim congress until legislative elections were held in 1995. In a parliamentary system, the executive always needs the backing of the majority of the legislative. Hence, while Mečiar was not the single executive, and even had to share executive power with other parties, he did have broad support in the parliament and the best organized political party in the country. Perhaps this gave him less incentive to leave the democratic arena, despite some minor infringements, as he was less frustrated in his legislative attempts.

10.2   From 'empirics' to 'theory': Unexpected findings

The eight case studies discussed in this edited volume are extremely valuable not only due to the answers that they give to the questions raised in the introductory framework, but also because they offer new insights into several aspects that we did not consider or anticipate beforehand. Without the aim of developing a detailed list of unexpected findings, we will proceed to focus on the following four aspects: (1) populism at the sub-national level; (2) reactions to populism; (3) the relationship between populism and competitive authoritarianism; and (4) populism and the international arena.

10.2.1   *Populism at the sub-national level*

In her chapter on Mexico Bruhn shows that we can assess the impact of populism on the quality of democracy not only at the national, but also at the local level. In fact, Andrés Manuel López Obrador is a populist leader who was the mayor of Mexico City between 2000 and 2005, one of the most populated metropolitan areas of the world. The chapter convincingly demonstrates that López Obrador's trajectory as mayor was rather positive, since he implemented several policies in favour of poor and marginalized groups. In addition, his economic management was responsible and did not cause any major criticisms. His negative impact on the quality of democracy came to the fore during his presidential campaign, particularly when he lost the elections in 2006. López Obrador claimed fraud, did not accept the official results, and mobilized his supporters in order to block important streets and places of Mexico City. In addition, he proclaimed himself 'the Legitimate President of Mexico' and attacked anyone who accepted that Felipe Calderón was in fact the real president of the country. In clear populist fashion, he maintained that the existing institutions were corrupted and appealed to the power of 'the people' as the only source capable of restoring democracy.

In his chapter on Austria Franz Fallend analyses the province of Carinthia under Governor Jörg Haider in the period 1999–2008. His analysis shows that Haider tried to circumvent the rights of certain minorities, particularly the Slovenian population. For instance, he criticized the existence of bilingual (German and Slovenian) local signs in the ethnically mixed districts of Carinthia. Nevertheless, the constitutional court of Austria forced Haider to respect the law. This means that the coming to power of the FPÖ at the local level did not represent a real challenge to the quality of Austrian democracy, since institutions like the constitutional court acted as 'checks and balances' against the popular sovereignty endorsed by Haider.

What can we learn from these cases of populism in government at the local level? As these examples illustrate, populism is much less threatening to the quality of democracy at the sub-national than at the national level. The reasons for this are at least two. On the one hand, while being mayor of a capital city or governor of a province does represent a powerful position, it is a position that is inevitably under control of certain institutions at the national level (e.g. parliament or constitutional court). On the other hand, populist actors – as almost all political leaders – usually aspire to obtain increasing quotas of power and, in consequence, they see the sub-national level only as a step towards achieving a more powerful position. Accordingly, populist leaders might show more respect to the rules of public contestation at the sub-national level, since this would permit them to demonstrate their 'democratic credentials' and hence improve their chances of obtaining a political position at the national level in the near future.

10.2.2 Reactions to populism

Although we did not explicitly raise the question about how to deal with 'the populist challenge' in the introductory framework, almost all chapters refer to this issue. Since there is little research to determine whether certain strategies are more successful and/or more democratic than others when it comes to coping with populism, it is worth looking into the findings of the case studies. In this regard, it is possible to identify four general strategies: isolation, confrontation, adaptation, and socialization. Of course, these different strategies rarely appear in pure form, as in most cases populists are confronted with a combination of strategies.

Those who adhere to the logic of *isolation* simply deny the legitimacy of the claims of the populist actors. The latter are seen as pathological expressions of the democratic order (Rosanvallon 2008; Taggart 2002). Accordingly, the established political parties construct a discourse, which makes a clear distinction between us and them: While the establishment is (self) proclaimed as 'good democrats,' the populists are drawn as 'evil forces.' It is worth noting that this reaction is quite similar to the populist language, since it assumes that the political world should be seen as a moral battle, which is (almost) impossible to solve through democratic channels. Not surprisingly, one of the main policies of the strategy of isolation is the formation of a *cordon sanitaire*, which, as de Lange and Akkerman demonstrate for the case of Belgium, has mixed effects on the quality of democracy.

Another option is *confrontation*, in which case the established political actors not only deny the legitimacy of the claims of the populist actors, but also decide to attack them. Arguing that there must be limits to the 'tolerance for the intolerant,' segments of the establishment might be tempted to transgress the rules of public contestation in order to extirpate the 'populist syndrome.' For instance, Roberts illustrates in his chapter that large parts of the Venezuelan (former) elites tried to boycott Chávez's government via extra-institutional mechanisms in at least two occasions: first, by supporting a military coup in 2002, and second, by backing a general strike in the national oil company in 2002–3.

In contrast to the strategy of isolation and confrontation, the strategy of *adaptation* does not rely on a moralization of politics. By contrast, it is based on the assumption that the claims made by the populist forces have a certain degree of legitimacy. Accordingly, those who adhere to the logic of adaption either implicitly or explicitly accept that populism can function as a democratic corrective, since it may well direct the attention of the establishment to certain topics that they have left aside of the political agenda. Consequently, as paradoxical as it might appear, populism can trigger a sort of learning process by which established political parties renew their programmes and policies in order to reduce the gap between governed and governors. This is to a large extent what the Austrian Christian Democratic ÖVP did in Austria before and during its coalition with the FPÖ. And, as Fallend shows, they did it with great success, largely marginalizing the populists and regaining the initiative in Austrian politics.

Finally, the strategy of *socialization* can be seen as complementary to adaptation. Whereas adaptation relates to the mainstream actors, socialization refers to short-term and long-term tactics that aim to include the populist forces in the political establishment. This implies a sort of pacification by de-radicalization of the populist actors, particularly in terms of accepting the rules of public contestation inherent to liberal democracy. The analysis by Fallend offers a possible example of this, as the coalition government triggered a division within the populist forces: While the more radical sector withdrew from the government, the more pragmatic sector formed a new party and stayed in government. Another possible example of the strategy of socialization is the involvement of the Organization of American States (OAS) in Venezuela after the 2002 coup against Chávez. By using a multi-lateral approach called 'intervention without intervening' (Cooper and Legler 2005), the OAS paved the way for the establishment of a dialogue between government and opposition, whereby an agreement on the realization of a presidential recall referendum was reached.

The findings beg a broad variety of questions of how best to deal with populists from a liberal democratic perspective. This is a hot issue particularly in Western Europe, where the best way to deal with radical right parties and extreme right groups is debated fiercely (e.g. De Witte 1997; Eatwell and Mudde 2004; Van Donselaar 1995; for a historical perspective see Capoccia 2005). While the populist radical right, let alone the extreme right, threat is not identical to that of populism per se, much can be learned from that debate. At the same time, while much of the European debate is purely normative, that is, determining one best approach, academics should (also) look into the conditions that foster or inhibit the success of the different approaches.

10.2.3   *The Levitsky-Loxton thesis: Populism leads to*
competitive authoritarianism

Levitsky and Loxton's chapter is not just interesting because of their insightful analysis of the case of Fujimori. The authors also present a more general thesis, namely that populism leads to 'competitive authoritarianism.' They argue that this is a logical process because: (a) populists are political outsiders; (b) populists earn a mandate to bury the political establishment; and (c) the political elite that they mobilized against, and defeated in the election, continues to control these institutions after the populist leader comes to power. Without a doubt, this argument is valid for the case of Fujimori in Peru, but the evidence of the other cases in this edited volume challenges the general validity of their thesis.

First of all, not all populists are political outsiders. While this might often be the case, there are several examples of populist leaders who are part of the political establishment. For instance, Bruhn shows in her chapter on Mexico that leaders such as Cuauhtémoc Cárdenas and Andrés Manuel López Obrador cannot be labelled as 'political outsiders.' Indeed, both are well-trained politicians socialized into the functioning of political parties and who had been in power at the local or regional level before their national bid. A similar argument could be made for Haider in Austria, even though he was at times confronted with political ostracism, and certainly Silvio Berlusconi in Italy and Pim Fortuyn in the Netherlands.

According to Barr, the populist leader is usually a 'maverick,' 'a politician who rises to prominence within an established, competitive party but then either abandons his affiliation to compete as an independent or in association with an outsider party, or radically reshapes his own party' (2009: 34). Alternatively, populists like López Obrador and Haider can be seen as 'outsider-elites, *connected to* the elites, but not *part of* them' (Mudde 2004: 560). In any case, many populists are not true political outsiders; they might be outside the political establishment, but they are inside the political game. Hence, many populists do have some kind of allegiance to the political game, even if they tend to oppose some rules and compete with most key players.

Second, Levitsky and Loxton rightly note that populist leaders aim to get rid of the establishment (i.e. the key players). In effect, it is not an exaggeration to say that populism, particularly in Latin America, can be seen as an important driver of processes of elite circulation and renewal (Rovira Kaltwasser 2009: 299–303). However, the interaction between populist leaders and different segments of the establishment can show a great level of variance, going from important degrees of cooperation (e.g. Fujimori in Peru or the FPÖ/BZÖ in Austria) to radical conflict (e.g. Chávez in Venezuela or VB in Belgium).

To understand this variance, particularly within the Latin American context of presidential systems, it is important to stress that populism can take divergent organizational forms in different national settings. Accordingly, populist leaders invest energy in forming a solid mass organization only when the reforms that they aim to embark on are fervently resisted by the establishment, since then they can effectively mobilize the masses in order to undertake the reforms in question (Roberts 2006). This implies that populism does not always intend to get rid of the *whole* establishment. By contrast, populists in power and in opposition try to maintain relations of cooperation with segments of the establishment that are more proximate in ideological terms (or strategic aims). It is not a coincidence that several European countries have seen the formation of coalition governments with and minority governments tolerated by populist radical right parties (De Lange 2008).

10.2.4. Populism and the international arena

The chapters of this edited volume have shown that the ambivalent relationship between populism and democracy can also be studied from an international perspective. Transnational actors and supranational institutions are aware of the 'populist challenge.' For instance, the agreements of the European Union (EU) and the Organization of American States (OAS) contain a democratic clause, which has been invoked to denounce the alleged anti-democratic character of certain populist actors (e.g. the coalition between the FPÖ and ÖVP in Austria, Fujimori's decision to close Congress, or Mečiar's increasingly authoritarian and nationalist third government).

Nevertheless, 'defending democracy' at the international level has proven to be anything but a straightforward task. Supranational institutions usually apply double standards when it comes to establishing sanctions based on democratic principles. For instance, the European Union reacted vigorously to the formation of a government that included a populist radical party in Austria, but it said nothing when Silvio Berlusconi formed a coalition with Gianfranco Fini's National Alliance and Umberto Bossi's Northern League. At the same time, the Organization of American States (OAS) has tried to deal with certain anti-democratic practices of Fujimori in Peru and Chávez in Venezuela, but did not complain about G. W. Bush's anti-terrorist measures. In fact, the OAS doctrine is focused on addressing interruptions and alternations of democracy, not of the quality of democracy (Boniface 2007: 53). This means that democracy promotion implies a reactive rather than a proactive endeavour for the OAS. Indeed, the OAS tends to intervene only when a major crisis comes to the fore; it does not have clear criteria and tools for action when it comes to dealing with a process of 'slow death of democracy' (O'Donnell 1992: 19), such as the ones that Peru and Venezuela have experienced with the rise of Fujimori and Chávez, respectively.

Put simply, there are good reasons to believe that when supranational institutions try to take sanctions based on democratic principles, they are not capable of overcoming the existent power asymmetries at the global level. This, in turn, gives more visibility and to a certain extent more legitimacy to the populist forces, since they can portray themselves as David fighting against Goliath (Mouffe 2005b: 64). This happened, for example, in Austria, where many right-wing people rallied behind the government mainly to protest the perceived illegitimate and hypocritical EU interference. In Latin America, on the other hand, many populists have made their struggle against the clearly self-serving U.S. interference in the region a key part of their populist struggle of *Americanismo*. The problem is that democracy promotion is based on the idea of non-partisanship. Consequently, the involvement of outside actors in democratically elected governments inevitably raises suspicion of the existence of a partisan agenda (Carothers 2010: 69). In other words, dealing with populism is a complicated task because it usually implies the defence of a particular model of democracy, which is not necessarily shared by the governed all over the world. Certainly, this opens the question about the normative and historical underpinnings of the very concept of liberal democracy (Koelble and Lipuma 2008).

Finally, it would be erroneous to think that populist forces operate only at the sub-national and national levels. While Jean-Marie Le Pen's efforts to build a strong EU-wide populist radical right bloc, which could play an important role in the European Parliament, have failed miserably, Venezuelan president Chávez has become a serious regional player within Latin America. Backed by the highest oil prices in history, he has used his (relative) wealth to reward allies in other countries in the region, such as Bolivian president Evo Morales and Ecuadorian president Rafael Correa, and to undermine U.S. influence in Latin America (Ellner 2008). Moreover, the current wave of Latin American radical left-wing populism is characterized by the attempt to redefine both democracy and democracy promotion along lines that are more meaningful for 'the people' (Legler, Lean, and Boniface 2007: 11). Although it is too early to evaluate the impact of this attempt, there is little doubt that contemporary populism is not only changing the meaning of the very concept of democracy in the Latin American region, but it is also spark-ing a public and academic debate on the shortcomings of the neoliberal policies that the U.S. and the International Financial Institutions have promoted in Latin America in the last decades.

10.3   Future paths of inquiry on populism and democracy

Although this volume is the first to study the relationship between popu-lism and democracy cross-regionally and according to an integrated theoretical framework and has produced significant new findings, there remains much to be done. In this last section we suggest a few avenues of further study which we believe are particularly relevant to the better understanding of the nature of populism in general and of the complex relationship between populism and democracy in particular.

First, a topic that several chapters in this volume touched upon, but few truly studied in detail: the diffusion of populism. In other words, in what way, and under which circumstances, can populism spread from one society to another? Not by coincidence, scholars working on Latin America have identified the existence of different 'waves of populism,' such as the rise of neopopulist leaders in the 1990s and the formation of radical left-wing populist forces since the first decade of the new millen-nium (Freidenberg 2007; Gratius 2007). Similarly, the rise of populist radical right parties in Europe has often been described as a 'wave' (e.g. Von Beyme 1988) or a 'contagious' phenomenon (e.g. Rydgren 2005). As these examples suggest, there are good reasons to think that the emer-gence of populism in one country is partly related to similar develop-ments in neighbouring countries. This would mean that populism, as well as democracy, is affected by the regional and international context.

Although we do not intend to develop a detailed argument about the diffusion of populism here, it is worthwhile indicating a possible starting point for further studies. Following the terminology of Simmons and her collaborators (2008), there are at least three mechanisms of diffu-sion which can influence the (re)appearance of populism: competition, learning, and emulation. The mechanism of *competition* came indirectly to the fore in various chapters of this book, where it was shown that the rise of populist forces challenges the mainstream parties, which, under certain conditions, are tempted to copy the populist discourse. At the same time, mainstream parties can adapt their agendas in order to pre-vent the formation of populist competitors (Mudde 2007: 281–2). In contrast to competition, the mechanism of *learning* refers to a change in beliefs, resulting either from observation and interpretation or from acquisition of new frames or theories. This process of social learning is normally facilitated by the exchange of information via networks in which both technocrats and 'organic intellectuals' are operating, developing new ideas and policies that can be raised by populist leaders and parties. Finally, the mechanism of *emulation* alludes not so much to the supply side, but rather to the demand side of the populist phenomenon. From this angle, the electorate of one country is aware of the political development of neighbouring countries, and in consequence, the emergence of a populist actor in one place can trigger a 'demonstration effect' in other places.

A second research agenda refers to the relationship between the type of organization promoted by the populist forces and the model of democracy that they (aim to) construct. Much Latin American literature assumes that populism includes the lack of strong party organizations and direct communication between leader and followers (e.g. Weyland 2001, 1996; Roberts 1995). At the same time, some North American scholars consider grassroots mobilization a key feature of populism (e.g. Formisano 2007). Finally, European populism entails both highly personalized parties (e.g. Forza Italia or List Pim Fortuyn) and some of the best organized parties in their respective countries (e.g. Flemish Interest, Movement for a Democratic Slovakia, or Swiss People's Party). The advantage of using our *ideological* minimal definition is that it enables us to use this definition across regions and also allows us to study the effect of party organization on the relationship between populism and democracy. Do non-organized populists indeed inflict more harm on democracy, as Levitsky and Loxton argue in this book, or do better institutionalized populist parties form a larger threat?

In addition, the relationship between the populist ideology and the kind of institutional setting that populist actors prefer is closely related to a topic raised by many scholars, namely, the transformation of the organization of political parties and the possible impact of this transformation on the democratic regime (e.g. Katz and Mair 1995; Von Beyme 1993). For instance, Mair (2002, 2006) has argued that the erosion of 'party democracy' paves the way for the rise of a sort of 'populist democracy' in which political parties are replaced by strong leaders who develop a direct and unmediated linkage with 'the people.' Seen in this light, the rise of populist forces goes hand in hand with the constitution of a new political scenario marked by the formation of 'cartel parties' and the increasing influence of the mass media, particularly television. However, while the previously mentioned new political scenario has been gaining momentum in many countries, we have not seen the emergence of populist forces in all of them (important exceptions are, for example, Spain in Europe and Chile in Latin America). At the same time, it is an exaggeration to say that *all* populist forces are at odds with the creation and maintenance of institutional apparatuses (Hawkins 2010a: 169–75). Accordingly, further studies on populism and democracy should devote more attention to the *type of organization* promoted by populist leaders and the impact that these organizations do have on the quality of democracy.

Although it seems that populism tends to foster a kind of 'Macho' politics, little has been written about the relationship between populism and gender. This is a third research agenda. After all, there are good reasons to think that specific regional or historical manifestations of populism develop different approaches towards gender. Indeed, Kampwirth's (2011) recent edited volume shows that in Latin America there has been a variety of populist projects defending particular models of masculinity and femininity. For instance, Evo Morales represents a case of populism from below, in which several grassroots organizations – including women's rights associations – play an important role in terms of the policy agenda of the government (Rousseau 2011). By contrast, Hugo Chávez comes closer to a case of populism from above, in which the government has developed several policies in favour of women, such as the introduction of a college-level work-study programme that aims to improve the qualification of women, and the creation of soup kitchens run by women, where needy children and single mothers from the shanty towns receive one free meal a day (Fernandes 2007: 108–12). As these examples reveal, the government of Chávez does promote policies for *poor* women rather than for women as such, and in consequence, it does not defend a feminist agenda.

Fourth, there is little in-depth research on the complex links between populism and the media. Particularly within the European context, many authors have argued that the increasing importance and commercialization of the mass media is one of the main drivers of the growing rise of populism (e.g. Mazzoleni 2003; Meyer 2006; Peri 2004; Puhle 2003). However, there are no comparative studies that empirically and/ or theoretically explicate the ways in which different media landscapes favour or hinder the emergence of populism. There are some interesting country studies though, that develop new insights into the relationship between populism and the media, and which contribute to the generation of hypotheses that can be tested in future studies. For instance, Art (2006) explains the different levels of success of populist radical right parties in Austria and Germany in part by the collective memory of each of these countries and their impact on the public debate and the media. Another interesting example is a recent article written by Bale, Taggart, and Van Kessel (2011), which examines the vernacular understandings of populism. Based on an empirical analysis of the main print media in the United Kingdom the authors demonstrate that populism tends to receive a negative connotation in the media and that the adjective 'populist' is often used as a synonym for 'popular.'

Within the Latin American context, populists in power do not only attack the media for its defence of the status quo and the interests of the elites, but they also push for political reforms that aim to create new media companies in tune with the populist ideology. In essence, populism does not believe in the existence of independent media, but rather perceives the media landscape through the Manichean distinction between 'the pure people' and 'the corrupt elite': On the hand, there is the honest and legitimate media that expresses the 'will of the people,' and on the other hand, there is a fraudulent and anti-democratic media that defends the interests of the elite (Waisbord 2011: 100). Not by coincidence, as Kitzberger (2010) has analysed in detail, the level of media activism of the current leftist administrations in Latin America seems to be related to their proximity to the populist ideology: The more the leftist government adheres to populism, the greater its critique of the media and the greater the state's intervention to ensure the 'democratization' of access and voice in the media sphere.

A fifth topic for future analysis is the development of a genuine comparative approach to populism in general and to the ambivalent relationship between populism and democracy in particular. While we have focused on contemporary populism in this volume, further studies can provide new insights by undertaking cross-temporal comparisons either within regions (e.g. Latin America) or across regions (e.g. South America and North America). From a historical point of view, it would be interesting to analyse whether populist forces, such as Peronism in Argentina and/or the Populist Party in the United States, have triggered episodes of institutional change that promoted democratization or de-democratization. This implies, as Capoccia and Ziblatt (2010) have suggested, that the institutional building blocks of democracy usually emerge asynchronically. Consequently, it is relevant to examine if, and in which ways, the emergence of populism has affected the historical development of single democratic institutions (e.g. the extension of suffrage, anti-electoral fraud rules, the approval of a new constitution, etc.). Furthermore, it would be interesting to reconsider the 'transitology' literature in order to study the impact of populism on the three stages of democratization: liberalization, transition, and consolidation (e.g. Mudde and Rovira Kaltwasser 2010).

With regard to contemporary cross-regional comparisons, future research could study different types or sub-families of populism or compare them explicitly. We think particularly about the more inclusionary populism in Latin America and the more exclusionary populism in Europe (Mudde and Rovira Kaltwasser 2011). Moreover, although there is little doubt that the Tea Party in the United States can be seen as a populist movement, no academic studies have so far tried to compare this movement to populist movements outside of the United States. Does the use of different definitions of 'the pure people' and 'the corrupt elite' have an effect on the relationship between populism and democracy? Do neoliberal populists affect the relationship between populism and democracy in similar ways in Europe and in Latin America? Does the Tea Party in the United States have a similar agenda, for instance in terms of anti-immigration, as the populist radical right parties in Europe?

Since populism represents a challenge for (liberal) democracy, future studies should focus on the factors that might hinder the (re)appearance of populism and thus take into account negative cases. For instance, some scholars have contended that the way national elites dealt with the Nazi past had a profound effect on the electoral success of the populist radical right in Europe (e.g. Art 2006; Decker 2008). In a similar vein, in those countries of Latin America where the left has experienced a learning process due to the authoritarian past and has adapted its programme in accordance with liberal democracy (e.g. Brazil, Chile, and Uruguay), the 'specter of (left-wing) populism' has not come to the fore (Lanzaro 2006). Finally, it has been argued that Latin American countries with a strong party system and solid political institutions can avoid populist reactions, since in these cases the proper functioning of the institutions of democratic representation leave little space for the (re)emergence of populism (e.g. Mainwaring and Scully 1995; Navia and Walker 2009). At the same time, in Europe various scholars have linked the rise of populist actors to the strength (or better: inertia) of party systems and political institutions, arguing that populist parties do particularly well in consensus democracies (e.g. Hakhverdian and Koop 2007; Kitschelt 2002), implying that more majoritarian and pluralist societies, like the United Kingdom, would be better protected against populists. As these illustrations suggest, when it comes to studying the factors that impede the (re)appearance of populism, many arguments have been put forward, and most can only be assessed on the basis of cross-regional and cross-temporal analyses.

Bibliography

Abts, K. and S. Rummens (2007) 'Populism versus Democracy,' *Political Studies* 55(2): 405–24.

Academy of Sciences of the Czech Republic Institute of Sociology (1990) *Economic Expectations and Attitudes Survey I-XI* [Computer file].

Ackerman, J. M. (2009) 'El que se enoja pierde,' *Proceso* 1699: 69.

Alarcón González, D. (1994) *Changes in the Distribution of Income in Mexico and Trade Liberalization.* Tijuana: El Colegio de la Frontera Norte.

Albertazzi, D. and D. McDonnell (eds.) (2007) *Twenty-First Century Populism: The Spectre of Western European Democracy.* Basingstoke: Palgrave.

Alonso, S., J. Keane, and W. Merkel (eds.) (2011) *The Future of Representative Democracy.* New York, Cambridge University Press.

Alvarez, A. E. (2003) 'State Reform Before and After Chávez's Election,' in S. Ellner and D. Hellinger (eds.), *Venezuelan Politics in the Chávez Era: Class, Polarization, and Conflict.* Boulder, CO: Lynne Rienner, 147–60.

Ames, R., E., Bernales, S. López, and R. Roncagliolo (2001) *Situación de la Democracia en el Perú.* Lima: Universidad Católica del Peru.

Angell, A. (1998) 'The Left in Latin America since c. 1920,' in L. Bethell (ed.), *Latin America. Politics and Society since 1930.* Cambridge: Cambridge University Press, 75–144.

Archer, K. and F. Ellis (1994) 'Opinion Structure of Party Activists: The Reform Party of Canada,' *Canadian Journal of Political Science* 27(2): 277–308.

Arditi, B. (2004) 'Populism as a Spectre of Democracy: A Response to Canovan,' *Political Studies* 52(1): 135–43.

  (2005) 'Populism as an Internal Periphery of Democratic Politics,' in F. Panizza (ed.), *Populism and the Mirror of Democracy.* London: Verso, 72–98.

Armony, A. and H. Schamis (2005) 'Babel in Democratization Studies,' *Journal of Democracy* 16(4): 113–28.

Art, D. (2006) *The Politics of the Nazi Past in Germany and Austria.* New York, Cambridge University Press.

  (2008) 'The Organizational Origins of the Contemporary Radical Right: The Case of Belgium,' *Comparative Politics* 40(4): 421–40.

  (2011) *Inside the Radical Right: The Development of Anti-Immigrant Parties in Western Europe.* Cambridge: Cambridge University Press.

Auer, S. (2003) *Liberal Nationalism in Central Europe.* London: Routledge.

Avendaño, J. (2001) 'La Perpetuidad en el Poder a Través del Congreso (La Corrupción del Poder Judicial y del Sistema Electoral),' in C. M. Batres (ed.), *Como Fujimori Jodió al Perú.* Lima: Editorial Mill Batres, 125–40.

Aviles, J. (2006) 'El plantón espera hoy un triunfo o más sacrificios,' *La Jornada*, 4 September.

Bailer-Galanda, B. and W. Neugebauer (1996) 'Right-Wing Extremism: History, Organisations, Ideology,' in B. Bailer-Galanda and W. Neugebauer (eds.), *Incorrigibly Right: Right-Wing Extremists, 'Revisionists' and Anti-Semites in Austrian Politics Today*. Vienna and New York: Stiftung Dokumentationsarchiv des österreichischen Widerstandes and Anti-Defamation League, 5–22.

Bakvis, H. and S. B. Wolinetz (2005) 'Canada: Executive Dominance and Presidentialization,' in T. Pogunte and P. Webb (eds.), *The Presidentialization of Politics: A Comparative Study of Modern Democracies*. New York: Oxford University Press, 199–220.

Bale, T. (2003) 'Cinderella and Her Ugly Sisters: The Mainstream and Extreme Right in Europe's Bipolarising Party Systems,' *West European Politics* 26(3): 67–90.

(2007) 'Are Bans on Political Parties Bound to Turn Out Badly? A Comparative Investigation of Three "Intolerant" Democracies,' *Comparative European Politics* 5(2): 141–57.

Bale, T., P. Taggart, and S. van Kessel (2011) 'Thrown Around with Abandon? Popular Understandings of Populism as Conveyed by the Print Media: A UK Case Study,' *Acta Politica* 46(2): 111–31.

Barney, D. D. (1996) 'Push-button Populism: The Reform Party and the Real World of Teledemocracy,' *Canadian Journal of Communication* 21(3): 381–413.

Barney, D. D. and D. Laycock (1999) 'Right-Populists and Plebiscitary Politics in Canada,' *Party Politics* 5(3): 317–39.

Barr, R. R. (2009) 'Populists, Outsiders and Anti-Establishment Politics,' *Party Politics* 15(1): 29–48.

Becerril, A. and E. Mendez (2006) 'Llama AMLO al Ejército a no Cumplir Órdenes de Represión,' *La Jornada*, 4 September.

Bélanger, E. and K. Aarts (2006) 'Explaining the Rise of the LPF: Issues, Discontent, and the 2002 Dutch Election,' *Acta Politica* 41(1): 4–20.

Belohradský, V. (1992) *Kapitalismus a občanské ctnosti*. Prague: Československý spisovatel.

Benoit, K. and M. Laver (2006) *Party Policy in Modern Democracies*. London: Routledge.

Berezin, M. (2009) *Illiberal Politics in Neoliberal Times: Cultures, Security, and Populism in a New Europe*. Cambridge: Cambridge University Press.

Berlin, I., R. Hofstadter, and D. MacRae et al. (1968) 'To Define Populism,' *Government and Opposition* 3(2): 137–80.

Betz, H-G. and S. Immerfall (eds.) (1998) *The New Politics of the Right: Neo-Populist Movements and Parties in Established Democracies*. New York: St. Martin's.

Billiet, J. (1995) 'Church Involvement, Ethnocentrism, and Voting for a Radical Right-Wing Party: Diverging Behavioral Outcomes of Equal Attitudinal Dispositions,' *Sociology of Religion* 56(3): 303–26.

(2002) 'Opkomstplicht of Vrijheid om al of niet te Gaan Stemmen in Vlaanderen: Het Verkiezingsonderzoek van 1999,' in M. Swyngedouw and J. Billiet (eds.), *De Kiezer Heeft zijn Redenen: 12 Juni 1999 en de Politieke Opvattingen van Vlamingen*. Leuven: Acco, 129–46.

Billiet, J. and H. De Witte (1995) 'Attitudinal Dispositions to Vote for a "New" Extreme Right-Wing Party: The Case of "Vlaams Blok,"' *European Journal of Political Research* 27(2): 181–202.

(2001) 'Wie Stemde in Juni 1999 voor het Vlaams Blok en Waarom?,' *Tijdschrift voor Sociologie* 22(1): 5–35.

(2008) 'Everyday Racism as Predictor of Political Racism in Flemish Belgium,' *Journal of Social Issues* 64(2): 253–67.

Blanco Muñoz, A. (1998) *Del 04F-92 al 06D-98: Habla el Comandante Hugo Chávez Frías. Testimonios Violentos 12*. Caracas: Fundación Cátedra Pío Tamayo.

Blais, A. and E. Gidengil (1991) *Making Representative Democracy Work: The Views of Canadians*. Toronto: Dundurn.

Blais, A., E. Gidengil, N. Nevitte, and R. Nadeau (1999) *Unsteady State: The 1997 Canadian Federal Election*. Don Mills, ON: Oxford University Press.

(2002) *Anatomy of a Liberal Victory: Making Sense of the Vote in the 2000 Canadian Election*. Peterborough, ON: Broadview.

Blommaert, J., E. Corijn, M. Holthof, and D. Lesage (2004) *Populisme*. Berchem: EPO.

Blondet, C. M. (2002) *El encanto del dictador: Mujeres y política en la década de Fujimori*. Lima: Instituto de Estudios Peruanos.

Boas, T. C. (2005) 'Television and Neopopulism in Latin America: Media Effects in Brazil and Peru,' *Latin American Research Review* 40(2): 27–49.

Bobbio, N. (1987) *The Future of Democracy*. Cambridge: Polity.

(1990) *Liberalism and Democracy*. London: Verso.

Bobošíková, J. (2010) 'Volby 2010 – naděje pro Českou republiku, projev lídra Suverenity Jany Bobošíkové na programové konferenci,' available at: http://www.suverenita.cz/aktuality/_zobraz=volby-2010--nadeje-pro-ceskou-republiku,-projev-lidra-suverenity-jany-bobosikove-na-programove-konfer-enci (accessed 15 November 2010).

Boniface, D. S. (2007) 'The OAS's Mixed Record,' in T. Legler, S. F. Lean, and D. S. Boniface (eds.), *Promoting Democracy in the Americas*. Baltimore: Johns Hopkins University Press, 40–62.

Bowen, S. and J. Holligan (2003) *El espía imperfecto: la telaraña siniestra de Vladimiro Montesinos*. Lima: Peisa.

Brems, E. (2006) 'Belgium: The Vlaams Blok Political Party Convicted Indirectly of Racism,' *International Journal of Constitutional Law* 4(4): 702–11.

Breuning, M. and J. T. Ishiyama (1998) 'The Rhetoric of Nationalism: Rhetorical Strategies of the Volksunie and Vlaams Blok in Belgium, 1991–1995,' *Political Communication* 15: 5–26.

Brewer-Carías, A. R. (2010) *Dismantling Democracy in Venezuela: The Chávez Authoritarian Experiment*. New York: Cambridge University Press.

Bruhn, K. (2009) 'López Obrador, Calderón, and the 2006 Presidential Campaign,' in J. I. Domínguez, C. Lawson and A. Moreno (eds.), *Consolidating Mexico's Democracy: The 2006 Presidential Campaign in Comparative Perspective*. Baltimore: The Johns Hopkins University Press, 169–88.

Bruhn, K. and K. F. Greene (2007) 'Elite Polarization Meets Mass Moderation in Mexico's 2006 Elections,' *PS: Political Science and Politics* 40(1): 33–8.

(2009) 'The Absence of Common Ground between Candidates and Voters,' in J. I. Domínguez, C. Lawson, and A. Moreno (eds.), *Consolidating Mexico's Democracy: The 2006 Presidential Campaign in Comparative Perspective*. Baltimore: The Johns Hopkins University Press, 109–28.

Budge, I. and D. Robertson (1987) 'Do Parties Differ, and How? Comparative Discriminant and Factor Analyses,' in I. Budge, D. Robertson, and D. Hearl (eds.), *Ideology, Strategy, and Party Change: Spatial Analyses of Post-war Election Programmes in 19 Democracies*. Cambridge: Cambridge University Press, 388–416.

Buelens, J. (2009) 'Volksraadplegingen: Kan België Wat Leren van Nederland?' *Res Publica* 51(1): 13–31.

Burt, J.-M. (2007) *Political Violence and the Authoritarian State in Peru: Silencing Civil Society*. New York: Palgrave MacMillan.

Bútora, M., G. Mesežnikov, and M. Kollár (eds.) (2009) *Slovakia 2008: Trends in Quality of Democracy*. Bratislava: Institute for Public Affairs.

Cameron, M. A. (1994) *Democracy and Authoritarianism in Peru: Political Coalitions and Social Change*. New York: St. Martin's.

(1997) 'Political and Economic Origins of Regime Change in Peru: The *Eighteenth Brumaire* of Alberto Fujimori,' in M. A. Cameron and P. Mauceri (eds.), *The Peruvian Labyrinth: Polity, Society, Economy*. University Park: The Pennsylvania State University, 37–69.

(2006) 'Endogenous Regime Breakdown: The *Vladivideo* and the Fall of Peru's Fujimori,' in J. Carrión (ed.), *The Fujimori Legacy: The Rise of Electoral Authoritarianism in Peru*. University Park: Pennsylvania State University Press, 268–93.

Camp, R. A. (2009) 'Democracy Redux? Mexico's Voters and the 2006 Presidential Race,' in J. I. Domínguez, C. Lawson and A. Moreno (eds.), *Consolidating Mexico's Democracy: The 2006 Presidential Campaign in Comparative Perspective*. Baltimore: The Johns Hopkins University Press, 29–49.

Canadian Alliance (2000) *A Time for Change*, at http://www.poltext.org/upload/can2000all_plt_en._14112008_173717.pdf.

Canovan, Margaret (1981) *Populism*. London: Junction Books.

(1999) 'Trust the People: Populism and the Two faces of Democracy,' *Political Studies* 47(1): 2–16.

(2002) 'Taking Politics to the People: Populism as the Ideology of Democracy,' in Y. Mény and Y. Surel (eds.), *Democracies and the Populist Challenge*. Basingstoke: Palgrave, 25–44.

(2004) 'Populism for Political Theorists?' *Journal of Political Ideologies* 9(3): 241–52.

(2005) *The People*. Cambridge: Polity.

Capoccia, G. (2005) *Defending Democracy: Reactions to Extremism in Interwar Europe*. Baltimore: The Johns Hopkins University Press.

Capoccia, G. and D. Ziblatt (2010) 'The Historical Turn in Democratization Studies: A New Research Agenda for Europe and Beyond,' *Comparative Political Studies* 43(8–9): 931–68.

Carothers, T. (2010) 'The Continuing Backlash against Democracy Promotion,' in P. Burnell and R. Youngs (eds.), *New Challenges to Democratization*. London: Routledge, 59–72.

Carpenter, M. (1997) 'Slovakia and the Triumph of Nationalist Populism,' *Communist and Post-Communist Studies* 30(2): 205–19.

Carrión, J. F. (1996) 'La opinón pública: ¿de identidades a intereses?' in F. Tuesta Soldevilla (ed.), *Los enigmas del poder: Fujimori 1990–1996*. Lima: Fundacion Friedrich Ebert, 277–302.

(2006) 'Public Opinion, Market Reforms, and Democracy in Fujimori's Peru,' in J. Carrión (ed.), *The Fujimori Legacy: The Rise of Electoral Authoritarianism in Peru*. University Park: Pennsylvania State University Press, 126–49.

Carter, E. (2005) *The Extreme Right in Western Europe: Success or Failure?* Manchester: Manchester University Press.

Carty, R. K., W. Cross, and L. Young (2000) *Reforming Canadian Party Politics*. Vancouver: University of British Columbia Press.

Castañeda, J. G. (1995) *The Mexican Shock: Its Meaning for the United States*. New York: The New Press.

Castles, F. G. and P. Mair (1982) 'Left-Right Political Scales: Some "Expert" Judgements,' *European Journal of Political Research* 12(1): 73–88.

Castro Rea, J., G. Ducatenzeiler, and P. Faucher (1990) 'La tentación populista: Argentina, Brasil, México y Perú,' *Foro Internacional* 31(2): 252–85.

Cerqueirová, A. (1999) *Republikáni: Šokující odhalení*. Unknown: Unholy Cathedral.

Cheibub, J. A. and F. Limongi (2002) 'Democratic Institutions and Regime Survival: Parliamentary and Presidential Democracies Reconsidered,' *Annual Review of Political Science* 5: 151–79.

Clarke, H. D., A. Kornberg, F. Ellis, and J. Rapkin (2000) 'Not for Fame or Fortune: A Note on Membership and Activity in the Canadian Reform Party,' *Party Politics* 6: 75–93.

Coffé, H. (2005a) *Extreem-Rechts in Vlaanderen en Wallonië: Het Verschil*. Roeselare: Roularta.

(2005b) 'The Adaptation of the Extreme Right's Discourse: The Case of the Vlaams Blok,' *Ethical Perspectives* 12(2): 205–30.

(2005c) 'Do Individual Factors Explain the Different Success of the Two Belgian Extreme Right Parties?' *Acta Politica* 40(1): 74–93.

Coffé, H., B. Heyndels, and J. Vermeir J. (2007) 'Fertile Grounds for Extreme Right-Wing Parties: Explaining the Vlaams Blok's Electoral Success,' *Electoral Studies* 26(1): 142–55.

Collier, R. B. and D. Collier (1991) *Shaping the Political Arena: Critical Junctures, the Labor Movement, and Regime Dynamics in Latin America*. Princeton: Princeton University Press.

Collier, D. and J. Gerring (eds.) (2009) *Concepts and Method in Social Science. The Tradition of Giovanni Sartori*. New York: Routledge.

Collier, D. and S. Levitsky (1997) 'Democracy with Adjectives: Conceptual Innovation in Comparative Research,' *World Politics* 49(3): 430–51.

Collier, D. and J. Mahon (1993) 'Conceptual "Stretching" Revisited: Adapting Categories in Comparative Analysis,' *The American Political Science Review*, 87(4): 845–55.

Conacher, Duff (2011) 'Don't Cut Vote Subsidy, Make it More Democratic,' *The Tyee*, 9 June 2011.

Conaghan, C. M. (2000) 'The Irrelevant Right: Alberto Fujimori and the New Politics of Pragmatic Peru,' in K. J. Middlebrook (ed.), *Conservative Parties, the Right, and Democracy in Latin America*. Baltimore: The Johns Hopkins University Press, 255–84.

(2005) *Fujimori's Peru: Deception in the Public Sphere*. Pittsburgh: University of Pittsburgh Press.

Conniff, M. L. (ed.) (1999): *Populism in Latin America*. Tuscaloosa: University of Alabama Press.

Consulta Mitofsky (2007) 'La limpieza percibida de las elecciones y la intención de participar en ellas,' available at: http://www.consulta.mx/Estudio.aspx?Estudio=limpieza-elecciones (accessed 18 October 2010).

(2008) 'Dos años despues de la elección presidencial en México,' available at: http://www.consulta.mx/Estudio.aspx?Estudio=dos-anios-2-julio (accessed 19 August 2010).

(2010) 'Monitor Mitofsky: Economía, Política, y Gobierno,' available at: http://www.consulta.mx/Estudio.aspx?Estudio=monitor-mitofsky (accessed 19 August 2010).

Conway, J. F. (1978) 'Populism in the United States, Russia, and Canada: Explaining the Roots of Canada's Third Parties,' *Canadian Journal of Political Science* 11(1): 99–124.

Cooper, A. F. and Legler, T. (2005) 'A Tale of Two Mesas: The OAS Defence of Democracy in Peru and Venezuela,' *Global Governance* 11(4): 425–44.

Coppedge, M. (2008) 'Venezuela: Popular Sovereignty versus Liberal Democracy,' in J. Dominguez and M. Shifter (eds.), *Constructing Democratic Governance in Latin America*. Baltimore: Johns Hopkins University Press, third edition, 165–92.

(1994) *Strong Parties and Lame Ducks: Presidential Partyarchy and Factionalism in Venezuela*. Stanford, CA: Stanford University Press.

Coppedge, M., A. Alvarez, and C. Maldonado (2008) 'Two Persistent Dimensions of Democracy: Contestation and Inclusiveness,' *The Journal of Politics* 70(3): 632–47.

Corrales, J. (2002) *Presidents Without Parties: The Politics of Economic Reform in Argentina and Venezuela in the 1990s*. University Park: Pennsylvania State University Press.

Corrales, J. and M. Penfold (2010) *Dragon in the Tropics: Hugo Chávez and the Political Economy of Revolution in Venezuela*. Washington, DC: Brookings Institution Press.

(2007) 'Venezuela: Crowding Out the Opposition,' *Journal of Democracy* 18(2): 99–115.

Cotler, J. (1994) *Política y Sociedad en el Perú*. Lima: Instituto de Estudios Peruanos.

(2000) 'La Gobernabilidad en el Perú: Entre el Autoritarismo y la Democracia,' in J. Cotler and R. Grompone (eds.), *El Fujimorismo: ascenso y caída de un régimen autoritario*. Lima: Instituto de Estudios Peruanos, 13–75.

Crisp, B. F. (2000) *Democratic Institutional Design: The Powers and Incentives of Venezuelan Politicians and Interest Groups*. Stanford, CA: Stanford University Press.

Cross, W. (2002) 'Changes in the Party System and Anti-party Sentiment,' in W. Cross (ed.), *Political Parties, Representation, and Electoral Democracy in Canada*, Don Mills, ON: Oxford University Press, 68–86.

Cross, W. and L. Young (2002) 'Policy Attitudes of Party Members in Canada: Evidence of Ideological Politics,' *Canadian Journal of Political Science*, 35(4): 859–80.

Cruz González, R. (2006) 'El grupo de Ebrard se lanza contra Cárdenas,' *La Jornada*, 7 September.

Csergő, Z. and K. Deegan-Krause (2011) 'Liberalism and Cultural Claims in Central and Eastern Europe: Toward a Pluralist Balance,' *Nations and Nationalism* 17(1): 85–107.

(2003) 'Liberalism, Nationalism and Cultural Rights in Central and Eastern Europe,' paper presented at the annual American Political Science Association meeting, Philadelphia, September 29.

Czesnik, M. (2009) 'Voter Turnout in Post-communist Europe,' paper presented at the International Workshop "European Elections 2009–Europeanization: Parties, Institutions, Member States," *Budapest*, 22–23 May.

Daeschner, J. (1993) *The War of the End of Democracy: Mario Vargas Llosa vs. Alberto Fujimori*. Lima: Peru Reporting.

Dahl, R. (1956) *A Preface to Democratic Theory*. New Haven: Yale University Press.

(1970) *After the Revolution? Authority in a Good Society*. New Haven: Yale University Press.

(1971) *Polyarchy: Participation and Opposition*. New Haven, CT: Yale University Press.

(1982): *Dilemmas of Pluralist Democracy*. New Haven: Yale University Press.

(1989) *Democracy and Its Critics*. New Haven: Yale University Press.

(1998) *On Democracy*. New Haven: Yale University Press.

(2000) How Democratic is the American Constitution? New Haven: Yale University Press, 2nd edition.

(2001) 'Democracy,' in N. J. Smelser and P. B. Baltes (eds.), *International Encyclopedia of Social and Behavioral Sciences*. Oxford: Elsevier, 3405–8.

(2006) *On Political Equality*. New Haven: Yale University Press.

Damen, S. (2001) 'Strategieën tegen extreem-rechts. Het cordon sanitaire onder de loep,' *Tijdschrift voor Sociologie* 22(1): 89–110.

Decker, F. (ed.) (2006) *Populismus: Gefahr für die Demokratie oder nützliches Korrektiv?*. Wiesbaden: VS Verlag für Sozialwissenschaften.

(2008) 'Germany: Right-wing Populist Failures and Left-wing Successes,' in D. Albertazzi and D. McDonnell (eds.), *Twenty-First Century Populism. The Spectre of Western European Democracy*. Basingstoke: Palgrave Macmillan, 119–34.

De Cleen, B. (2009) 'Popular Music Against Extreme Right Populism: The Vlaams Belang and the 0110 concerts in Belgium,' *International Journal of Cultural Studies* 12(6): 577–95.

De Cleen, B. and N. Carpentier (2010) 'Contesting the Populist Claim on "The People" Through Popular Culture: The 0110 Concerts versus the Vlaams Belang,' *Social Semiotics* 20(2): 175–96

De Decker, P., C. Kesteloot, F. De Maarschalck, and J. Vranken (2005) 'Revitalizing the City in an Anti-Urban Context: Extreme Right and the

Rise of Urban Policies in Flanders, Belgium,' *International Journal of Urban and Regional Research* 29(1): 152–71.

Deegan-Krause, K. (2000) *Accountability and Party Competition in Slovakia and the Czech Republic*. South Bend, IN: University of Notre Dame.

(2003) 'The Ambivalent Influence of the European Union on Democratization in Slovakia,' in P. Kubicek (ed.), *The European Union and Democratization*. London: Routledge, 56–86.

(2004) 'Uniting the Enemy: Politics and the Convergence of Nationalisms in Slovakia,' *East European Politics and Societies* 18(4): 651–96.

(2006) *Elected Affinities: Democracy and Party Competition in Slovakia and the Czech Republic*. Palo Alto, CA: Stanford University Press.

Deegan-Krause, K. and T. Haughton. (2008) 'Live Fast, Die Young? Populist Appeals in Slovak Politics in Comparative Perspective', paper prepared for the ECPR Joint Sessions, Rennes, France, 16 April.

(2009) 'Toward a More Useful Conceptualization of Populism: Types and Degrees of Populist Appeals in the Case of Slovakia,' *Politics & Policy* 37(4): 821–41.

Degregori, C. I. (2000) *La década de la antipolítica: auge y huida de Alberto Fujimori y Vladimiro Montesinos*. Lima: Instituto de Estudios Peruanos.

(2003) 'Peru: The Vanishing of a Regime and the Challenge of Democratic Rebuilding,' in J. I. Domínguez and M. Shifter (eds.), *Constructing Democratic Governance in Latin America*. Baltimore: Johns Hopkins University Press, 220–43.

Degregori, C. I. and C. Meléndez (2007) *El nacímiento de los otorongos: el congreso de la república durante los gobiernos de Alberto Fujimori (1990–2000)*. Lima: Instituto de Estudios Peruanos.

Degregori, C. I. and R. Grompone (1991) *Demonios y redentores en el Nuevo Perú: una tragedia en dos vueltas*. Lima: Instituto de Estudios Peruanos.

Dekker, P. and T. van der Meer (2004) 'Politiek vertrouwen 1997–2004,' *Tijdschrift voor de Sociale Sector* 58(12): 33–5.

Dekker, P., L. Halman, and T. van der Meer (2006) 'Ontwikkelingen in Politiek Vertrouwen in Europa, 1981–2004,' in A. Korsten and P. de Goede (eds.), *Bouwen aan Vertrouwen in het Openbaar Bestuur: Diagnoses en Remedies*. Den Haag: Elsevier Overheid, 61–78.

De Lange, S. (2008) *From Pariah to Power: Explanations for the Government Participation of Radical Right-Wing Populist Parties in West European Parliamentary Democracies*. Antwerp: University of Antwerp.

de la Torre, C. (2010) *Populist Seduction in Latin America*, Athens, OH: Ohio University Press, 2nd ed.

(2000) *Populist Seduction in Latin America. The Ecuadorian Experience*. Athens, OH: Ohio University Press.

de la Torre, C. and E. Peruzzotti (eds.) (2008): *El retorno del pueblo: populismo y nuevas democracias en América Latina*. Quito: FLACSO-Ecuador.

Deschouwer, K. (2001) 'De Zorgeloze Consensus. De Statuten van het Vlaams Blok en de Partijtheorie,' *Tijdschrift voor Sociologie* 22(1): 63–87.

Detant, A. (2005) 'The Politics of Anti-Racism in Belgium: A Qualitative Analysis of the Discourse of the Anti-Racist Movement Hand in Hand in the 1990s,' *Ethnicities* 5(2): 183–215.

De Winter, L. and J. Ackaert (1998) 'Compulsory Voting in Belgium: A Reply to Hooghe and Pelleriaux,' *Electoral Studies* 17(4): 425–8.

De Witte, H. (ed.) (1997) *Bestrijding van racism and rechts-extremisme: wetenschappelijke bijdragen aan het maatschappelijk debat*. Leuven: Acco.

De Witte, H. and P. L. H. Scheepers (1997) 'Twintig jaar Vlaams Blok: herkomst, evolutie en toekomst van partij en kiezers,' *Internationale Spectator* 51: 420–8.

Diamond, L. and L. Morlino (2005) 'Introduction,' in L. Diamond and L. Morlino (eds.), *Assessing the Quality of Democracy*. Baltimore: The Johns Hopkins University Press, ix–xliii.

Dietz, H. A. and D. J. Myers (2007) 'From Thaw to Deluge: Party System Collapse in Venezuela and Peru,' *Latin American Politics and Society* 49(2): 59–86.

Di Tella, T. (1965) 'Populism and Reform in Latin America,' in C. Véliz (ed.), *Obstacles to Change in Latin America*. Oxford: Oxford University Press, 47–74.

Dornbusch, R. and S. Edwards (eds.) (1991) *The Macroeconomics of Populism in Latin America*. Chicago: University of Chicago Press.

Doorenspleet, R. and P. Kopecký (2008) 'Against the Odds: Deviant Cases of Democratization,' *Democratization* 15(4): 697–713.

Doorenspleet, R. and C. Mudde (2008) 'Upping the Odds: Deviant Democracies and Theories of Democratization,' *Democratization* 15(4): 815–32.

Drake, P. (1978) *Socialism and Populism in Chile, 1932–52*. Urbana: University of Illinois Press.

(2009) *Between Tyranny and Anarchy. A History of Democracy in Latin America, 1800–2006*. Stanford: Stanford University Press.

Durand, F. (2003) *Riqueza económica y pobreza política: reflexiones sobre las elites del poder en un país inestable*. Lima: Universidad Católica.

Dvořáková, V. (1991) 'The Politics of Anti-Politics? The Radical Right in the Czech Republic: Past and Present,' in L. B. Sørensen and L. Eliason (eds.), *Fascism, Liberalism and Social Democracy in Central Europe*. Aarhus: Aarhus University Press, 166–79.

(2003) 'Civil Society in the Czech Republic: "Impulse 99" and "Thank You, Time To Go,"' in P. Kopecký and C. Mudde (eds.), *Uncivil Society? Contentious Politics in Post-Communist Europe*. London: Routledge, 134–56.

Easton, D. (1965) *A Systems Analysis of Political Life*. New York: Wiley.

Eatwell, R. and C. Mudde (eds.) (2004) *Western Democracies and the New Extreme Right Challenge*. London: Routledge.

Economic Commission for Latin America and the Caribbean (1999) *Statistical Yearbook for Latin America and the Caribbean*. Santiago, Chile: United Nations.

(2000) *Statistical Yearbook for Latin America and the Caribbean*. Santiago, Chile: United Nations.

Edwards, S. (2010) *Left Behind: Latin America and the False Promise of Populism*. Chicago: Chicago University Press.

Ellner, S. (2008) 'The Hugo Chávez Phenomenon: Anti-imperialism from Above or Radical Democracy from Below?,' in F. Rosen (ed.), *Empire and Dissent. The United States and Latin America*. Durham and London: Duke University Press, 205–27.

Ellner, S. and D. Hellinger (eds.) (2003) *Venezuelan Politics in the Chávez Era: Class, Polarization, and Conflict*. Boulder, CO: Lynne Rienner.

Enriquez, S. (2006a) 'Tribunal's Ruling Not Likely to End Crisis,' *Los Angeles Times*, 6 September: A8.

(2006b) 'Calderón Shifts Attention to the Poor,' *Los Angeles Times*, 7 September: A9.

Erk, J. (2005) 'From Vlaams Blok to Vlaams Belang: The Belgian Far-Right Renames Itself,' *West European Politics* 28(3): 493–502.

European Commission (2003) *Eurobarometer: Public Opinion in the European Union* 58, available at: http://ec.europa.eu/public_opinion/archives/eb/eb58/eb58_en.pdf.

Evans, R. (1998) *Desnutrición en Venezuela: Periodo 1990–1996*. Caracas: Instituto Nacional de Nutrición.

Fabrý, J. (1997) 'Lze rozpustit republikány?' *Nová Přítomnost* 5: 26–7.

Falkner, G. (2006) 'Österreich als EU-Mitglied: Kontroversen auf internationaler und nationaler Ebene,' in E. Tálos (ed.), *Schwarz-Blau: Eine Bilanz des Neu-Regierens*. Vienna/Münster: LIT, 86–101.

Fallend, F. (2001) 'Austria,' *European Journal of Political Research* 40(3–4): 238–53.

(2002) 'Austria,' *European Journal of Political Research* 41(7–8): 906–14.

(2003) 'Austria,' *European Journal of Political Research* 42(7–8): 887–99.

(2004a) 'Austria,' *European Journal of Political Research* 43(7–8): 934–49.

(2004b) 'Are Right-Wing Populism and Government Participation Incompatible? The Case of the Freedom Party of Austria,' *Representation* 40(2): 115–30.

(2005) 'Austria,' *European Journal of Political Research* 44(7–8): 940–56.

(2006) 'Austria,' *European Journal of Political Research* 45(7–8): 1042–54.

(2007) 'Austria,' *European Journal of Political Research* 46(7–8): 876–90.

Farney, J. (2009) *Social Conservatives and the Boundaries of Politics in Canada*. Ph.D. Dissertation, Department of Political Science, University of Toronto.

Fawn, R. (2001) 'Czech Attitudes Towards Roma: "Expecting More of Havel's Country,"' *Europe-Asia Studies* 53(8): 1193–219.

Fernandes, S. (2007) 'Barrio Women and Popular Politics in Chávez's Venezuela,' *Latin American Politics & Society* 49(3): 97–127.

Ferrero Costa, E. (1993) 'Peru's Presidential Coup,' *Journal of Democracy* 4(1): 28–40.

Filc, D. (2010) *The Political Right in Israel. Different Faces of Jewish Populism*. London: Routledge.

Flanagan, T. (1995) *Waiting for the Wave: The Reform Party and Preston Manning*. Toronto: Stoddart.

(2008) *Harper's Team*. Montreal: McGill-Queen's University Press.

(2010) '"Something Blue….": Conservative Organization in an Era of Permanent Campaign,' paper presented at the Annual Meetings of the Canadian Political Science Association, Montreal, 3 June.

Flores-Macias, F. (2009) 'Electoral Volatility in 2006,' in J. I. Domínguez, C. Lawson, and A. Moreno (eds.), *Consolidating Mexico's Democracy: The 2006 Presidential Campaign in Comparative Perspective*. Baltimore: The Johns Hopkins University Press, 191–208.

FOCUS (1992–2000). *Public opinion survey* [Computer file].

Formisano, R. P. (2007) *For the People: American Populist Movements from the Revolution to the 1850s*. Chapel Hill: The University of North Carolina Press.

Fossum, J.-E. and D. Laycock (2010) 'Representative Democracy in the EU and Canada Compared,' paper presented at the Annual Meeting of the Canadian Political Science Association, Montreal, 3 June.

— (2011) 'Representation and Democratic Legitimacy: Comparing the European Union and Canada,' paper presented at the seminar "Challenging Democracy: Matchpoints," *Aarhus*, May.

Fowks, J. (2000) *Suma y resta de la realidad: medios de comunicación y elecciones generales 2000 en el Perú*. Lima: Fundación Friedrich Ebert.

FPÖ (1997) *The Programme of the Freedom Party of Austria*. Vienna: FPÖ.

Freeden, M. (1998) 'Is Nationalism a Distinct Ideology?' *Political Studies* 46(4): 748–65.

Freidenberg, F. (2007) *La tentación populista: una vía al poder en América Latina*. Madrid: Editorial Síntesis.

Friesen, J. (2010) 'The "Smiling Buddha" and his multicultural charms,' *The Globe and Mail*, 29 January.

Friesen, J. and J. Ibbitson (2010) 'Conservative Immigrants boost Tory Fortunes,' *The Globe and Mail*, 4 October.

Friesl, C., T. Hofer, and R. Wieser (2009) 'Die Österreicher/-innen und die Politik,' in C. Friesl, R. Polak and U. Hamachers-Zuba (eds.), *Die Österreicher/-innen: Wertewandel 1990–2008*. Vienna: Czernin, 205–93.

García Calderón, E. (2001) 'Peru's Decade of Living Dangerously,' *Journal of Democracy* 12(2): 46–58.

García-Guadilla, M. P. (2003) 'Civil Society: Institutionalization, Fragmentation, Autonomy,' in S. Ellner and D. Hellinger (eds.), *Venezuelan Politics in the Chávez Era: Class, Polarization, and Conflict*. Boulder, CO: Lynne Rienner, 179–96.

Garner, T. I. and K. Terrell (1998) 'A Gini Decomposition Analysis of Inequality in the Czech Republic and Slovakia During the Transition,' *Economics of Transition* 6(1): 23–46.

Gates, Leslie C. (2010) *Electing Chávez: The Business of Anti-Neoliberal Politics in Venezuela*. Pittsburgh: University of Pittsburgh Press.

Gehler, M. (2003) 'Kontraproduktive Intervention: Die 'EU 14' und der Fall Österreich oder vom Triumph des 'Primats der Innenpolitik' 2000–2003,' in M. Gehler, A. Pelinka and, and G. Bischof (eds.), *Österreich in der Europäischen Union: Bilanz seiner Mitgliedschaft*. Vienna et al.: Böhlau, 121–81.

Germani, G. (1978) *Authoritarianism, Fascism, and National Populism*. New Brunswick: Transaction.

Geys, B., B. Heyndels, and J. Vermeir (2006) 'Explaining the Formation of Minimal Coalitions: Anti-System Parties and Anti-Pact Rules,' *European Journal for Political Research* 45: 957–84.

Geysels, J. (2008) 'Over het Cordon Sanitaire en Andere Soepelheden,' *Res Publica* 50(1): 50–4.

Gidengil, E., A. Blais, N. Nevitte, and R. Nadeau (2001) 'The Correlates and Consequences of Anti-Partyism in the 1997 Canadian Election,' *Party Politics* 7(4): 491–513.

Gidengil, E., J. Everitt, P. Fournier, and N. Nevitte (2008) *Canadian Election Study, 2008*. Toronto, ON: York University Institute for Social Research (ISR).

Gijsels, H. (1992) *Het Vlaams Blok*. Leuven: Kritak.

(1994) *Open je ogen voor het Vlaams Blok ze sluit*. Leuven: Kritak.

Goldfrank, B. (2011) 'The Left and Participatory Democracy: Brazil, Uruguay, and Venezuela,' in S. Levitsky and K. M. Roberts (eds.), *The Resurgence of the Left in Latin America*. Baltimore: Johns Hopkins University Press, 162–183.

Gorman, S. M. (1997) 'Antipolitics in Peru,' in B. Loveman and T. M. Davies (eds.), *The Politics of Antipolitics: The Military in Latin America*. Lanham, MD: SR Books, 300–26.

Gould, J. and K. Krause (1998) 'Ked volby znamenaju prilis vela ...,' *OS: Forum obcianskej spolocnosti* 2(6): 51–4

Gratius, S. (2007) 'La "tercera ola populista" de América Latina,' *FRIDE Working Paper*, 45.

Grayson, G. (2006) *Mexican Messiah: Andrés Manuel López Obrador*. University Park, PA: Penn State Press.

Green, A. and C. S. Leff (1997) 'The Quality of Democracy: Mass-Elite Linkages in the Czech Republic,' *Democratization* 4(4): 63–87.

Green, J. (2006) 'The Rebirth of Populism in Latin America Poses a Powerful Challenge to the Neoliberal Order,' available at: venezuelanalysis.com/analysis/1903.

Grompone, R. (1991) *El velero en el viento: política y sociedad en Lima*. Lima: Instituto de Estudios Peruanos.

Guillermoprieto, A. (1995) *The Heart that Bleeds: Latin America Now*. New York: Vintage.

Hacker, J. and P. Pierson (2010) *Winner-Take-All Politics. How Washington Made the Rich Richer – and Turned Its Back on the Middle Class*. New York: Simon and Schuster.

Hakhverdian, A. and C. Koop (2007) 'Consensus Democracy and Support for Populist Parties,' *Acta Politica* 42(4): 401–20.

Handlin, S. and R. B. Collier (2011) 'Left Party Linkages: Partisanship, Direct Contact, and Social Organization,' in S. Levitsky and K. M. Roberts (eds.), *The Resurgence of the Left in Latin America*. Baltimore: Johns Hopkins University Press, 139–161.

Hanley, S. (2007) 'Klaus Thinktank Warns of Islamicisation,' available at: http://drseansdiary.wordpress.com/2007/08/20/klaus-thinktank-newsletter-warns-of-islamicization (accessed 1 December 2010).

(2008) *The New Right in the New Europe: Czech Transformation and Right-Wing Politics, 1989–2006*. London: Routledge.

Harper, S. (2004) 'One Conservative Voice, Notes for Address by Stephen Harper,' *Ottawa Leadership Launch*, 12 January.

(2006) 'Notes for an Address by the Right Honourable Stephen Harper, Prime Minister of Canada, In Support of the Measures Contained in the Speech from the Throne: "Turning a New Leaf"'

Haughton, T. (2005) *Constraints and Opportunities of Leadership in Post-Communist Europe*. Aldershot: Ashgate.

Hawkins, K. (2009) 'Is Chávez Populist? Measuring Populist Discourse in Comparative Perspective,' *Comparative Political Studies*, 24(6): 1040–67.

(2010a) *Venezuela's Chavismo and Populism in Comparative Perspective*. Cambridge: Cambridge University Press.

(2010b) 'Who Mobilizes? Participatory Democracy in Chávez's Bolivarian Revolution,' *Latin American Politics and Society* 52(3): 31–66.

Heinisch, R. (2003) 'Success in Opposition – Failure in Government: Explaining the Performance of Right-Wing Populist Parties in Public Office,' *West European Politics* 26(3): 91–130.

(2008) 'Austria: The Structure and Agency of Austrian Populism,' in D. Albertazzi and D. McDonnell (eds.), *Twenty-First Century Populism: The Spectre of Western European Democracy*. Basingstoke: Palgrave Macmillan, 67–83.

(2010) 'Determinants of Success and Failure of Populists in Public Office: Preliminary Evidence from the Experience of Austrian Populist Parties in Government at the State and National Level,' paper prepared for the ECPR Joint Sessions, Münster, March 22–27.

Held, D. (1996) *Models of Democracy*. Cambridge: Polity.

Hellinger, D. (2003) 'Political Overview: The Breakdown of *Puntofijismo* and the Rise of *Chavismo*,' in S. Ellner and D. Hellinger (eds.), *Venezuelan Politics in the Chávez Era: Class, Polarization, and Conflict*. Boulder, CO: Lynne Rienner, 27–54.

Henderson, K. (2002) *Slovakia: The Escape from Invisibility*. London: Routledge.

Hermet, G. (2003) 'El populismo como concepto,' *Revista de Ciencia Política* XXIII(1): 5–18.

Higley, J. and M. Burton (2006) *Elite Foundations of Liberal Democracy*. Lanham: Rowman & Littlefield.

Hindess, B. and M. Sawer (eds.) (2004) *Us Against Them: Anti-Elitism in Australia*. Bentley: API Network.

Hofstadter, R. (1969) 'North America,' in G. Ionescu and E. Gellner (eds.), *Populism. Its Meanings and Characteristics*. London: Weidenfeld and Nicolson, 9–27.

Hooghe, M., S. Marien, and T. Pauwels (2009) 'Where Do Distrusting Voters Go To If There is No Exit or Voice Option,' paper presented at the ECPR General Conference, Potsdam, 10–12 September.

Hooghe, M. and K. Pelleriaux (1998) 'Compulsory Voting in Belgium: An Application of the Lijphart Thesis,' *Electoral Studies* 17(4): 419–24.

Howe, P. and D. Northrup (2000) 'Strengthening Canadian Democracy: The Views of Canadians,' *Policy Matters* 1(5): 104.

Huber, J. and R. Inglehart (1993) 'Expert Interpretations of Party Space and Party Locations in 42 Societies,' *Party Politics* 1(1): 73–111.

Human Rights Watch (2008) *A Decade under Chávez: Political Intolerance and Lost Opportunities for Advancing Human Rights in Venezuela*. Washington, DC: Human Rights Watch.

Human Rights Watch(2010) 'Venezuela: End Prosecutions of Dissenters,' available at: http://www.hrw.org/en/news/2010/03/25/venezuela-end-prosecutions-dissenters (accessed 25 July 2010).

Ibbitson, J. (1997) *Promised Land: Inside the Mike Harris Revolution*. Scarborough, ON: Prentice Hall Canada.

(2010) 'Placating Tory Base on the Census Causes Harper Government Grief,' *The Globe and Mail*, 19 July.

IFE (1991) *Contienda electoral en las elecciones presidenciales*. Mexico City: Instituto Federal Electoral.

IMAS (2000) 'Unter dem Eindruck des EU-Unrechts: Österreicher rücken zusammen', *IMAS-Report* 10, available at: http://www.imas.at/content/download/404/1518/version/1/file/10–04%5B1%5D.pdf.

Innes, A. (2001) *Czechoslovakia: The Short Goodbye*. New Haven, CT: Yale University Press.

Intercampus (1990) *El debate. Versión completa del debate realizada entro los Candidatos a la Presidencia de la República, en el Centro Cívico de Lima, el 3 de junio de 1990*. Lima: Universidad del Pacífico.

International Labour Organisation (1998) *1998 Labour Overview: Latin America and the Caribbean*. Lima: International Labour Organisation.

Ionescu, G. (1969) 'Eastern Europe,' in G. Ionescu and E. Gellner (eds.), *Populism: Its Meanings and Characteristics*. London: Weidenfeld and Nicolson, 97–121.

Ionescu, G. and E. Gellner (eds.) (1969) *Populism: Its Meanings and National Characteristics*. London: Weidenfeld and Nicolson.

Jagers, J. (2002) 'Eigen Democratie Eerst! Een Comparatief Onderzoek naar het Intern Democratisch Gehalte van de Vlaamse Politieke Partijen,' *Res Publica* 44(1): 73–96.

(2006) *De Stem van het Volk! Populisme als Concept Getest bij Vlaamse Politieke Partijen*. Antwerp: University of Antwerp.

Jagers, J. and S. Walgrave (2007) 'Populism as Political Communication Style: An Empirical Study of Political Parties' Discourse in Belgium,' *European Journal of Political Research* 46: 319–45.

Johnston, R. (2008) 'Polarized Pluralism in the Canadian Party System,' *Canadian Journal of Political Science* 41(4): 815–34.

Johnston, R., A. Blais, E. Gidengil, and N. Nevitte (1995) *The Challenge of Direct Democracy: The 1992 Canadian Referendum*. Montreal: McGill-Queen's University Press.

Jun, U. (2006) 'Populismus als Regierungsstil in westeuropäischen Parteiendemokratien: Deutschland, Frankreich und Großbritannien,' in F. Decker (ed.), *Populismus. Gefahr für die Demokratie oder nützliches Korrektiv?* Wiesbaden: VS Verlag, 233–54.

Kalyvas, A. (2005) 'Popular Sovereignty, Democracy, and the Constituent Power,' *Constellations* 12(2): 223–44.

Kampwirth, K. (ed.) (2011) *Gender and Populism in Latin America. Passionate Politics*. University Park: Pennsylvania State University.

Katz R. S. and P. Mair (1995) 'Changing Models of Party Organization and Party Democracy. The Emergence of the Cartel Party,' *Party Politics* 1(5): 5–28.

(1998) *The Populist Persuasion: An American History*. Ithaca, NY: Cornell University Press.

(1995) *The Populist Persuasion: An American History*. New York: Basic Books.

Keane, J. (2009): *The Life and Death of Democracy*. New York: Norton.

Keman, H. (2009) 'Comparative Research Methods,' in D. Caramani (ed.), *Comparative Politics*. Oxford: Oxford University Press, 63–82.

Kenney, C. (1996) '¿Por qué el autogolpe? Fujimori y el congreso, 1990–1992,' in F. Tuesta Soldevilla (ed.), *Los enigmas del poder: Fujimori 1990–1996*. Lima: Fundación Friedrich Ebert, 75–104.

(2004) *Fujimori's Coup and the Breakdown of Democracy in Latin America*. Notre Dame: University of Notre Dame Press.

Khol, A. (1996) 'Die FPÖ im Spannungsfeld von Ausgrenzung, Selbstausgrenzung, Verfassungsbogen und Regierungsfähigkeit,' *Österreichisches Jahrbuch für Politik* 1995: 193–221.

(2010) 'Veritas filia temporis – die Wahrheit ist eine Tochter der Zeit: Die Nationalratswahlen am 3. Oktober 1999 im Rückblick,' *Österreichisches Jahrbuch für Politik* 2009: 379–97.

Kirchheimer, O. (1965) 'Der Wandel des westeuropäischen Parteisystems,' *Politische Vierteljahresschrift* 6: 20–41.

Kitschelt, H. (2002) 'Popular Dissatisfaction with Democracy: Populism and Party Systems,' in Y. Meny and Y. Surel (eds.), *Democracies and the Populist Challenge*. Basingstoke: Palgrave, 179–96.

Kitschelt, H., Z. Mansfeldová, R. Markowski, and G. Tóka (1999) *Post-Communist Party Systems: Competition, Representation and Inter-Party Cooperation*. Cambridge: Cambridge University Press.

Kitschelt, H. and S. Wilkinson (2007) 'Citizen-politician Linkages: An Introduction,' in H. Kitschelt and S. Wilkinson (eds.), *Patrons, Clients, and Policies. Patterns of Democratic Accountability and Political Competition*. New York: Cambridge University Press, 1–49.

Kitzberger, P. (2010) 'The Media Activism of Latin America's Leftist Governments: Does Ideology Matter?' *German Institute of Global Area Studies (GIGA) Working Papers*, No 151.

Kleis Nielsen, R. (2006) 'Hegemony, Radical Democracy and Populism,' *Distinktion: Scandinavian Journal of Political Theory* 18: 77–97.

Knopff, R. and F. L. Morton (2000). *The Charter Revolution and the Court Party*. Peterborough, ON: Broadview.

Koeble T. and E. Lipuma (2008) 'Democratizing Democracy: A Postcolonial Critique of Conventional Approaches to the "Measurement of Democracy,"' *Democratization* 15(1): 1–28.

Kopeček, L. (2008) 'Czech Social Democracy and its "Cohabitation" with the Communist Party: The Story of a Neglected Affair,' *Communist and Post-Communist Studies* 41(3): 317–38.

Knight, A. (1998) 'Populism and Neo-Populism in Latin America, especially Mexico,' *Journal of Latin American Studies* 30(2): 223–48.

Krastev, I. (2007) 'The Strange Death of the Liberal Consensus,' *Journal of Democracy* 18(4): 56–63.

Kreidl, M. and K. Vlachová (2000) 'Rise and Decline of Right-Wing Extremism in the Czech Republic in the 1990s,' *Czech Sociological Review* 8(1): 69–91.

Krouwel, A. (2003) 'Otto Kirchheimer and the Catch-All Party,' *Western European Politics* 26(2): 23–40.

Kymlicka, W. (1996) *Multicultural Citizenship*. Don Mills, ON: Oxford University Press.

(1998) *Finding Our Way: Rethinking Ethnocultural Relations in Canada*. Don Mills, ON: Oxford University Press.

Laclau, Ernesto (1977) *Politics and Ideology in Marxist Theory*. London: New Left Books.

(2005a) *On Populist Reason*. London: Verso.

(2005b) 'Populism: What's in a Name?,' in F. Panizza (ed.), *Populism and the Mirror of Democracy*. London: Verso, 32–49.

Laclau, E. and C. Mouffe (1985) *Hegemony and Socialist Theory: Towards a Radical Democratic Politics*. London: Verso.

Laird, G. (1998) *Slumming It at the Rodeo: The Cultural Roots of Canada's Right-wing Revolution*. Vancouver: Douglas and Macintyre.

Lanzaro, J. (2006) 'La "tercera ola" de las izquierdas latinoamericanas,' in P. P. Herrero (ed.), *La "izquierda" en América Latina*. Madrid: Editorial Pablo Iglesias, 47–81.

Latinobarómetro (1998) *Informe de prensa: encuesta Latinobarómetro 1998*. Santiago: Corporación Latinobarómetro.

(2005) *Informe Latinobarómetro 2005*. Santiago: Corporación Latinobarómetro.

Laver, M. and W. B. Hunt (1989) *Policy and Party Competition*. London: Routledge.

Laycock, D. (1990) *Populism and Democratic Thought in the Canadian Prairies, 1910–1945*. Toronto: University of Toronto Press.

(2001) *The New Right and Democracy in Canada*. Don Mills, ON: Oxford University Press.

(2005a) 'Populism and the New Right in English Canada,' in F. Panizza (ed.), *Populism and the Mirror of Democracy*. London: Verso, 172–201.

(2005b) 'Reconfiguring Popular Sovereignty in Post-Charter Canada: The View from the Canadian New Right,' in J.-E. Fossum (ed.), *Constitutional Processes in Canada and the EU Compared*. Oslo: Centre for European Studies, University of Oslo, 225–58.

Laycock, D. and D. D. Barney (1999) 'Right-populists and Plebiscitary Politics in Canada,' *Party Politics* 5(3): 317–40.

Leff, C. S. (1997) *The Czech and Slovak Republics: Nation versus State*. Boulder, CO: Westview.

Legler, T., S. F. Lean, and D. S. Boniface (2007) 'The International and Transnational Dimensions of Democracy in the Americas,' in T. Legler, S. F. Lean, and D. S. Boniface (eds.), *Promoting Democracy in the Americas*. Baltimore: Johns Hopkins University Press, 1–18.

Levitsky, S. and M. A. Cameron (2003) 'Democracy Without Parties? Political Parties and Regime Change in Fujimori's Peru,' *Latin American Politics and Society* 45(3): 1–33.

Levitsky, S. and K. M. Roberts (eds.) (2011) *The Resurgence of the Left in Latin America*. Baltimore: Johns Hopkins University Press.

Levitsky, S. and L. Way (2002) 'The Rise of Competitive Authoritarianism,' *Journal of Democracy* 13(2): 61–75.

(2010) *Competitive Authoritarianism: Hybrid Regimes after the Cold War*. New York: Cambridge University Press.

Levy, D. C. and K. Bruhn, with E. Zebadua (2006) *Mexico: The Struggle for Democratic Development*. Berkeley, CA: University of California Press, 2nd edition.

Lewis, P. G. (2008) 'Changes in the Party Politics of the New EU-Member States in Central Europe: Patterns of Europeanization and Democratization,' *Journal of Southern Europe and the Balkans* 10(2): 151–65.

Lijphart, A. (1999) *Patterns of Democracy: Government Forms and Performance in Twenty-Six Countries*. New Haven, CT: Yale University Press.

Linz, J. J. (1978) *The Breakdown of Democratic Regimes: Crisis, Breakdown, and Reequilibration*. Baltimore: Johns Hopkins University Press.

Lipset, S. M. (1960) *Political Man. The Social Bases of Politics*. Garden City: Doubleday.

López Maya, M. (2003) 'Hugo Chávez Frías: His Movement and His Presidency,' in S. Ellner and D. Hellinger (eds.), *Venezuelan Politics in the Chávez Era: Class, Polarization, and Conflict*. Boulder, CO: Lynne Rienner, 73–91.

——— (2005) *Del viernes negro al referendo revocatorio*. Caracas: Alfadil.

López Obrador, A. M. (2005a) '50 compromisos para recuperar el orgullo nacional,' available at: www.lopezobrador.org.mx (accessed 26 February 2006).

——— (2005b) 'Por una verdadera purificación de la vida pública,' speech in Apan, Hidalgo, 3 November, available at: www.lupaciudadana.com.mx (accessed 9 September 2010).

——— (2005c) 'Arriba los de abajo, abajo los de arriba,' speech in Tezontepec, Hidalgo, 4 November, available at: www.lupaciudadana.com.mx (accessed 9 September 2010).

——— (2005d) 'Se renovarán todas las instituciones de la República,' speech in Córdoba, Veracruz, 12 November, available at: www.lupaciudadana.com. mx (accessed 9 September 2010).

——— (2006a) 'Suprema Corte de Justicia o Supremo Corte de Derecho?' speech to Consejo Consultivo para un Proyecto Alternativo de Nación, Mexico City, 9 March, available at: www.lupaciudadana.com.mx (accessed 9 September 2010).

——— (2006b) 'Los elitistas dicen que no respetamos el Estado de derecho [...] lo que queremos nosotros es que haya verdaderamente legalidad,' speech in Tepeaca, Puebla, 10 March, available at: www.lupaciudadana.com.mx (accessed 9 September 2010).

——— (2006c) 'Las elecciones del Estado de México y la elección presidencial están muy relacionadas,' speech in Luvianos, Estado de México, 1 May, available at: www.lupaciudadana.com.mx (accessed 9 September 2010).

——— (2006d) 'La democracia no termina en lo electoral,' speech in Salamanca Guanajuato, 6 May, available at: www.lupaciudadana.com.mx (accessed 9 September 2010).

——— (2006e) 'Ya es tiempo de que el pueblo gobierne nuestro país, que sea el pueblo el que se beneficie,' speech in Huautla, Oaxaca, 13 May, available at: www.lupaciudadana.com.mx (accessed 9 September 2010).

——— (2006f) 'El 2 de julio vamos a demostrar que nunca va a poder el dinero con la dignidad y con la moral de nuestro pueblo,' speech in Guasave, Sinaloa, 17 May, available at: www.lupaciudadana.com.mx (accessed 9 September 2010).

——— (2006g) 'El triunfo de la derecha es moralmente imposible,' campaign closing speech in Queretaro, Queretaro, 21 June, available at: www.lupaciudadana. com.mx (accessed 9 September 2010).

——— (2006h) 'No habrá "terrorismo fiscal,"' campaign closing speech in León, Guanajuato, 23 June, available at: www.lupaciudadana.com.mx (accessed 9 September 2010).

——— (2007) *La mafia nos robó la Presidencia*. Mexico City: Editorial Grijalbo.

López Rodríguez, D. (2008) 'Evangelicals and Politics in Fujimori's Peru,' in P. Freston (ed.), *Evangelical Christianity and Democracy in Latin America*. New York: Oxford University Press, 131–61.

Lubbers, M. (2001) *Exclusionistic Electorates: Extreme Right-Wing Voting in Western Europe*. Nijmegen: Katholieke Universiteit Nijmegen.

Lubbers, M., P. Scheepers, and J. Billiet (2000) 'Multilevel Modeling of Vlaams Blok Voting: Individual and Contextual Characteristics of the Vlaams Blok Vote,' *Acta Politica* 35(4): 363–98.

Lucardie, P. (2010) 'Tussen establishment en extremisme: Populistische partijen in Nederland en Vlaanderen,' *Res Publica* 52(2): 149–72.

Luengo D., N. L. and M. G. Ponce Z. (1996) 'Lectura oblicua del proceso electoral de 1995,' *Politeia* 19: 63–80.

Luther, K. R. (2003) 'The Self-Destruction of a Right-Wing Populist Party? The Austrian Parliamentary Election of 2002,' *West European Politics* 26(2): 136–52.

(2006a) 'Die Freiheitliche Partei Österreichs (FPÖ) und das Bündnis Zukunft Österreich (BZÖ),' in H. Dachs et al. (eds.), *Politik in Österreich: Das Handbuch*. Vienna: Manz, 364–88.

(2006b) 'Strategien und (Fehl-)Verhalten: Die Freiheitlichen und die Regierungen Schüssel I und II,' in E. Tálos (ed.), *Schwarz-Blau: Eine Bilanz des "Neu-Regierens."* Vienna/Münster: LIT, 19–37.

(2008) 'Electoral Strategies and Performance of Austrian Right-wing Populism, 1986–2006,' in G. Bischof and F. Plasser (eds.), *The Changing Austrian Voter*. New Brunswick, NJ: Transaction, 104–22.

(2010) 'Governing with Right-Wing Populists and Managing the Consequences: Schüssel and the FPÖ,' in G. Bischof and F. Plasser (eds.), *The Schüssel Era in Austria*. New Orleans: University of New Orleans Press, 79–103.

Machonin, P. (1996) *Strategie sociální transformace české společnosti*. Brno: Doplněk.

Maingón, T. and T. Patruyo (1996) 'Las elecciones locales y regionales de 1995: tendencias políticas,' *Cuestiones Políticas* 16: 91–136.

Mainwaring, S. and T. R. Scully (1995) 'Introduction: Party Systems in Latin America,' in S. Mainwaring and T. R. Scully (eds.), *Building Democratic Institutions. Party Systems in Latin America*. Stanford: Stanford University Press, 1–34.

Mair, P. (2002) 'Populist Democracy vs Party Democracy,' in Y. Mény and Y. Surel (eds.), *Democracies and the Populist Challenge*. Basingstoke: Palgrave, 81–98.

(2006) 'Ruling the Void? The Hollowing of Western Democracy,' *New Left Review*, 42(6): 25–51.

Manning, E. C. and E. P. Manning (1967) *Political Realignment*. Toronto: McClelland and Stewart.

Manning, P. (1992) *The New Canada*. Toronto: Macmillan Canada.

Manning Centre for Building Democracy (2010) *The State of Canada's Conservative Movement*. Ottawa, ON: Manning Centre for Building Democracy.

March, L. and C. Mudde (2005) 'What's Left of the Radical Left? The European Radical Left after 1989: Decline and Mutation,' *Comparative European Politics* 3(1): 23–49.

Mareš, M. (2003) *Pravicový extremismus a radikalismus v ČR*. Brno: Barrister & Principal.

Martin, L. (2010) *Harperland: The Politics of Control*. Toronto: Viking Canada.

Matsuzatu, K. (2004) 'A Populist Island in an Ocean of Clan Politics: The Lukashenka Regime as an Exception among CIS Countries,' *Europe-Asia Studies* 56(2): 213–39.

Mauceri, P. (1996) *State Under Siege: Development and Policy Making in Peru*. Boulder, CO: Westview.

(2006) 'Electoral Authoritarian versus Partially Democratic Regimes: The Case of the Fujimori Government and the 2000 Elections,' in J. Carrión (ed.), *The Fujimori Legacy: The Rise of Electoral Authoritarianism in Peru*. University Park: The Pennsylvania State University Press, 150–77.

Mazzuca, S. (2010) 'Access to Power Versus Exercise of Power: Reconceptualizing the Quality of Democracy in Latin America,' *Studies in Comparative and International Development* 45(3): 334–57.

Mazzoleni, G. (2003) 'The Media and the Growth of Neo-Populism in Contemporary Democracies,' in G. Mazzoleni, J. Stewart and B. Horsfield (eds.), *The Media and Neo-Populism. A Contemporary Comparative Analysis*. Westport: Praeger, 1–20.

McClintock, C. (1996) 'La voluntad política presidencial y la ruptura constitucional de 1992 en el Perú,' in F. Tuesta Soldevilla (ed.), *Los enigmas del poder: Fujimori 1990–1996*. Lima: Fundación Friedrich Ebert, 53–74.

(2006a) 'Electoral Authoritarian Versus Partially Democratic Regimes: The Case of the Fujimori Government and the 2000 Elections,' in J. Carrión (ed.), *The Fujimori Legacy: The Rise of Electoral Authoritarianism in Peru*. University Park: Pennsylvania State University Press, 242–67.

(2006b) 'An Unlikely Comeback in Peru,' *Journal of Democracy* 17(4): 95–109.

McClintock, C. and F. Vallas (2003) *The United States and Peru: Cooperation – At a Cost*. New York: Routledge.

Meguid, B. (2005) 'Competition between Unequals: The Role of Mainstream Party Strategy in Niche Party Success,' *American Political Science Review* 99(3): 347–59.

Meissner, D. (2010) 'B.C. Will Dump HST If Voters Demand,' available at: http://www.saynotohstinbc.ca/news-articles/b-c-will-dump-hst-if-voters-demand (accessed 22 October 2010).

Méndez, P. and F. Valor (2002) 'Impulsan políticas sociales la popularidad de AMLO,' *Reforma*, 9 May: 4B.

Mény, Y. and Y. Surel (eds.) (2000) Par le Peuple, Pour le Peuple: le populisme et les démocraties. Paris: Editions Fayard.

(2002a) *Democracies and the Populist Challenge*. Basingstoke: Palgrave.

(2002b) 'The Constitutive Ambiguity of Populism,' in Y. Mény and Y. Surel (eds.), *Democracies and the Populist Challenge*. Basingstoke: Palgrave, 1–21.

Merkel, W. (2010) *Systemtransformation. Eine Einführung in die Theorie und Empirie der Transformationsforschung*. Wiesbaden: VS Verlag.

Merlingen, M., C. Mudde, and U. Sedelmeier (2001) 'The Right and the Righteous? European Norms, Domestic Politics and the Sanctions against Austria,' *Journal of Common Market Studies* 39(1): 59–77.

Meyer, T. (2006): 'Populismus und Medien,' in F. Decker (ed.), *Populismus. Gefahr für die Demokratie oder nützliches Korrektiv?* Wiesbaden: VS Verlag, 81–96.

Minkenberg, M. (2001) 'The Radical Right in Public Office: Agenda-Setting and Policy Effects,' *West European Politics* 24(4): 1–21.

Møller, J. and S. Skaaning (2011) 'Stateness first?' *Democratization* 18(1): 1–24.

Molina Vega, J. E. and C. Pérez Baralt (1996) 'Elecciones regionales de 1995: la consolidación de la abstención, el personalismo, y la desalineación,' *Cuestiones Políticas* 16: 73–90.

Morgan, J. (2007) 'Partisanship during the Collapse of Venezuela's Party System,' *Latin American Research Review* 42(1): 78–98.

Morlino, L. (2004) 'What Is a "Good" Democracy?' *Democratization* 11(5): 10–32.

Morrow, D. (2000) 'Jörg Haider and the New FPÖ: Beyond the Democratic Pale?' in P. Hainsworth (ed.), *The Politics of the Extreme Right: From the Margins to the Mainstream*. London: Pinter, 33–63.

Morton, F.L. (1998) 'The Charter of Rights: Myth and Reality,' in W. Gairdner (ed.), *Against Liberalism: Essays in Search of Freedom, Virtue and Order*. Toronto: Stoddart, 33–61.

Mouffe, C. (2000) *The Democratic Paradox*. London: Verso.

(2005a) 'The "End of Politics" and the Challenge of Right-wing Populism,' in F. Panizza (ed.), *Populism and the Mirror of Democracy*. London: Verso, 50–71.

(2005b) *On the Political*. London: Routledge.

Mouzelis, N. (1978) 'Ideology and Class Politics: A Critique of Ernesto Laclau,' *New Left Review* 112(6): 45–61.

(1985) 'On the Concept of Populism: Populist and Clientelist Modes of Incorporation in Semiperipheral Polities,' *Politics and Society* 14(3): 329–48.

Mudde, C. (1995) 'One against All, All against One! A Portrait of the Vlaams Blok,' *Patterns of Prejudice* 29(1): 5–28.

(2002): 'In the Name of the Peasantry, the Proletariat, and the People: Populisms in Eastern Europe,' in Y. Mény and Y. Surel (eds.), *Democracies and the Populist Challenge*. Basingstoke: Palgrave, 214–32.

(2004) 'The Populist *Zeitgeist*,' *Government & Opposition* 39(3): 541–63.

(2007) *Populist Radical Right Parties in Europe*. Cambridge: Cambridge University Press.

(2010) 'The Populist Radical Right: A Pathological Normalcy,' *West European Politics* 33(6): 1167–86.

Mudde, C. and C. Rovira Kaltwasser (2010) 'Populism and Democratization: From Friend to Foe?' paper presented at the workshop "Comparing Transitions across Regions," Oxford, UK, 6 November.

(2011) 'Voices of the Peoples: Populism in Europe and Latin America Compared,' *Kellogg Institute Working Paper*, 378.

(forthcoming) 'Populism', in M. Freeden, M. Stears, and L. Tower (eds.), *The Oxford Handbook of Political Ideologies*. Oxford: Oxford University Press.

Müller, W. C. (2000a) 'Austria: Tight Coalitions and Stable Government,' in W. C. Müller and K. Strøm (eds.), *Coalition Governments in Western Europe*. Oxford: Oxford University Press, 86–125.

(2000b) 'The Austrian Elections of October 1999: A Shift to the Right,' *West European Politics* 23(3): 191–200.

(2002) 'Evil or the "Engine of Democracy"? Populism and Party Competition in Austria,' in Y. Mény and Y. Surel (eds.), *Democracies and the Populist Change*. Basingstoke: Palgrave, 155–75.

(2004) 'The Parliamentary Election in Austria, November 2002,' *Electoral Studies* 23(2): 346–53.

Müller, W. C. and F. Fallend (2004) 'Changing Patterns of Party Competition in Austria: From Multipolar to Bipolar System,' *West European Politics* 27(5): 801–35.

Müller, W. C. and M. Jenny (2000) 'Abgeordnete, Parteien und Koalitionspolitik: Individuelle Präferenzen und politisches Handeln im Nationalrat,' *Österreichische Zeitschrift für Politikwissenschaft* 29(2): 137–56.

Murakami, Y. (2007) *Perú en la era del chino: la política no institucionalizada y el pueblo en busca de un salvador*. Peru: CIAS Center for Integrated Area Studies, Kyoto University.

Murphy, H. (2006) 'The Presidential Candidates,' *Washington Post*, 9 June.

Näsström, S. (2007) 'The Legitimacy of the People,' *Political Theory* 35(5): 624–58.

(2011) 'The Challenge of the All-Affected Principle,' *Political Studies* 59(1): 116–34.

Navia, P. and P. Walker (2009) 'Political Institutions, Populism, and Democracy in Latin America,' in S. Mainwaring and T. R. Scully (eds.), *Democratic Governance in Latin America*. Stanford: Stanford University Press, 246–65.

Nedelsky, N. (2009) *Defining the Sovereign Community: The Czech and Slovak Republics*. Philadelphia: University of Pennsylvania Press.

Nevitte, N. and S. White (2008) 'Citizen Expectations and Democratic Performance: The Sources and Consequences of Democratic Deficits from the Bottom Up,' paper presented at the conference 'Comparing the Democratic Deficit in Canada and the U.S.: Defining, Measuring, and Fixing,' Harvard University, Cambridge, MA, 8–10 May.

Norden, D. (2003) 'Democracy in Uniform: Chávez and the Venezuelan Armed Forces,' in S. Ellner and D. Hellinger (eds.), *Venezuelan Politics in the Chávez Era: Class, Polarization, and Conflict*. Boulder, CO: Lynne Rienner, 93–112.

Norris, P. (2005) *Radical Right: Parties and Voters in the Electoral Market*. New York: Cambridge University Press.

(2011) *Democratic Deficit. Critical Citizens Revisited*. New York: Cambridge University Press.

Nozick, R. (1974) *Anarchy, State, and Utopia*. New York: Basic Books.

Odbor verejnej mienky Kancelárie HZDS (1996) *5 rokov HZDS v tlači*. Bratislava: HZDS.

O'Donnell, G. (1992) 'Transitions, Continuities and Paradoxes' in G. O'Donnell and S. Valenzuela (eds.), *Issues in Democratic Consolidation: The New South American Democracies in Comparative Perspective*. Notre Dame: University of Notre Dame Press, 17–56.

(1994) 'Delegative Democracy,' *Journal of Democracy* 5(1): 55–69.

(1996) 'Illusions about Consolidation,' *Journal of Democracy* 7(2): 34–51.

Offe, C. (2003) 'Reformbedarf und Reformoptionen der Demokratie,' in C. Offe (ed.), *Demokratisierung der Demokratie. Diagnosen und Reformvorschläge*. Frankfurt: Campus, 9–23.

Oxhorn, P. (1998) 'The Social Foundations of Latin America's Recurrent Populism: Problems of Popular Sector Class Formation and Collective Action,' *Journal of Historical Sociology* 11(2): 212–46.

Panfichi, A. (1997) 'The Authoritarian Alternative: "Anti-Politics" in the Popular Sectors of Lima,' in D. Chalmers et al. (eds.), *The New Politics of Inequality in Latin America: Rethinking Participation and Representation.* New York: Oxford University Press, 217–36.

Panizza, F. (2005) 'Introduction: Populism and the Mirror of Democracy,' in F. Panizza (ed.), *Populism and the Mirror of Democracy.* London: Verso, 1–31.

(2009) *Contemporary Latin America. Development and Democracy beyond the Washington Consensus.* London: Zed.

Pankowski, R. (2010) *The Populist Radical Right in Poland: The Patriots.* London: Routledge.

Patten, S. (1996) 'Preston Manning's Populism: Constructing the Common Sense of the Common People,' *Studies in Political Economy* 50: 95–132.

Pauwels, T. (2010) 'Explaining the Success of Neo-Liberal Populist Parties: The Case of Lijst Dedecker in Belgium,' *Political Studies* 58(5): 1009–29.

Pease García, H. (2003) *La autocracia Fujimoriista: del estado intervencionista al estado mafioso.* Lima: Fondo Editorial del Pontificia Universidad Católica del Perú.

Peeler, J. (1992) 'Elites Settlements and Democratic Consolidation: Colombia, Costa Rica and Venezuela,' in J. Higley and R. Gunther (eds.), *Elites and Democratic Consolidation in Latin America and Southern Europe.* New York: Cambridge University Press, 81–111.

Pehe, J. (1991) 'The Emergence of Right-Wing Extremism,' *Report on Eastern Europe*, 28 June: 1–6.

(2010) *Demokracie bez demokratů: Úvahy o společnosti a politice.* Prague: Prostor.

Peri, Y. (2004) *Telepopulism. Media and Politics in Israel.* Stanford: Stanford University Press.

Pithart, P. and V. Klaus (1996) 'Rival Visions,' *Journal of Democracy* 7(1): 12–23.

Pitkin, H. (1967) *The Concept of Representation.* Berkeley and Los Angeles: University of California Press.

Planas, P. (2000) *La democracia volátil: movimientos, partidos, líderes políticos y conductas electorales en el Perú contemporáneo.* Lima: Fundación Friedrich Ebert.

Plasser, F. and P. A. Ulram (1995) 'Wandel der politischen Konfliktdynamik: Radikaler Rechtspopulismus in Österreich,' in W. C. Müller, F. Plasser, and P. A. Ulram (eds.), *Wählerverhalten und Parteienwettbewerb: Analysen zur Nationalratswahl 1994.* Vienna: Signum, 471–503.

(2000) 'Rechtspopulistische Resonanzen: Die Wählerschaft der FPÖ,' in F. Plasser, P. A. Ulram and F. Sommer (eds.), *Das österreichische Wahlverhalten.* Vienna: Signum, 225–41.

(2002) *Das österreichische Politikverständnis: Von der Konsens- zur Konfliktkultur?.* Vienna: WUV Universitätsverlag.

Plattner, M. F. (2010) 'Populism, Pluralism, and Liberal Democracy,' *Journal of Democracy* 21(1): 81–92.

Potůček, M. (1999) 'Havel vs. Klaus: Public Policy in the Czech Republic,' *Journal of Comparative Policy Analysis and Practice* 1(2): 163–96.

Priester, K. (2007) *Populismus. Historische und aktuelle Erscheinungsformen.* Frankfurt a.M./New York: Campus.

Przeworski, A. (1999) 'Minimalist Conception of Democracy: A Defense,' in S. Shapiro and C. Hacker-Cordón (eds.), *Democracy's Value*. Cambridge: Cambridge University Press, 23–55.

(2010) *Democracy and the Limits of Self-Government*. New York: Cambridge University Press.

Puhle, H. J. (2003) 'Zwischen Protest und Politikstil: Populismus, Neo-Populismus und Demokratie,' in N. Werz (ed.): *Populismus. Populisten in Übersee und Europa*. Opladen: VS Verlag, 15–44.

Quintelier, E. (2008) 'Changing Determinants of Party Membership in Flanders,' paper presented at the Poletmaal, Nijmegen 29–30 May.

Qvortrup, M. (2005) *A Comparative Study of Referendums: Government by the People*. Manchester: Manchester University Press, 2nd edition.

Reed, Q. (2006) *Political Corruption, Privatisation and Control in the Czech Republic: A Case Study of Problems in Multiple Transition*. Oxford: Ph.D. Thesis Oxford University.

Reform Party of Canada (RPC) (1990) *Principles and Policies*. Calgary, AB: Reform Party of Canada.

(1996a) *Blue Sheet*. Calgary, AB: Reform Party of Canada.

(1996b) *Charter of Rights and Freedoms Task Force Report*. Calgary, AB: Reform Party of Canada.

(1997) *A Fresh Start for Canadians*. Calgary, AB: Reform Party of Canada.

Report (2000) Report of Martti Ahtisaari, Jochen Frowein, Marcelino Oreja. Adopted in Paris on 8 September 2000, available at: www.mpil.de/shared/data/pdf/report.pdf.

Riedlsperger, M. (1998) 'The Freedom Party of Austria: From Protest to Radical Right Populism,' in H.-G. Betz and S. Immerfall (eds.), *The New Politics of the Right: Neo-Populist Parties and Movements in Established Democracies*. New York: St. Martin's, 27–43.

Rink, N., K. Phalet, and M. Swyngedouw (2009) 'The Effects of Immigrant Population Size, Unemployment, and Individual Characteristics on Voting for the Vlaams Blok in Flanders 1991–1999,' *European Sociological Review* 25(4): 411–24.

Roberts, A. (2003) 'Demythologizing the Czech Opposition Agreement,' *Europe-Asia Studies* 55(8): 1273–303.

Roberts, K. M. (1995) 'Neoliberalism and the Transformation of Populism in Latin America: The Peruvian Case,' *World Politics* 48(1): 82–116.

(1998) *Deepening Democracy? The Modern Left and Social Movements in Chile and Peru*. Stanford: Stanford University Press.

(2006) 'Populism, Political Conflict, and Grass-Roots Organization in Latin America,' *Comparative Politics* 38(2): 127–48.

(2008) 'Social Correlates of Party System Demise and Populist Resurgence in Venezuela,' *Latin American Politics and Society* 45(3): 35–57.

Romero, A. (1997) 'Rearranging the Deck Chairs on the Titanic: The Agony of Democracy in Venezuela,' *Latin American Research Review* 32(1): 7–36.

Rosanvallon, P. (2008) *Counter-Democracy: Politics in an Age of Distrust*. New York: Cambridge University Press.

Rospigliosi, F. (2000) *Montesinos y las fuerzas armadas: cómo controló durante una década las instituciones militares*. Lima: Instituto de Estudios Peruanos.

Rousseau, S. (2011) 'Indigenous and Feminist Movements at the Constituent Assembly in Bolivia. Locating the Representation of Indigenous Women,' *Latin American Research Review* 46(2): 5–28.

Rovira Kaltwasser, C. (2009) *Kampf der Eliten. Das Ringen um gesellschaftliche Führung in Lateinamerika, 1810–1982.* Frankfurt a.m./New York: Campus.

  (2012) 'The Ambivalence of Populism: Threat and Corrective for Democracy.' *Democratization* 19(2): 184–208.

Roxborough, I. (1984) 'Unity and Diversity in Latin American History,' *Journal of Latin American Studies* 16(1): 1–26.

Russell, P. H. and L. Sossin (eds.) (2009) *Parliamentary Democracy in Crisis.* Toronto: University of Toronto Press.

Rybář, M. and K. Deegan-Krause (2009) 'Party Democracy and Party Competitiveness in Slovakia: Is There A Trade-Off?' paper presented at the ECPR Joint Session of Workshops, Lisbon, Portugal, April 16.

Rydgren, J. (2005) 'Is Extreme Right-Wing Populism Contagious? Explaining the Emergence of a New Party Family,' *European Journal of Political Research*, 44(3): 413–37.

Sachs, J. (1989) 'Social Conflict and Populist Policies in Latin America,' *National Bureau of Economic Research*, Working Paper 2897.

Sanchez, O. (2008) 'Transformation and Decay: The De-institutionalization of Party Systems in South America,' *Third World Quarterly* 29(2): 315–37.

Santos, B. and L. Avritzer (2005) 'Introduction: Opening Up the Canon of Democracy,' in B. Sousa and L. Avritzer (eds.), *Democratizing Democracy: Beyond the Liberal Democratic Canon.* New York: Verso, xxxiv–lxxiv.

Sartori, G. (1970) 'Concept Misformation in Comparative Politics,' *American Political Science Review* 64(4): 1033–53.

Sawer, M. and B. Hindess (eds.) (2004) *Us and Them: Anti-Elitism in Australia.* Perth: API Network.

Sawer, M. and D. Laycock. (2009) 'Down with Elites and Up with Inequality: Market Populism in Australia and Canada,' *Commonwealth & Comparative Politics* 47(2): 133–50.

Schady, N. R. (2000) 'The Political Economy of Expenditures by the Peruvian Social Fund (FONCODES), 1991–95,' *American Political Science Review* 94(2): 289–304.

Schedler, A. (1998) 'What is Democratic Consolidation?,' *Journal of Democracy* 9(2): 91–107.

Scheuch, E. K. and H. D. Klingemann (1967) 'Theorie des Rechtsradikalismus in westlichen Industriegeselllschaften,' *Hamburger Jahrbuch für Wirtschafts- und Gesellschaftspolitik* 12: 11–29.

Schmidt, G. D. (1996) 'Fujimori's 1990 Upset Victory in Peru: Electoral Rules, Contingencies, and Adaptive Strategies,' *Comparative Politics* 28(3): 321–54.

  (2006) 'All the President's Women: Fujimori and Gender Equity in Peruvian Politics,' in J. F. Carrión (ed.), *The Fujimori Legacy: The Rise of Electoral Authoritarianism in Peru.* University Park: The Pennsylvania State University Press, 150–77.

Schmitt, C. (1932) *Der Begriff des Politischen.* Berlin: Duncker & Humblot.

Schmitter, P. (2010) 'Twenty-Five Years, Fifteen Findings,' *The Journal of Democracy* 21(1): 17–28.

Schumpeter, J. A. (1949) *Capitalism, Socialism and Democracy*. New York: Harper.

Sikk, A. (2009) *Parties and Populism*. London: Center for European Politics, Security and Integration (CEPSI) Working Paper No.1.

Simmons, B. A., F. Dobbin, and G. Garrett (2008) 'Introduction: The Diffusion of Liberalization,' in B. A. Simmons, F. Dobbin, and G. Garrett (eds.), *The Global Diffusion of Market and Democracy*. New York: Cambridge University Press, 1–63.

Simpson, J. (2010) 'PM's Census Policy Senseless But Great for the Party', *The Globe and Mail*, 17 July.

Skinner, Q. (1973) 'The Empirical Theorists of Democracy and Their Critics: A Plague on Both Their Houses,' *Political Theory* 1(3): 287–306.

Sládek, M. (1992).... *tak to vidím já.*, Brno: SPR-RSČ.

(1995) *To, co mám na mysli, je svoboda*. Brno: SPR-RSČ.

SORA (2002) *Nationalratswahl 2002: Analyse des Wahlergebnisses und des Wahlkampfes*. Vienna: SORA/Institute for Social Research and Analysis.

SPR-RSČ (1990) 'Hlavní referát přednesený předsedou Sdružení pro republiku – Republikánské strany Československa,' in *Materiály z ustavujícího sjezdu*. Prague: SPR-RSČ, 1–10.

Spruyt, M. (1995) *Grove borstels: Stel dat het Vlaams Blok morgen zijn programma realiseert, hoe zou Vlaanderen er dan uit zien?* Leuven: Van Halewijck.

(2000) *Wat het Vlaams Blok verzwijgt*. Leuven: Van Halewijck.

Stanley, B. (2008) 'The Thin Ideology of Populism,' *Journal of Political Ideologies* 13(1): 95–110.

Stavrakakis, Y. (2004) 'Antinomies of Formalism: Laclau's Theory of Populism and the Lessons from Religious Populism in Greece,' *Journal of Political Ideologies* 9(3): 253–67.

Stokes, S. C. (2001) *Mandates and Democracy: Neoliberalism By Surprise in Latin America*. Cambridge: Cambridge University Press.

Swyngedouw, M. and J. Billiet (2002) *De kiezer heeft zijn redenen: 13 juni 1999 en de politieke opvattingen van Vlamingen*. Leuven: Acco.

Swyngedouw, M. and G. Ivaldi (2001) 'The Extreme Right Utopia in Belgium and France: The Ideology of the Flemish Vlaams Blok and the French Front National,' *West European Politics* 24(3): 1–22.

Tácha, D. (1998) 'Živili jsme Sládka,' *Týden* 37: 37–9.

Taggart, P. (2000) *Populism*. Buckingham: Open University Press.

(2002) 'Populism and the Pathology of Representative Politics,' in Y. Meny and Y. Surel (eds.), *Democracies and the Populist Challenge*. Basingstoke: Palgrave, 62–80.

Taguieff, P. A. (1995) 'Political Science Confronts Populism: From a Conceptual Mirage to a Real Problem,' *Telos* 103:9–43.

Tálos, E. (2006) 'Politik in Schwarz-Blau/Orange: Eine Bilanz,' in E. Tálos (ed.), *Schwarz-Blau: Eine Bilanz des "Neu-Regierens"*. Wien/Münster: LIT, 326–43.

Tännsjö, T. (1992) *Populist Democracy: A Defense*. London: Routledge.

Tanaka, M. (1998) *Los espejismos de la democracia: el colapso del sistema de partidos en el Perú*. Lima: Instituto de Estudios Peruanos.

(2005) 'Peru 1980–2000: Chronicle of a Death Foretold? Determinism, Political Decisions, and Open Outcomes,' in F. Hagopian and S. P. Mainwaring (eds.), *The Third Wave of Democratization in Latin America. Advances and Setbacks*. New York: Cambridge University Press, 261–88.

Thijssen, P. and S. L. de Lange (2005) 'Explaining the Varying Electoral Appeal of the Vlaams Blok in the Districts of Antwerp,' *Ethical Perspectives* 12(2): 231–58.

Tilly, C. (2007) *Democracy*. Cambridge: Cambridge University Press.

Učen, P. (1999) 'A Decade of Conflict within Slovak Polity: Party Politics Perspective,' in V. Dvořáková (ed.), *Success or Failure? Ten Years After*. Prague: Česká společnost pro politické vědy a Slovenské združenie pre politické vedy, 80–103.

Urbinati, N. and M. E. Warren (2008) 'The Concept of Democratic Representation in Contemporary Democratic Theory,' *The Annual Review of Political Science* 11: 387–412.

Vachudová, M. (2005) *Europe Undivided: Democracy, Leverage, and Integration after Communism*. Oxford: Oxford University Press.

(2008) 'Centre – Right Parties and Political Outcomes in East Central Europe,' *Party Politics* 14(4): 387–405.

Van der Brug, W. (2003) 'How the LPF Fuelled Discontent: Empirical Tests of Explanations of LPF Support,' *Acta Politica* 38(1–2): 89–106.

Van Donselaar, J. (1995) *De staat paraat? De bestrijding van extreem-rechts in West Europa*. Amsterdam: De Geus.

Van Spanje, J. (2010) 'Contagious Parties. Anti-Immigration Parties and Their Impact on Other Parties' Immigration Stances in Contemporary Western Europe,' *Party Politics* 16(5): 563–86.

Vargas Llosa, M. (1993) *El pez en el agua*. Buenos Aires: Alfaguara.

(1994) *A Fish in the Water: A Memoir*. New York: Fabrar Straus Giroux.

VB (1996) 'Minutes of the Vlaams Blok Congress "Vlaanderen Werkt,"' held in Den Haan on 30 November–1 December.

(2003) *Een toekomst voor Vlaanderen. Programma en standpunten van het Vlaams Blok*. Brussels: Vlaams Blok

(2004a) *Beginselverklaring*. Brussesl: Vlaams Belang.

(2004b) *Een toekomst voor Vlaanderen. Programma en standpunten van het Vlaams Blok*. Brussels: Vlaams Blok.

(2004c) *Vlaamse staat, Europese natie*. Brussels: Vlaams Blok.

(2010) *Verkiezingsprogramma 13 juni 2010*. Brussels: Vlaams Belang.

Vibert, F. (2007) *The Rise of the Unelected. Democracy and the New Separation of Powers*. New York: Cambridge University Press.

Von Beyme, K. (1988) 'Right-Wing Extremism in Europe,' *West European Politics* 11(2): 1–18.

(1993) *Die politische Klasse im Parteienstaat*. Frankfurt a.M.: Suhrkamp.

VV (2010) *Veci veřejné politický program*, available at: http://www.veciverejne.cz/ politicky-program.html (accessed 5 May 2010).

Waisbord, S. (2011) 'Between Support and Confrontation: Civic Society, Media Reform, and Populism in Latin America,' *Communication, Culture & Critique* 4(1): 97–117.

Walgrave, S. and K. De Swert (2004) 'The Making of the (Issues of the) Vlaams Blok,' *Political Communication* 21: 479–500.

(2007) 'Where Does Issue Ownership Come From? From the Party or from the Media? Issue-Party Identifications in Belgium, 1991–2005,' *Press/Politics* 12(1): 37–67.

Walicki, A. (1969) 'Russia,' in G. Ionescu and E. Gellner (eds.), *Populism. Its Meanings and Characteristics*. London: Weidenfeld and Nicolson, 62–96.

Warmenbol, L. (2010) *Wijken voor het VB: Een Etnografische Studie van de Steun voor Radicaal-Rechts op Lokaal Niveau*. Antwerp: Ph.D. Thesis University of Antwerp.

Warren, M. E. and H. Pearse (eds.) (2008) *Designing Deliberative Democracy: the British Columbia Citizens' Assembly*. New York: Cambridge University Press.

Weffort, F. (1978) *O populismo na política brasileira*. Rio de Janeiro: Editora Paz e Terra.

Weyland, K. (1996) 'Neopopulism and Neoliberalism in Latin America: Unexpected Affinities,' *Studies in Comparative International Development* 32: 3–31.

(1998) 'Swallowing the Bitter Pill: Sources of Popular Support for Neoliberal Reform in Latin America,' *Comparative Political Studies* 31(5): 539–68.

(2001) 'Clarifying a Contested Concept: Populism in the Study of Latin American Politics,' *Comparative Politics* 34(1): 1–22.

(2006) 'The Rise and Decline of Fujimori's Neopopulist Leadership,' in J. F. Carrión (ed.), *The Fujimori Legacy: The Rise of Electoral Authoritarianism in Peru*. University Park: The Pennsylvania State University Press, 13–38.

Weyland, K., R. L. Madrid, and W. Hunter (eds.) (2010) *Leftist Governments in Latin America: Successes and Shortcomings*. New York: Cambridge University Press.

Whitehead, L. (2002) *Democratization. Theory and Experience*. Oxford: Oxford University Press.

Williams, K. (2000) *Slovakia after Communism and Mečiarism*. London: School of Slavonic and East European Studies.

(2003) 'Lustration as the Securitization of Democracy in Czechoslovakia and the Czech Republic,' *Journal of Communist Studies and Transition Politics* 19(4): 1–24.

Wilpert, G. (2006) *Changing Venezuela by Taking Power: The History and Policies of the Chávez Government*. London: Verso.

Youngers, C. A. (2000) *Deconstructing Democracy: Peru under President Alberto Fujimori*. Washington, DC: Washington Office on Latin America.

Žižek, S. (2008) *In Defense of Lost Causes*. London: Verso.

Zúquete, J. P. (2008) 'The Missionary Politics of Hugo Chávez,' *Latin American Politics and Society* 50(1): 91–121.

Index

CPSIA information can be obtained
at www.ICGtesting.com
Printed in the USA
LVHW042008200819
628316LV00014B/326